Butoh America

Butoh America unearths the people and networks that popularized Butoh dance in the Americas through a focused look at key artists, producers, and festivals in the United States and Mexico.

This is the first book to gather these histories into one narrative and look at the development of American Butoh. From its inception in San Francisco in 1976, American Butoh aligned with avant-garde performance art in alternative venues such as galleries and experimental theaters. La MaMa in New York and the Festival Internacional Cervantino (FIC) in Guanajuato both served to legitimize the form as esteemed experimental performance. A crystallizing moment in each of the three locations—San Francisco, New York, and Mexico City—has been a grand-scale festival featuring prominent Japanese and numerous other international artists which also fostered local communities.

This book stitches together the flow of people and ideas, highlights the connections in the Butoh diaspora, and incorporates interviewee perspectives regarding future directions for the genre in the Americas.

Tanya Calamoneri is a dancer, choreographer, and Assistant Professor of Dance at Texas Tech University. Her primary area of research is Butoh dance. She also writes about issues concerning the migration of forms across cultural boundaries in a globalized world. Her writing has been published in Routledge's *Theatre, Dance and Performance Training Journal, Dance Chronicle, Journal of Dance Education*, and *Movement Research Journal*, as well as a chapter on Butoh pedagogy in the Routledge *Butoh Companion* and a chapter in Routledge's *Intercultural Actor and Performer Training*.

Routledge Advances in Theatre & Performance Studies

This series is our home for cutting-edge, upper-level scholarly studies and edited collections. Considering theatre and performance alongside topics such as religion, politics, gender, race, ecology, and the avant-garde, titles are characterized by dynamic interventions into established subjects and innovative studies on emerging topics.

Dance Data, Cognition and Multimodal Communication
Carla Fernandes, Vito Evola and Cláudia Ribeiro

Theatre and the Virtual
Genesis, Touch, Gesture
Zornitsa Dimitrova

Old Norse Poetry in Performance
Brian McMahon & Annemari Ferreira

Shakespeare's Contested Nations
Race, Gender, and Multicultural Britain in Performances of the History Plays
L. Monique Pittman

Performing the Wound
Practicing a Feminist Theatre of Becoming
Niki Tulk

Butoh America
Butoh Dance in the United States and Mexico from 1970 to the early 2000s
Tanya Calamoneri

Deburau
Pierrot, Mime, and Culture
Edward Nye

Performance at the Urban Periphery
Insights from South India
Cathy Turner, Sharada Srinivasan, Jerri Daboo and Anindya Sinha

Australian Metatheatre on Page and Stage
An Exploration of Metatheatrical Techniques
Rebecca Clode

For more information about this series, please visit: www.routledge.com/Routledge-Advances-in-Theatre-Performance-Studies/book-series/RATPS

Butoh America

Butoh Dance in the United States and
Mexico from 1970 to the early 2000s

Tanya Calamoneri

Routledge
Taylor & Francis Group
LONDON AND NEW YORK

First published 2022
by Routledge
4 Park Square, Milton Park, Abingdon, Oxon OX14 4RN

and by Routledge
605 Third Avenue, New York, NY 10158

Routledge is an imprint of the Taylor & Francis Group, an informa business

British Library Cataloguing-in-Publication Data
A catalogue record for this book is available from the British Library

Library of Congress Cataloging-in-Publication Data
A catalog record for this book has been requested

ISBN: 978-0-367-13760-1 (hbk)
ISBN: 978-1-032-22562-3 (pbk)
ISBN: 978-0-429-02847-2 (ebk)

DOI: 10.4324/9780429028472

Typeset in Bembo
by Apex CoVantage, LLC

For Jack and Stella

Contents

Figures

A Note About Spanish and Japanese Names and Words

I follow the *Real Academia Española* for Spanish words, titles, and proper names. For proper names written in the context of English, such as Mexico City, I write them as they are commonly seen in English, rather than with the proper diacritical marking: México. When Mexico appears in an official title that is otherwise written in Spanish, as in Ballet Nacional de México, the accent is included. All translations from Spanish to English are my own.

I follow the *Monumenta Nipponica* stylesheet with the following exceptions: I have chosen to list all Japanese names with the given name first and family name second. As this book primarily engages with Japanese artists in the context of American performance, I use this convention across the board to avoid confusion. I also write commonly accepted words such as butoh and Ohno with the "oh" rather than with the diacritical mark for a long "o," consistent with the majority of English-language publications and reviews. I do keep diacritical marks when they are written as such in a title or direct quotation. When referring to artists with the same last name, for example, Hiroko and Koichi Tamano, I will sometimes refer to them by their first name to distinguish the references.

Acknowledgments

Shinichi Iova-Koga was my first butoh teacher and the one who got me started on this journey back in 2000 when he asked me to join inkBoat's production of *Cockroach*. I have to thank him for thoroughly confusing me and sending me off in search of answers.

More artists than I could fit into one book gave me their time and told me their stories. I am grateful for their trust and hope to chronicle their work one day if I could not fit it all here: Alenka Mullin, Aura Arreola, Brechin Flournoy, Carlos Ivan Cruz Islas, Crow, Dana Iova-Koga, Diego Piñón, Espartaco Martínez, Eugenia Vargas, Gustavo Emilio Rosales, Hiroko Tamano, Jeff Janisheshki, Joan Laage, Jonathan Caudillo, José Bravo, Joshua Kohl, Kinji Hayashi, Koichi Tamano, Leigh Evans, Marilú Macareno, Maureen Fleming, Molly Barrons, paige starling sorvillo, Shige Moriya, Shinichi Iova-Koga, Tania Galindo, Teresa Carlos, Vangeline, and Ximena Garnica. Their energy and spirit is the entire reason for this text.

Brechin Flournoy generously opened her archives on the San Francisco Butoh Festival to me, and I spent many days pouring over her materials. Ximena Garnica did the same with the New York Butoh Festival, sifting through materials along with me. Ozzie Rodriguez and Shigeko Suga graciously assisted me with the treasure trove of materials at La MaMa Archives in New York and patiently answered many emails clarifying details.

Drs. Bruce Baird, Rosemary Candelario, Megan Nicely, and Zack Fuller, and Michael Sakamoto co-organized our first butoh panels at conferences, and all were instrumental in giving me the skills, confidence, and opportunity to write this book. Dr. Katherine Mezur connected me to Mexican butoh artists at a PSI conference in Aomori, Japan, and Eugenia Vargas accepted my request to engage in the Mexican butoh community and welcomed me with open arms.

Dr. Luke Kahlich served as my dissertation advisor at Temple University and continues to be my steadfast mentor throughout my research and career. My PhD cohort at Temple University, especially Drs. Takiyah Nur Amin, Nyama McCarthy Brown, and Jennifer Conley, are a constant source of inspiration, and they have endured countless conversations about butoh and still want to talk to me. Dr. Martha Eddy supervised my Somatic Movement Therapy Training and Dynamic Embodiment certification and has helped me make connections between her work and the goals and methods in butoh.

Texas Tech University has generously supported my work with a Faculty Research Grant, Humanities Council Faculty Grant, Alumni College Research Grant, and additional support for travel to archives, digitization of archival materials, and open-access publication support. Additionally, my colleagues in the School of Theatre and Dance have encouraged me along the way, particularly those who have served as official mentors: Drs. Ali Duffy and Dorothy Chansky, and Dean Genevieve Durham Decesaro. SOTD Chair Mark Charney has provided steady encouragement as well. The Women's Writing Group at Texas Tech has given me a quiet place to think among other dedicated scholars, particularly Dr. Cassie Christopher who pushed me toward a daily word count goal. TTU Librarian Robert Weiner never failed to produce a resource I needed. I am also thankful to Drs. Chris Smith and Roger Landes at Texas Tech University for interviewing me for Voices from the Vernacular Music Center, allowing me to talk through some of the bridges in avant-garde performance across genres. And Dr. Jorge Zamora generously reviewed the Spanish text and references to artists and institutions, patiently correcting my lack of proper accents. The TTU graduate students who have assisted me have been absolutely invaluable: Abigail Bugh scanned and catalogued my first archive hauls and patiently built a database of performances and workshops by touring Japanese artists, Charles Hughes tracked down obscure poetry references for me, Paul Kortemeier assisted with historical research, Bailey Patterson organized the photos, and Anne Wharton did the painstaking work of editing the citations. I could not be more grateful to have the support of Texas Tech University at my back.

I had the opportunity to work on many of the ideas in this book at various conferences, including the 2019 Cuerpos en Revuelta butoh festival in Mexico City at which I presented about the history of butoh in the United States, and the 2019 Butoh Next Symposium at CUNY Graduate Center, at which I co-presented with Tania Galindo on the history of butoh in Mexico. I was invited to write a chapter for the *Routledge Butoh Companion* (2019), edited by Bruce Baird and Rosemary Candelario, that enabled me to collect my thoughts on this material, particularly the unique communities in San Francisco and New York.

And finally I am grateful to my parents who, when told that I was a hyperactive child, thought that dance was the best solution.

Abbreviations

BAM	Brooklyn Academy of Music
BRM	Butoh Ritual Mexicano; Body Rhythm Movement
DAE	Degenerate Art Ensemble
ETW	Experimental Theater Wing (in Tisch School of the Arts, New York University)
FIC	Festival Internacional Cervantino, also referred to as Cervantino
FONCA	Fondo Nacional para la Cultura y las Artes
INBA/L	Instituto Nacional de Las Bellas Artes/y Literaturas
LEDTR	Laboratorio Escenica Danza Teatro Ritual
MB	Mind/Body; Muscle/Bone
NEA	National Endowment for the Arts
NYBF	New York Butoh Festival
NYBK	New York Butoh-Kan
NYT	*The New York Times*
OTB	On The Boards
SFBF	San Francisco Butoh Festival
SFBG	*San Francisco Bay Guardian*
SFMOMA	San Francisco Museum of Modern Art
SFSU	San Francisco State University
SOGEM	Sociedad General de Escritores de México
SNDD	School for New Dance Development
TAI	Taller de Arte e Idealogia
TIP	Taller de Investigación Plastica
TYCC	The Young Composers Collective
UC	University of California (as in UC Riverside, UC San Diego)
UNAM	La Universidad Nacional Autónoma de México

1 Introduction

A man in a black suit jacket is stuck in a tree. With his arm wedged in between two skinny branches, his bare feet dangle above the ground. An invisible gale-force wind blows from one side, pinning him to his perch. Eventually, a cross-current hits his leg, causing it to spiral around his stuck form. The twisting frees him from his trap, and he continues on his windswept way, staggering out of sight.

The man was Shinichi Iova-Koga. The occasion was an improvisational performance at Mendocino Arts Center in California in 2000. As a dancer new to butoh, I found the short dance to be simple yet profound. It evoked metaphors about the nature of life, attachment, and suffering. The audience watched from inside the gallery, peering out large glass windows that surrounded the tree and dancer on two sides. It was like a little forgotten alley that was activated into a performance event by a hapless passerby. The glass surrounding the space made it feel like a strange snow globe, silent to those outside with a deafening squall inside. We could watch each other watching him and see the recognition of his plight in our own, as well as that of the stranger watching from the other side.

I mention this memory to begin a discussion about the changing modes of performance that began in the 1970s with the advent of performance art. Concomitant with shifting schools of thought within American performance, the venues also began to change. Galleries, living rooms, music clubs, and outdoor spaces all became viable performance arenas. The first butoh artist to arrive in the United States in 1976,[1] Koichi Tamano performed in the Japan Now Exhibition in Los Angeles and then received an invitation to perform at the San Francisco Museum of Modern Art (SF MOMA). Though these were established institutions, and performance art moved purposefully outside of such structures, the alignment of dance and visual arts was a significant pairing with repercussions for future events. Butoh's initial entry point through galleries and other alternative spaces is an important element of butoh's place in the Americas. This placement effectively identified it as performance art, with all of the associations with body experimentation, extreme experiences for performers and audience alike, and radical redefinitions of existing artistic genres. The American artists and students that adopted Japanese butoh's aesthetics and

DOI: 10.4324/9780429028472-1

methods aligned with the goals of avant-garde performance artists; they weren't looking to make new dance, new theater, new music, new visual art, or redefine any one discipline. They were trying to make new expression, and butoh provided many vital keys to that quest.

The resulting movement vocabulary in performance that emerged in the 1980s and 1990s drew from these multifaceted encounters and inspirations and developed a common, shared approach. That is not to say that all artists worked in one specific style, in fact, quite the contrary. Nonetheless, their work was legible as of the same ilk, because they were engaged in similar social and artistic questions: how could they resist normative structures?

Dance scholar Ramsay Burt elaborates a notion of contemporary performance knowledge as "a shared resource—a commons—rather than a commodity from which to generate financial profit" (Burt 2017, 71). Drawing from Judith Revel's 2008 essay "Resistance, Subjectivities, Common," Burt writes, "the common [is] a space where the community of the common can work together in ways that respect and value their singular differences from one another rather than being reduced to uniformity and sameness" (Burt 2017, 60). Burt notes the shift in counter-cultural movements toward nonhierarchical alternatives to mainstream structures, thus creating a more pluralistic community. Dancers were searching for authenticity, and "the new forms and approaches which emerged in the 1970s valued individuality and personal autonomy alongside meaningful communal engagement" (Burt 2017, 36). More than just a demonstration of personal expression, Burt casts these tendencies in a decidedly political light. He refers to participating in the commons as a means of "ungoverning." He writes:

> Ungoverning is continually engaging in the maintenance and protection of the commons through opening up spaces that are relatively free from the effects of control, regulation, or normalization.
>
> (Burt 2017, 23)

In other words, an independent community of artists can co-exist and is most healthy with a diversity of perspectives, aesthetics, identities, and approaches. However, how can dance gain "independence from institutional constraints through aesthetic deconstruction" (Burt 2017, 4)? How does one move independently, outside of standards and values, particularly in a neoliberal economy where value must be measured and quantified?

Burt is speaking specifically about European contemporary dance since the mid-1990s. However, his references to Judson Church dancers would suggest that his analysis is applicable to the shifting mode of producing art the world over which began as a result of social unrest in the 1960s and spilled into social action from the 1970s forward. The ungoverning he describes happening in 1990s concert dance is related if not the same as the ungoverning of the 1960s as early experimental performance artists wrenched the doorways and gatekeepers of mainstream performance from their proverbial hinges. I argue that upon interaction with the Americas, butoh both supported the existing movement-specific methodology and provided a new language for emerging modes of creating performance that emphasized transformative experiences for performer and audience alike.

In Latin America, butoh situates the narrative of "ungoverning" within the discourse on colonialism. It is significant that the connection to Japanese artists allows Latin America to circumvent the typical route of cultural production as flowing through the West. For example, Anna Pavlova's 1919 tour linked the notion of modernity in dance to European tradition, with ballet as the hallmark of civilized society. When dance students study dance history at al Universidad Autónomo de México (UNAM), for example, they study the history of Western dance, not indigenous dance. Butoh, on the other hand, cultivates a modernity that is not Western but, in fact, is anti-Western. A rich example of Burt's concept of ungoverning in practice, butoh in Mexico bolsters the community of artists who have established outside the mainstream "Westernized" performance styles and modes of production. It allows them to be utterly contemporary and non-Western at the same time.

There is a danger of the romanticized trope of Japan: it represents either timeless beauty or tragic loss. The discussion of butoh in the Americas also falls into one of two categories: the Orientalist discourse, through which butoh is read as an exotic Other akin to what Barbara Thornbury calls "America's kabuki" (Thornbury 2013), and what Rosemary Candelario refers to as a "nuclear narrative" (Candelario 2016), through which butoh is read as an expression of trauma, aligned with grotesque and horrific subjects and aesthetics. Both narratives explain butoh's frequent employment in outwardly exotic, often horrifying characters in American performance, for example, the three witches in Tony Taccone's 1994 Macbeth at Berkeley Repertory Theater.[2]

The artists profiled in this book, I suggest, propose a third discourse that considers butoh's role in providing a distinctive form to aspects of the existing avant-garde movement. Butoh is an integral part of the American performance commons, established by alternative performance artists who rejected not only the boundaries of artistic genre but also neoliberalism and the art world's modes of production. Butoh contributed form and method to an existing conversation on how to change performance expression. It clearly impacted future generations of performing artists, as evidenced by the successful artists and companies profiled in this book who continue to straddle disciplinary boundaries and eschew categorization. Their defiance is not without its costs, however. When one is outside legibility and institutional structures in contemporary society, one is often without funding. It is a precarious position to exist in "a neoliberal economy in which a smokescreen of freedom belies profound financial insecurity" (Frankfurter 2019, 98). A query I had of each artist I interviewed was how they managed to knit together a life outside of the normative system. Each had a unique path, many of them with crooked twists and turns that made their work what it is today. It is the multiplicity of these renegade histories that form the *butoh commons*.

Scope of the Study

Butoh America traces the history of butoh in the United States and Mexico from the 1970s to early 2000s as artists migrated across American soil, from Canada to Chile and Argentina. In particular, this study looks at the seeds butoh has sewn across this region through key producers and festivals, and several subsequent homegrown American butoh artists and companies that have risen to prominence in the last 20 years.

The starting point for this text is the 1970s in the Americas. As such, it assumes the reader's knowledge and understanding of butoh history, from Tatsumi Hijikata's *Kinjiki* (1959), Kazuo Ohno's collaborations with Hijikata and successful solo career, through the formation of Akaji Maro's Dairakudakan, and the many second-generation companies that arose from that entity. Many other scholars have covered this terrain so I will refer readers to their work: Baird (2005, 2006, 2012), Baird and Candelario (2019), Blakely Klein (1988), Fraleigh (1999), and Fraleigh and Nakamura (2006).

Though I do engage in discussions of methodology and meaning-making with the artists interviewed in this text, it is not the focus of my current project. Again, numerous scholars and artists have attempted to capture the "live fish" of butoh in words, myself included. It is a slippery fish, indeed.

What I *have* attempted in this text is a history of a migration and the cross-fertilization of Japanese artists with artists and communities in the Americas, specifically the United States and Mexico. Three locales provide insight into the imprint of Japanese butoh dancers on American artistic communities: New York, San Francisco/Seattle, and Mexico City. A major international festival arose in each location: The San Francisco Butoh Festival (1993–2003), The New York International Butoh Festival (2003–2009), Cuerpos en Revuelta: Festival Internacional de Danza Butoh en America Latina (Mexico City, 2016–present), and the New York Butoh Institute Festival (2017–present). Each festival has its antecedents from which it gained knowledge, network, and a public inclined toward the work. Supporting the birth of the aforementioned festivals is a gradually increasing influx of touring artists who found connections with the performance art scene of the 1970s and experimental theatre practitioners of the 1980s.

The reason I highlighted the festivals as a source of analysis is because they indicate a critical mass of students, teachers, performers, audience, producers, and funders willing to designate butoh as a movement. Interestingly, each of the primary festival fomenters was students themselves. Flournoy was exposed to Maureen Fleming and Sankai Juku in college and then discovered the Tamanos after moving to the Bay Area. Ximena Garnica was a student of Atsushi Takenouchi and Diego Piñón and participated in a San Francisco Butoh Festival as a student and a performer before she and a team of savvy producers/students launched the New York Butoh Festival. Eugenia Vargas was a student of Diego Piñón and also Natsu Nakajima before her work coalesced into Cuerpos en Revuelta. All were performers prior to their encounter with butoh, and all have continued their artistic work throughout their producing. This distinguishes them from the Ellen Stewarts of this study and the Festival Internacional Cervantino (FIC) producers, who unquestionably made bold choices and introduced new art forms. However, the unique shape of the butoh festivals that included pedagogical components was designed by dancers who wanted to know more for the purposes of their own art.

A complete history is nearly impossible as there are so many people who have played a role in this story, and so I hope that readers will see this as a beginning and an invitation to contribute to the growing archive. Due to restrictions of time and space, this text focuses on the stories of seminal Japanese artists as they toured and/or emigrated to the United States and Mexico, and describes the artists and communities that met them here. Drag queens, radical performance artists, experimental musicians, and visionary presenters emerged to greet them, drawing butoh into the fabric of cutting-edge American arts. I follow these roots through the crucibles of the festivals and then spotlight prominent companies and performers that emerged.

A Note on "America"

The title *Butoh America* sounds as if it would address the regional boundaries of the Americas—North, South, and Central—and there certainly are artists working in a butoh-informed idiom throughout the entire continent. However, I focus this study more narrowly to capture the ports of entry beginning in the early 1970s, through the cities of San Francisco, New York, and Mexico City.

Methodology

My goal of mapping the growth and development of butoh in the United States and Mexico was achieved through piecing together a timeline from reviews, programs, photographs, and typed resumes on yellowing paper. My research assistant and I developed a database of 1,400 discrete performances by Japanese butoh artists in the United States and Mexico from 1970 to 2010 and cross-referenced the artists involved as well as connections among presenters. These were all touring productions that were well supported by funding and institutions. If we were to include the American-based artists in this database, that number would increase exponentially.

This text is the result of four years of research in archives, basements, tucked away filing cabinets, and overflowing closets. The artists profiled herein generously opened their spaces and lives to me, and shared their histories. I watched numerous performances at La MaMa Archives, including the exquisite *After Eros* with Yoshito Ohno and Maureen Fleming, Min Tanaka's epic choreography for Ellen Stewart's *Oedipus*, and the ribald Poppo and the GoGo Boys. Through the San Francisco Butoh Festival's archive, I had a chance to revisit many pieces I had seen live before I had a scholarly lens for butoh, among them

Akira Kasai's otherworldly *Exusiai* and the Japanese New Wave company Op-Eklekt. Actor and Harupin-Ha dancer Kinji Hayashi had a rare copy of Koichi Tamano in Hijikata's choreography, *Fin Back Whale*, that I was able to obtain from him before he sadly passed away in 2018. As I was in New York pursuing my masters and writing a thesis on butoh throughout the entire New York Butoh Festival, I watched the majority of those performances live and kept all of the programs, though I also spent time in the archives at CAVEArtspace as well. In Mexico, I saw performances and symposiums from the first two Cuerpos en Revuelta through video archives and then participated in the third festival live. I also saw Espartaco Martínez live at the FIC in Guanajuato. Many more performances I watched online through artist websites and video platforms such as YouTube and Vimeo, some publicly available, and others with permission from the artists through their own digital archives.

Ethnographic research and participant observation support my analysis of the artistic trajectories and choreographic works. The artists that are profiled most extensively in this text are like nodes through which many currents have passed. I interviewed more people than I could have fit into one book, and it will hopefully spill over into other writing one day.

While I foreground the archival research, interviews, and analysis of performances, I acknowledge that I was involved in the butoh communities in San Francisco and New York as a dancer, student, choreographer, teacher, and producer. I have known many of the people involved in this history in multiple capacities. Brechin Flournoy, director of the San Francisco Butoh Festival, was the Associate Director of Dancers' Group when I was just a program assistant there signing students into classes back in 1997, before I even knew what butoh was. When I went through the festival rosters that she had meticulously preserved, I saw my own handwriting on the pages. I joined a butoh company almost by accident because they were touring a show to Berlin and I wanted to travel to Germany; that was Shinichi Iova-Koga's inkBoat, which was my introduction to this brave new world. In 2000, inkBoat toured to the Seattle Butoh Festival where I first met Joan Laage. In 2002, I attended ImPulstanz in Vienna and had the chance to study with Carlotta Ikeda and Ko Murobushi, the latter of whom I would follow for many years in New York and through his collaboration with inkBoat. I moved to New York in 2003 right when CAVE was launching the New York Butoh Festival. I volunteered to help and got cast in one of their pieces, *In Illo Tempore*. They were my entrée into a new group of artists working in this form and also a chance to continue studying with several people I had met previously, namely, SU-EN, Murobushi, and Yuko Kaseki. I have also been fortunate to travel to Tokyo, Kyoto, Aomori, and Berlin to study and research in archives and museums. I have met many people along the way and have them to thank for answering my questions and connecting me to still more artists. At a Performance Studies International (PSI) conference in Aomori, Japan, Katherine Mezur paired me with Eugenia Vargas, Teresa Carlos, and Aura Arreola in an improvisational performance. The very next year they started the Cuerpos en Revuelta butoh festival in Mexico City. I invited myself down in 2018 and, with their gracious support, met a plethora of artists actively engaging with butoh in and around Mexico City. I then returned in 2019 to give a talk about butoh history in the United States as part of the third Cuerpos en Revuelta.

I offer my history to register that this selection of artists is from my own perspective. Had I landed in Chicago, Durham, Portland, or Boston, where there are also long-standing butoh communities, I might have a different view of the networks that have crisscrossed this continent. Had I spent more time in Guanajuato and had a chance to work with Lola Lince or Pájaro de Nube, perhaps I would have drawn other parallels to experimental performance. *Butoh America* is by no means a definitive history. It is an invitation to share in the wealth of the butoh community and a prompt to other authors to write more. If nothing else, I hope that I have shown in these pages the vital work that butoh artists have brought to contemporary performance in the United States and Mexico: work that is at once raw and healing, boundary-breaking, and activist. The artists involved continue to change the way we see bodies and existence, and the value and potential of performance. And while many are avant-garde and perhaps appear to be fringe, their aesthetics and methods have influenced mainstream contemporary dance and theater undeniably, and thus their history needs to be entered into those archives to give credit where credit is due.

Overview of the Chapters

Chapter 1, "Introduction," proposes the notion of butoh as a commons, and part of a larger dialogue about existing outside institutionalized boundaries. I also suggest that butoh offered a movement language to an existing avant-garde praxis that valued physical presence in art.

Chapter 2, "Stranger in a Strange Land," outlines the contours of American performing arts that Japanese butoh artists encountered in the 1970s and lays the foundation for the touring networks that would develop in the Americas. La MaMa theater director Ellen Stewart brought Shuji Terayama to New York, Chilean filmmaker and provocateur Alejandro Jodorowsky settled in Mexico City by way of Paris. Both artists broke all the rules of propriety and performance in general, paving the way for experimentation to come. Major catalysts include Koichi and Hiroko Tamano, who relocated to the San Francisco Bay Area in 1976 at Hijikata's request to send butoh abroad, Ellen Stewart who also brought Min Tanaka and Kazuo Ohno to perform in New York in the 1970s and 1980s, and tours by Dairakudakan at the American Dance Festival (ADF) in 1984 and Sankai Juku tours in 1985. In Guanajuato, Mexico, the FIC presented Carlotta Ikeda in 1980, Sankai Juku in 1981, Natsu Nakajima in 1987 who by then became a regular presence in Mexico, teaching numerous workshops and collaborating with both dance and theater artists. Mexican theater director Abraham Oceransky has created a critical channel for butoh in Mexico, collaborating with Ko Murobushi and Nakajima frequently as well as Yumiko Yoshioka and Katsura Kan; many Mexican performers encountered butoh through connection to Oceransky.

Chapter 3, "American Anchor Artists and Festivals," highlights three key artists: Maureen Fleming, Joan Laage, and Diego Piñón. All have spent numerous years in Japan and worked with the Ohnos, and two have worked with Min Tanaka. Their teaching and performance is the foundation of American butoh. Additionally, Brechin Flournoy launched the San Francisco Butoh Festival launched in 1993, the first major American festival dedicated to butoh, which developed student communities, educated critics and audiences, and cultivated the funding community to support butoh in the Americas.

Chapter 4, "Gen X Butoh," features highly visible artists from the next generation of Americans, two of whom launched large-scale butoh festivals: Espartaco Martínez, Eugenia Vargas, Shinichi Iova-Koga/inkBoat, Crow and Joshua Kohl/Degenerate Art Ensemble, and Ximena Garnica and Shige Moriya/CAVE/LEIMAY. Several of these artists no longer refer to their work as butoh, but all acknowledge the profound impact their engagement with Japanese butoh artists has had on their work.

Chapter 5, "The Future of Butoh Is. . . ," offers a look at two distinct artists who both claim the mantel of butoh and change the narrative in their own ways. Vangeline/New York Butoh Institute has made it her mission to shed light on the women of butoh. Tania Galindo/Butoh Chilango is an activist from Mexico City who makes work that is both political and also engages with indigenous communities and stories. The closing discussion acknowledges that the diaspora is unfolding around us, and the butoh commons continues to evolve with the contribution of each new participant.

Notes

1 Japanese dancers Eiko and Koma also arrived this same year and performed in the same Japan Now Festival. Though they were students of both butoh founders Tatsumi Hijikata and Kazuo Ohno, they did not adopt the name butoh in their work and were careful in promotion to develop their own style of dance.
2 I have previously discussed butoh's use as a theatrical tool to portray the grotesque in theatre and film (Calamoneri 2016).

Works Cited

Baird, Bruce. 2012. *Hijikata Tatsumi and Butoh: Dancing in a Pool of Gray Grits*. New York: Palgrave Macmillan.

Baird, Bruce. 2006. "Structureless in Structure: The Choreographic Tectonics of Hijikata Tatsumi's Buto." In *Modern Japanese Theater and Performance*, edited by David Jortner, Keiko McDonald, and Kevin J. Wetmore Jr., 93–108. Lanham: Lexington Books.

Baird, Bruce. 2005. "Butō and the Burden of History: Hijikata Tatsumi and the Nihonjin." PhD diss., University of Pennsylvania.

Baird, Bruce, and Rosemary Candelario. 2019. *The Routledge Companion to Butoh Performance*. Routledge Theatre and Performance Companions. Routledge.

Blakely Klein, Susan. 1988. *Ankoku Butō: The Premodern and Postmodern Influences on the Dance of Utter Darkness*. Ithaca: Cornell East Asia Papers, Cornell University.

Burt, Ramsay. 2017. *Ungoverning Dance: Contemporary European Theatre Dance and the Commons*. New York: Oxford University Press.

Calamoneri, Tanya. 2016. "Dancing Hamlet in a world of frogs: butoh and the actor's inner landscape", *Theatre, Dance and Performance Training*, 7:3, 375–388.

Candelario, Rosemary. 2016. *Flowers Cracking Concrete*. Middletown, CT.: Wesleyan University Press.

Fraleigh, Sondra Horton. 1999. *Dancing Darkness: Butō, Zen, and Japan*. Pittsburg: University of Pittsburgh Press.

Fraleigh, Sondra, and Tamah Nakamura. 2006. *Routledge Performance Practitioners: Hijikata Tatsumi and Ohno Kazuo*. New York: Routledge.

Sariel, Golomb Frankfurter. 2019. "Ungoverning Dance: Contemporary European Theatre Dance and the Commons by Ramsay Burt (Review)." *Dance Research Journal* 51 (3) (12): 98–100.

Thornbury, Barbara E. 2013. *America's Japan and Japan's Performing Arts*. Ann Arbor: University of Michigan Press.

2 Stranger in a Strange Land

1970s Avant-Garde as Precursor to Butoh

Political Climate

The growth of counterculture in the Americas is related both directly and indirectly to the political climate of the 1960s and 1970s. In the United States, flags and military service draft cards were set on fire in defiant performances of protest. The Civil Rights movement in the United States played out in corporeal violence, with physical bodies crossing imaginary lines with real consequences.

Fueled by protest movements in France and the Civil Rights movement and protests against the Vietnam War in the United States, the Mexican student movement erupted in the summer of 1968. Mexican students presented a manifesto that demanded "basic liberties and rights: free speech, a halt to state violence, accountability for police and military abuses, the release of political prisoners and the beginning of a dialogue with the government" (Malkin 2018, 2). *The New York Times* journalist Elisabeth Malkin notes that even before 1968, there were social uprisings involving miners, railroad workers, students, and teachers, and that "a rural guerilla movement was forming in the Western mountains" (Malkin, 4). Student movement protests began in earnest in July 1968 and gained broad support by August, when Javier Barros Sierra, *rector* (equivalent to a university president in the United States) of al Universidad Nacional Autónoma de México (UNAM), marched with students to protest repression by an authoritarian government. The movement gained momentum throughout August culminating in a large-scale demonstration in Mexico City's central square, the Zócalo. Police forces responded by occupying universities, where student movement leaders had headquartered and commandeered university presses to produce their newspapers; however, this only served to make protesters organize an even larger march that collected in *La Plaza de las Tres Culturas* on October 2.

La Plaza de las Tres Culturas was conceived as a monument to contemporary Mexico, an amalgam of cultures layered in time. It is the site of an Aztec ruin, a colonial Spanish church, and the modern Tlatelolco apartments. The site marks "a peculiar union in destruction and survival" with a dedication plaque that signals "the painful birth of the mestizo people," where Hernán Cortés defeated Cuauhtémoc at the Aztec city Tlatelolco on August 13, 1592 (Steinberg 2016,

DOI: 10.4324/9780429028472-2

24). Eerily, the plaza became the site of yet another violent erasure, when the army opened fire on protesters, killing at least 200 people and arresting nearly 2,000 (Dillon 1998, 1), who were later tortured and detained, some for more than two years (Malkin 2018). Less than two weeks later, Mexico launched the opening ceremony of the 1968 Olympics. The event is remembered by many in Mexico as a "massacre" and a brutal demonstration of authoritarian control. Yet there were literal and figurative cracks in the foundation of modern Mexico, where counterculture grew and found outlet in social and artistic collectives.

An Aesthetics of Violence

Mexican dance scholar and journalist Gustavo Emilio Rosales notes the context of butoh's rise in popularity amid "a nation convulsed by internal violence" (2018, 306). Rosales is referring to a specific butoh performance in 2014 at Centro Cultural Los Talleres, against a backdrop of narcopolitics; however, this juxtaposition of avant-garde art and brutal political repression is clearly a recurrent theme.

Social and political violence was by no means limited to Mexico. The United States was host to race riots throughout the 1960s and 1970s (some might even say they continue today), and the decimation of communities in the name of progress and urban expansion. In 1971, then-president Richard Nixon declared a "war on drugs," which, according to research, has only exacerbated drug-related violence (see Castillo and Kronick 2020). Violence is woven into the fabric of our modern society, so much so that even schoolchildren in the United States undergo drills for active shooter situations.

Several artists interviewed for this text comment on an aesthetics of chaos and decay, and how their work intervenes with social commentary. An example of one such intervention by butoh artist José Bravo demonstrates how artists have linked performance and activism, through a community piece he made in Guerrero, where 43 students disappeared in the custody of Mexican police. Activists have adopted the phrase "*Vivos se los llevaron, vivos los queremos*" (*They were taken alive, we want them back alive*), which Bravo incorporated as a call and response with the audience in his performance work. For him, butoh is a philosophy that he calls "*teatro cuerpo social*," or social body theater, that has the value of "witnessing humanity" (José Bravo, pers. comm., September 15, 2018). Such a poignant experience of vulnerability and human fragility approaches the urgency which the early butoh artists might have felt in post–World War II Japan.

Japanese butoh artists found common ground with American artists when they arrived in the 1970s. At this time in many Westernized countries, the very conventions of performance were at stake. Amid the global movements protesting social injustice that began in earnest in 1968, artists challenged both societal and disciplinary norms, and the state institutions which maintained these boundaries. The means, method, and content of performance were fundamentally altered. Many artists began presenting work in nontraditional venues, where they were free from the rules of production and also content censorship.

In Mexico, Alejandro Jodorowsky and *Los Grupos*, or the Group Movement, radically re-defined performativity. Jodorowsky brought the influence of the European avant-garde to Mexico City and staged live events that were scandalous to common decency, while at the same time critiquing the state-sponsored institutions. In one event, his performance centered around a helicopter crashed in a pool at the Academy of San Carlos; in another, he smashed a piano on a live television arts program. Throughout all of his work, he cultivated a raw, irreverent aesthetic with nudity, violence, and destruction. Visual artists who were influenced by Jodorowsky's interventions formed artistic collectives that protested the norms of state-sponsored art—mainly figurative murals glorifying the Mexican state—with action painting, blank canvases, and new venues that intentionally stood outside of state sponsorship and control.

And in the United States, artists such as Carolee Schneemann, Allan Kaprow, Chris Burden, and many others ushered in a new mode of performance art. Kaprow coined the term "happenings" with his 1959 performance piece *Eighteen Happenings in Six Parts*, which staged a series of events in three adjoining rooms in a New York loft, Reuben Gallery. Events ranged from choreographed movement sequences to everyday actions like squeezing oranges, and also accounted for the movement of the audience as a part of the "choreography" (Deak 2006, 9). A painter by training, Kaprow credited painter Jackson Pollock for turning the audience into participants with his large-scale murals. He writes of Pollock and other visual artists in his era: "not only will these bold creators show us, as if for the first time, the world we have always had about us but ignored, but they will disclose of entirely unheard of happenings and events" (quoted in Deak 2006, 10), such as things that occur on city streets and go unnoticed every day. Kaprow's happenings sought to draw our attention to these subtleties in the same way that John Cage's *4'33"* (1952) did. Cage sat down at a piano as if intending to play and then remained motionless in silence for four minutes and 33 seconds, during which time the audience, with their hearing heightened for the expectation of a performance, was to listen to the environmental sounds of birds, sirens, and city streets.

In Schneemann's 1964 happening titled *Meat Joy*, performers slapped each other with fish and plucked chickens (*The Village Voice* 2005, 23). The painter-turned-performer unfolded poems from her vagina (*Scroll* 1967), made art objects with her menstrual blood (*Blood Work Diary* 1972), and "inserted her own body into painting's visual field" (Richard 2009).

In this era, the emphasis shifted from passive art appreciation to active art engagement. In the 1960s and 1970s, artists were concerned with "altering [art's] role in society from a vehicle directed toward entertainment to a vehicle for critical reflection," write Curtis Carter, scholar of aesthetics and philosopher focused on the role of art in society (Carter 2013, 292). They positioned bodies in new roles of agency, often by engaging those bodies outside the disciplinary field in which they worked. For example, dance scholar Sally Banes writes that during this time

> there were dances made by visual artists and composers as well as by dancers, films made by choreographers, performances by poets and visual artists, and all manner of undefinable events by people who were already defining themselves as unclassifiable intermedia artists.
>
> (Banes 1991, 157)

The goal of this intermixing had a philosophical bent toward a democratic community, as opposed to prior elitist, exceptionalist models. In dance, the Judson Church era of performances "invoked a new paradigm that understands art pluralistically and as anti-essentialist" (Carter, 292). In other words, anyone or anything could be material for art, rejecting notions that only certain bodies that adhered to subjective standards of beauty and technical prowess ought to appear on stage and be considered art. Yvonne Rainer's *We Shall Run* (1963) exemplified this with a group of 12 dancers and nondancers who simply ran for the course of the performance. There was no leader and no apparent structure save the one that emerged from the performers themselves in the moment. Banes writes "simplicity and grandeur met in an ethos of egalitarian community" (Banes 1991, 158).

Forms of expression emerged that blurred meaning, confused audiences, and emphasized the intersectional nature of human existence. Furthermore, dance contributed to performance art as a genre helping to usher in an action-oriented, visual bodily text (Carroll 2012, 126). Given such an artistic climate, it is relatively easy to see the appeal that a deeply visceral and often ineffable form such as butoh held for American artists, and the kinship Japanese avant-garde artists found there.

Perhaps the most direct invitation for butoh in the United States was offered by Ellen Stewart and La MaMa Experimental Theater in New York, where the Japanese avant-garde shattered America's previous notions of Japanese culture and performing arts. In particular, she brought Shuji Terayama and his collaborators who presented a violent, bold, genre-bending style of work that was a welcome aesthetic influence.

On the West Coast of the United States, another influence would take root. Hijikata-trained dancers Koichi and Hiroko Tamano landed in the late 1970s and slowly built a butoh company out of punk rock, drag, and other performers that they encountered along the way. They performed in galleries, music clubs, street festivals, parks, and a host of other locations, and also founded Country Station sushi restaurant. Their steadfast presence built a community of students. And from their work, San Francisco Butoh Festival curator Brechin Flournoy found fertile ground for the massive undertaking of an international festival that she grew in the 1990s, which is profiled in Chapter 3.

This chapter explores the influence of Jodorowsky, Ellen Stewart and La MaMa Experimental Theatre Club, and the Tamanos. It then looks at the explosion of butoh touring in the Americas in the late 1980s and early 1990s. Additionally, it highlights two pivotal figures that firmly established butoh artists in the United States and Mexico through collaborations: Ellen Stewart and Abraham Oceransky. In 1987, Stewart began collaborating with Min Tanaka on productions that performed in New York and traveled to Greece. In 1989, Mexican experimental director Abraham Oceransky invited Natsu Nakajima to work with his company, creating a platform for Mexican artists to study with her, Ko Murobushi, and other Japanese dancers. In so doing, they eventually built touring networks for butoh in the Americas.

Jodorowsky and the Mexican Avant-Garde in the 1960s and 1970s

In many Latin American countries, art interventions such as happenings and other means of disrupting institutional hierarchies took on an activist valence, where artists used these strategies to comment on government repression (Decker 2015, 19). At the time, Mexico was consolidating its national image as it rose to international prominence and became the first Latin American nation to be selected to host the Olympics. The public face was represented most strikingly through State-sponsored murals depicting a romantic notion of agrarian life and industrial progress, such as those by Diego Rivera and David Alfaro Siqueiros. El Palacio de Bellas Artes institutionalized Ballet Folklórico de México of Amalia Hernández in 1952, and the dance company represented Mexico at the Pan American games in Chicago in 1959.

Art historian Arden Decker (Associate Director, International Center for the Arts in the Americas, Museum of Fine Arts, Houston, TX) has done extensive investigation into the changes in artistic production in the 1960s and 1970s in Mexico. In her research on the emergence of Los Grupos, activist artist collectives that broke with institutional structures, she writes:

> The omission of radical, contemporary art practice in state museums and state-sponsored exhibitions coupled with an increasingly oppressive climate due to the student uprisings of the late 1960s fueled the desire for alternative exhibition spaces and a move toward artist collectives and collaboration.
>
> (Decker, 29)

Decker details the impact of cross-disciplinary work at this time, particularly events that were precursors to performance art. In one such event, she describes Mathias Goeritz's *Manifesto de Los (H)artos* as a "flat out rejection of continued artistic categorization" (Decker, 62). The exhibition opened on November 30, 1961, with a performance intervention that included action painting and a live chicken that laid an egg during the performance that was sold to a participating artist and crushed in the course of the event. In this same exhibition, painter José Luis Cuevas presented a blank "mural" entitled *Vision Panorámica de las*

Artes Plásticas [*Panoramic Vision of the Plastic Arts*] as an attempt to "satirize the stranglehold of muralism and the Mexican School" (Decker, 64).

Los Grupos, or artist collectives, began to form as a simple act of resistance against State-sponsored crackdowns on gatherings of suspected student activists and also as a supportive structure outside institutional means that could investigate form and content. Some of the more prominent groups included Tepito Arte Acá, Proceso Pentágono, Mira, Suma, Germinal, Taller de Arte e Ideología (TAI), El Colectivo, Tetradero, Março, Peyote y la Compañía, No-Grupo, Taller de Investigación Plástica (TIP), and Fotógrafos Independientes (Decker, 159).

Decker terms the formation of Los Grupos as a phenomenon, rather than a movement, as each group had distinct aims and methods (Decker, 159). She categorizes them broadly into two camps:

> Those [that were] highly polemical groups that considered themselves to be kin to "cultural workers" (and intentionally functioned together more like unions) and those groups that were comprised of individual artists utilizing power in numbers as a means for creating spaces for experimentation and critical approaches to art making.
>
> (Decker, 159)

In other words, some groups formed as part of a sociopolitical protest, and others more of a formalistic, artistic protest.

Chilean-born Alejandro Jodorowsky (b.1929 Tocapilla, Chile) established himself in Mexico City from Paris in 1960 and almost immediately became a beacon for Mexican counterculture artists—including visual artists, actors, dancers, theater directors, filmmakers—who were hungry for inspiration from the European avant-garde (Decker, 66). Among many artists, Jodorowsky had worked with Samuel Beckett and Antonin Artaud. Jodorowsky had also studied mime with Etienne Decroux and joined the theater troupe of Decroux's student, Marcel Marceau, and toured with him to Mexico in 1959. The young artist found an eager community and decided to stay. In Mexico, Jodorowsky began with a production of *Endgame*, by Beckett, which was panned by critics (Decker, 87). Jodorowsky nonetheless continued to introduce Theater of the Absurd (through Beckett and Ionesco, among others) and Artaud's Theater of Cruelty to the nascent experimental performance scene in Mexico.

By 1960, he developed his own theory of "panic theater" which he experimented with through "explosive cocktail parties" (Decker, 79), which were improvisational events staged for the artist to observe social interactions in extreme circumstances. He invited guests from all social strata, ranging from statesmen to prostitutes. One participant commented that Jodorowsky "knew how to organize people in a social game" (Decker, 79). Decker writes that musician Luis Urías characterized the structure of the ephemerals as "like jazz, with each individual reacting to create a collective production" (Decker, 79).[1] These events were often only one-time occurrences, as the human reaction element in each "score" would alter the outcome in each event. They were seen more as social performance research than theatrical pieces.

In 1965, Jodorowsky published *Teatro Pánico* (*Panic Theatre*), a text that encapsulated his work since his arrival in Mexico City in 1960. *Teoría de pánico* (*Panic theory*), as he termed his philosophical basis, manifested through *efímeros pánicos* (*panic ephemerals*), which were essentially one-time events, often improvised and seldom documented. There is some video footage remaining, however, which allows a glimpse of the work: in one rare documented event that occurred in 1965 in Paris, entitled *Melodrama Sacramental*, a ritualistic copulation yields strange results, at each turn amplifying its shock value. A woman dances atop a paper mâché breast and when she leaves her perch, two men kick and stomp on the breast sending plaster flying. A man in a Japanese samurai warrior outfit presides over a naked man strapped to a stretcher. An attendant appears to have spoons clipped to his naked skin in rows up and down his back, arms, and legs. Naked men and women jump, holler, yelp, and gyrate, as a clothed man waves a live chicken at them, sometimes hitting them with it in what appears to be a benediction. A frenzied drummer is encircled and urged on by onlookers, and it is difficult to tell if they are audience or performers. What starts out looking like two-dimensional bouffant performance (there was a cardboard cutout used in the aforementioned copulation) ends in pure chaos, with a man tied to a cross and draped with offal from a cow, another man entering a vaginal-shaped pool and then pushing live turtles back through the slit, which writhe on their backs in a heap. The audience can be heard laughing, perhaps out of nervousness or perhaps in recognition of the sheer absurdity of the spectacle.

Experimental instruments and music figured heavily in the *efimerals*. Luis Urías was a long-time associate of Jodorowsky in Mexico, and he constructed musical sets out of everyday objects, like a drum set out of trash cans, a makeshift "harp," and a *conocordio*: an arrangement of pipes, a bathtub, and a horn that when played made it appear that music "came out of the ass" (Decker, 83).

In April 1967, Jodorowsky staged a piano destruction[2] on a television talk show hosted by Juan López Moctezuma, a friend, collaborator, and fellow filmmaker. Broadcast to Mexican audiences through national television, the event evoked shock and elicited critical disdain. Jodorowsky's act was a literal and metaphorical attempt at breaking the norms of art. Whether intended or not, it was received as an attack on cultural institutions that tried to force a Mexican national identity through state-sponsored art, particularly that which chronicled Mexican culture.

Jodorowsky's work is rife with violence, primarily enacted on animals. Similar to the decapitated chicken floundering in the ocean waves in Eiko Hosoe's film *Navel and A-Bomb*, choreographed by Hijikata, there is a nod in Jodorowsky to Artaud's Theater of Cruelty and sacrifice that was intended to provide catharsis for the audience. In Hosoe's film, a goat is carried ceremoniously and strange dances are performed around a cow prior to the headless chicken haplessly splashing about, evoking the futility of humanity felt particularly keenly in post–World War II Japan. Unlike *Navel and A-Bomb*, however, in Jodorowsky's works, there is little sense of ritual and solemnity, and the sacrificial acts seem brutal and careless. In one *efimeral*, a character by the name of Monster-Monster bites the head off of a live dove and then proceeded to dismember it savagely (Decker, 84–85).

Jodorowsky claimed that there was a point to the brutality in his work: "there are two types of violence: creative and destructive" (quoted in Decker, 87). Presumably, he thought his work was the former, breaking boundaries in order to invent new worlds. However, it is important to critique Jodorowsky's objects of brutality and particularly his treatment of women. In *Melodrama Sacramental*, women were most often the performers with the least clothes and are often passive figures against whom violence is perpetrated. A man passes by a naked woman who is gyrating to music and nonchalantly squeezes and twists her nipple as if adjusting the volume on a radio. In other scenes, violence against women is perpetuated with surrogate objects. In one scene, two men stomp on and kick a paper mâché breast; in another, they hack female mannequins with an ax. The piece opens with two men pretending to rape a woman with a cardboard phallus. Queer sci-fi film critic Emily Asher-Perrin writes in a critique of Jodorowsky's failed *Dune* film, recounting an interview he gave in 1970 on his film *Fando y Lis*, "he actually insists on being beaten by his costar and then raping her for the purpose of the film" (Asher-Perrin 2017). For emphasis, Asher-Perrin includes Jodorowsky's actual words:

> After she had hit me long enough and hard enough to tire her, I said, "Now it's my turn. Roll the cameras." And I really . . . I really . . . I really raped her. And she screamed. Then she told me that she had been raped before . . . Fantastic scene. A very, very strong scene.
>
> (Asher-Perrin 2017)

Asher-Perrin critiques Jodorowsky's version of art as one of faux genius, that is, "glorious and unknowable yet ugly and obscene . . . that doesn't require trust or respect or basic human decency" (Asher-Perrin 2017). While Jodorowsky may have broken formal boundaries of art, he merely reinscribes tired gender dynamics that were at the heart of 1960s social protest movements.

Thankfully his and other misogynistic artists' activities are being called increasingly into question. And at the same time, Jodorowsky's formalistic transgressions became an accepted norm in the experimental arts. Decker suggests that Jodorowsky is often not mentioned in histories of Mexican conceptual art because his art was so outside comprehension. She argues that Jodorowsky was "one of the most significant forces in the introduction of conceptualism in Mexico" (Decker, 69). Felipe Ehrenberg of Grupo Proceso Pentágono concurs, calling attention to the impact of this artist on his and following generations: "The effects of Jodorowsky are very deep . . . Jodorowsky, as much as they do not say it, generally affected art in Mexico in an indescribable way" (Decker, 69).

Jodorowsky's reach extended to popular culture through television with a show called *1, 2, 3, 4, 5, a gogó*, created by him, "showman Alfonso Arau, and multi-cameraman Fernando Ge [González]" (Escoto 2021, 28). Arau and Jodorowsky met in the early 1960s when the former attended the show of Marcel Marceau's company on tour in Mexico, in which Jodorowsky performed. Arau subsequently traveled to France to study with L'Ecole international de théâtre Jacques LeCoq. When Arau returned to Mexico, he and Jodorowsky developed a one-man show called *Locuras Felices* (*Happy Follies*), which performed in both Mexico City and Paris (Escoto, 31). Arau also studied with Japanese ex-pat Stanislavskian teacher Seki Sano, a revolutionary Russian-trained Japanese specialist in Stanislavski and Michael Chekov methods who fled to New York and then to Mexico in 1939 due to political persecution for his work. Seki's goal was to promote "anti-Nazi-fascist consciousness" (Tanaka 1994, 59). Sano became an influential theater artist in the development of Mexican experimental performance; among his students were theater director José Luis Cruz.

Jodorowsky, Arau, and Ge were hired into *1, 2, 3, 4, 5, a gogó* once it was already in existence. It had been launched as a show for contemporary youth culture. The show aired in the 7–9 PM slot, intended for teenagers, on Canal 5 (Escoto 2021, 33) and was a pop-culture romp that aimed to capture the 1968 zeitgeist of excess and psychedelia. It was described as "hybrid musical spectacle that intermingled theatrical experimental values . . . in the midst of the psychedelic effervescence" (Escoto, 29). Numerous famous guests and members of the Mexican *La Maffia* (avant-garde artists and intelligentsia) graced the show, including Felipe Ehrenberg, José Luis Cuevas, and Carlos Monsiváis; José Agustín served as scriptwriter for a time (Escoto, 33). Absurd antics "bombarded the audience with poetic and subversive images such as a young woman inside a coffin and dancer Valerie Trumblay wearing a man's beard" (Escoto, 34), or one episode dedicated entirely to interviewing a cow. More than 100 costumed performers littered the set, and Ge's mobile camera work caught them from multiple angles, adding to the chaos, propelled further by loud rock music. Jodorowsky repeated his piano destruction on the show, which got him fired, and Arau was soon after fired for his parody of *El Monje Loco* (*The Mad Monk*), which was perceived by producer Telesistema as critical of the Church (Escoto, 39). The show was canceled less than a year after it began, but it still afforded the artists involved with media exposure that further bolstered their pop icon status.

Abraham Oceransky and Multi-disciplinary, Cross-Cultural Theater

Experimental theater director Abraham Oceransky emerged as both a precursor to and a direct conduit for butoh in Mexico. Oceransky had been a publicist and a rocker, playing guitar in the bands The Slippers, Los Locos del Ritmo, and Los Teen Tops. He encountered theater by accident, when he accompanied a friend to an audition. The director of the show was none other than Jodorowsky, who asked him to read for him. From that moment, Oceransky's life took on a new direction. He says: "I realized that there was a work of conscience, art is not a superfluous thing, it is not a vulgar matter, it is not a form of economic work, it is a monastery"[3] (Milenio 2020).

Oceransky studied at la Escuela de Arte Teatral del Instituto Nacional de Bellas Artes (INBA 2019) and had his directing debut in 1967 with *Gigantes de la montaña*, by Pirandello (Maya 2002). Oceransky was also involved in Happenings through UNAM and began his own experimental research in La Carpa Alicia (Alice Tent), a space where he rehearsed and hosted classes in a variety of performance forms. He has long been an aficionado of Japanese culture, especially physical practices like martial arts, Eastern philosophy, and controversial playwright Yukio Mishima. In his development of a theatrical aesthetic, he experiments with mime, physical theater, and site-specific theater in nontraditional settings. In an interview with Patricia Vega of *Letras Libre*, Oceransky discusses the fact that his aesthetics and methods were influenced by Jodorowsky, Artaud, and Japanese butoh. Nakajima was the first of several butoh artists that Oceransky would invite to work with his company; he worked closely with Ko Murobushi from 1999 to 2002, Yumiko Yoshioka from 2010 until present, and Katsura Kan in 2015 and 2017.

By 1971, he had won critical awards for his adaptation of Lewis Carroll stories, entitled *Conejo Blanco* (*White Rabbit*) (Maya 2002). At 29 years old, he began the first experimental theater in Mexico with little more than four clip lights and a group of friends that believed in his vision. He created a black box theater called El Galeón, which was incorporated in 1972 as an official space of Centro Cultural del Bosque, part of INBA. In its 50 years of existence, it has been the home of Oceransky's company Teatro T as well as other notable experimental directors including Peter Brook and Tadeus Kantor (INBA 2019). In 1985, he moved Teatro T to Xalapa, Veracruz, where he joined the faculty of the Teatro de la Universidad Veracruzana. Here, he established Estudio Cuarto T, then el Teatro La Libertad, and most recently a new space simply called La Libertad (Rodriguez 2020).

Oceransky met butoh dancer Natsu Nakajima in 1987. She was the second butoh artist invited to perform at the esteemed international theater festival, the Festival Internacional Cervantino (FIC), in Guanajuato, where she performed *Niwa* to critical acclaim. On this same tour, she performed the work at UNAM, where she met theater director Abraham Oceransky and also dancer/actress/sculptor Roció Sagaón, who was married to French photographer George Vinaver and was involved in Mexican intellectual circles with the likes of Luis Buñuel and José Luis Cuevas (Gomez 2015). Oceransky, who had long been interested in physical theater, Asian arts, and experimental creative practices, was taken with Nakajima's work and invited her back to work with his company and to teach public workshops numerous times between 1989 and 2005. Choreographer Lola Lince participated in one of these workshops and subsequently collaborated with Nakajima on several performances.

Oceransky cultivated a lasting relationship with both Nakajima and Ko Murobushi, bringing both of these artists more than a dozen times each to teach at UNAM and the University Veracruzana between the mid-1980s and present. Oceransky also introduced Berlin-based Yumiko Yoshioka to teach at Teatro T in 2010 and has presented a total of nine intensive workshops with her for his students and company. He has also hosted Katsura Kan a handful of times, following Kan's 2012 collaboration/commission from Isabel Beteta at Los Talleres in Mexico City.

La MaMa and Her Children: Shuji Terayama and the Japanese Avant-Garde in New York in the 1970s

Visionary curator Ellen Stewart opened the floodgates that brought Japanese avant-garde performance to New York. A decade before she brought the experimental dance of Japanese butoh with the US premiere of Kazuo Ohno, Stewart brought experimental Japanese theater in the 1970s. La MaMa first presented Yukata Higashi's *Golden Bat* directed by Itsuro Shimoda (performed in Japanese) in June 1970. The musical was extremely well received. The *Golden Bat* was immediately followed by Shuji Terayama's critically acclaimed play *La Marie Vision* (performed in English) in July 1970. Subsequently, in September of the same year, La MaMa presented Higashi's *Coney Island*, this time featuring the rock-theater performers singing in English, which eroded some of the exotic charms of *Golden Bat* but nonetheless was favorably received. These three productions ushered in a new era for New York audiences and artists alike, engaging directly with their contemporaries in Japan on current issues of social and political change.

Golden Bat director Higashi was an original member of Terayama's radically experimental company Tenjo Sajiki, the first and arguably the most important Japanese theater group in the international theater circuit in the 1960s and 1970s (Thornbury 2016, 106). Higashi went on to establish the experimental Japanese musical theater group Tokyo Kid Brothers, for which *Golden Bat* director Shimoda served as musical director. The group was featured in Terayama's acclaimed 1971 film *Throw away the Books, Rally in the Streets*. Both the film and Tokyo Kid Brothers' live shows embraced the psychedelic rock-heavy musical style of the wildly popular *Hair*, which was incubated just around the corner from La MaMa at Joseph Papp's Public Theater before it went to Broadway in 1968. The similarities in style drew comparisons, which garnered a place in the contemporary artistic dialogue and critical sphere, whereas previously Japanese artists had mainly been reviewed as cultural objects that were somehow fixed in tradition.

Japanese scholar Barbara Thornbury argues that La MaMa's "Downtown" New York status both "ushered Japan and its performing arts into new debates about cultural production and encounter, while at the same time solidifying the position of La MaMa as the leading voice in those debates" (Thornbury, 107). Further, she argues that La Mama's presentations rescued Japanese performing arts from the antiquated, exotified, Kabuki-associated reception that Japanese performing arts had been affiliated with in the United States, particularly New York, and put them on equal footing with their American contemporaries. Says Thornbury, "La MaMa was the first institution to incorporate Japan fully within New York's competitive performing arts environment" (Thornbury, 107), meriting critical review rather than merely polite cultural interest.[4] Demonstrating a commitment to this new cross-cultural dialogue with Japan, Stewart and La MaMa subsequently presented several of Terayama's films,[5] invited Tokyo Kid Brothers' Shimoda back to direct Ching Yeh's *Craving for Worldly Pleasures* in 1973, and that same year invited Higashi to direct his own play *The City*, with Shimoda again composing music.

Through these efforts, Stewart built an audience and cultivated critical reception that would begin to understand Japanese avant-garde performance in a new light. Moreover, says Mio Yoo, Stewart's successor and the current Artistic Director of La MaMa, "These young performers from Japan brought artists and audiences together at a time when there was still prejudice against Asians here in the US" (Yoo 2019).

The imprint Terayama and his proteges made in New York was significant for not only the reception of Japanese contemporary artists in the United States but also the aesthetic intervention it offered to American artists. Terayama's 1980 *Directions to Servants* featured deafeningly loud music and fire-breathing actors, and was performed in Japanese (Fowler 1983, 1). The performance also showcased music by punk/rock/opera and film composer J.A. Seazer, a frequent collaborator of Terayama. The play had all the makings of a cult classic: irreverent, genre-shattering, and decidedly obscure in that it was performed in Japanese.

Direction to Servants' cast included three bald-headed white paint-clad actors who, according to La MaMa archivist Ozzie Rodriguez, were also butoh dancers: Tadashi Ichikawa, Takeshi Wakamatsu, and Hajime Hirai. Wakamatsu and Dairakudakan director Akaji Maro were featured in a Toshinori Okada's Chelfitsch production of Kobo Abe's play *Tomodachi* (*Friend*). Those three dancers lead the physicality of the play: *The New York Times* review called them "stunningly grotesque" commenting on their "slavering at the audience," they move as a pack of beaten dogs, over whose heads one actress "savagely brandishes a dog leash" (Corry 1980). John Corry of *The New York Times* called Terayama "the Tokyo apostle" to Hal Prince for his style of concept-musical, albeit one that Corry likened in places to a grotesque Last Supper (Corry 1980). Though he criticized Terayama's *Servants* for being egotistical and self-indulgent, Corry nonetheless concedes that "it is still an important piece of work" (Corry 1980).

Terayama had certainly made an impression on the downtown New York performance scene. He also initiated New York audiences to butoh and its grotesque elements. A similar trajectory happened in France, where Terayama was presenting film and theater works in the 1960s and butoh arrived by the mid-1970s. Patrick DeVos, professor of French Theater at the University of Tokyo, notes that Terayama and his contemporaries in the experimental music scene influenced the reception of butoh in France thus: "Shuji Terayama were already known before butoh made its appearance in France, so a new image of Japan began to solidify-a Japan that was erotic, sophisticated, and a creator of what you might call the 'aesthetics of violence'" (Wochi Kochi 2013).

Other notable Japanese artist groups bear mentioning in the history of butoh in New York, even if their work was not termed butoh as such. Eiko and Koma first performed their version of butoh—"white dance" as they called it to distinguish it from Hijikata's dance of darkness—in 1976 presented by the Japan Society. The couple studied with Kazuo Ohno in Japan, Mary Wigman student Manja Chmiel in Germany, and Lucas Hoving (student of José Limon, Martha Graham, Doris Humphrey, and others) in the Netherlands. The pair have developed their own style that they call "delicious movement," and often present installation-like performances over several hours. They have collaborated with such numerous acclaimed artists as Anna Halprin and Kronos Quartet. The couple often tackles complex and sensitive themes, such as their collaboration with Cambodian painters presented in Cambodia and New York, that touches on life after the Killing Fields, and *Offering*, a mourning ritual presented near Ground Zero in New York. The duet has grown in prominence over the years, receiving such esteemed awards as two New York "Bessies," and Guggenheim and MacArthur fellowships. Their work is chronicled by Rosemary Candelario in her book *Flowers Cracking Concrete: Eiko & Koma's Asian/American Choreographies* (2016).

Kei Takei had studied with both Ohno and Hijikata in Japan and then relocated to New York in 1967 at the recommendation of Anna Sokolow (Kei Takei's Moving Earth, n.d.). She performed at various venues in New York including the seminal Dance Theater Workshop (1970) and Brooklyn Academy of Music's Leperq Space (1975). Takei rejected the "darkness of gloom aesthetic" (Kei Takei's Moving Earth, n.d.) of her early butoh teachers and instead made her own solemn work that has been described as "installments of spare, repetitive rituals" (New Yorker, 2021). As testament to her ability to create art as a ceremonial practice, from 1969 to 1996, Takei choreographed and staged no less than 31 installments of a piece titled *Light: Part X*.

Hisatoshi "Poppo" Shiraishi, a student of butō dancer Kunisaki Kamiryo, founded Poppo and the GoGo Boys in 1979 and began presenting ritualistic, punk, site-specific work in the East Village. He was known for daring, controversial work, including jumping on moving cars and dancing with toilets. Poppo also created works for the stage at La MaMa. In *A New Model of the Universe*, he carries a pig across stage, while a female dancer tears apart paper and throws it about the space. Dancers painted all in gold run laterally across the stage in lanes, performing acrobatic tricks. They increase the level of danger by adding 4x4 beams carried in the arms of one or two dancers and swinging them around so that the remaining dancers have to duck and dodge. There are arch moments of ballet vocabulary, in which dancers bourée offstage flapping their arms. The aesthetic is unruly and bold, drawing from the energy of the company's street performances. Several members of the GoGo Boys went on to form their own companies, including long-time principal dancer Celeste Hastings who has developed a rich solo career and in 2000 founded the Butoh Rockettes, which often performs in New York's club scene. Many performers filtered in and out of Poppo's GoGo Boys, including Zack Fuller, who has performed internationally and also worked extensively with Min Tanaka, and Sara Baird and Susan Lamberth, who went on to form Anemone Dance, which presented work in New York from 2002 to 2007.

Hijikata Sends Koichi Tamano to California

The first butoh performance that was termed as such in the United States happened on the West Coast in 1976, under the auspices of the Japan Now Festival, in two museums: first the Los Angeles Museum of Contemporary Art and then the San Francisco Museum of Modern Art. Through a connection with Japanese ex-pats living in the United States, Koichi Tamano traveled to California. He says he began touring at the behest of Hijikata, to bring butoh abroad (Koichi Tamano pers. comm., July 2018). He brought with him Mariko Ohno and Hiroshi Kasai (no relation to Kazuo Ohno or Akira Kasai) and performed at the two festivals, as well as several small galleries and music venues. Eiko and Koma, who had been at Asbestos-kan at the same time as the Tamanos, also performed in the San Francisco exhibition, with their work, *No Wave*.

I want to briefly address Tamano's history as it is significant for the lineage authenticity narrative that has permeated American butoh, at least on the US West Coast, and also reveals some of the linkages between the Tamanos and artists who subsequently toured to the United States.

In 1972, Hijikata choreographed *Nagasu kujira* (*Fin Back Whale*) for Koichi Tamano, which effectively founded the Harupin-Ha Company. The first performance included Yoko Ashikawa, Kazuo Aoyagi, and Yukio Waguri. Tamano had performed with these artists in *Shike no tame no niju nana ban* (*27 Nights for Four Seasons*), the development of which spanned 1970–72 in Tokyo. Saga Kobayashi had also danced in *27 Nights*, and it was through the Tamanos that the San Francisco Butoh Festival made her acquaintance. Tamano had been participating in Hijikata's Asbestos-kan studio since 1965, performing with Kazuo and Yoshito Ohno, Akira Kasai, Mitsutaka dancing or assisting in numerous important works including *Bara iro dance* (*Rose Colored Dance*) and *Nikutai no hanran* (*Rebellion of the Body*).

Hiroko Tamano had joined Hijikata's studio in 1972 with the production of *27 Nights*. She had come to Tokyo in 1970 to study art at Musashino Art College and then changed her course toward dance when she "met butoh" (pers. comm. July 2018). She remained at Asbestos-kan from 1972 to 1975, dancing in stage productions and late-night cabarets, and then followed Koichi as he formed his own company in Tokyo.

Harupin-Ha's second production was in 1975 with *Muen'Tan* (*Smokeless Coal*). Dancing in this performance were Anzu Furukawa, Mutsuko Tanaka, and Hiruta Sanae. Ushio Amagatsu served as stage crew. Furukawa and

Amagatsu were also dancing in Dairakurakan at the time and went on to found the companies DanceLoveMachine and Sankai Juku, respectively. (The Tamanos were the conduit for Furukawa connecting with the San Francisco Butoh Festival.) As further testament to how interwoven the international butoh community is, when Furukawa's company Dance Butter Tokyo performed at the San Francisco Butoh Festival, former Tamano dancer Shinichi Iova-Koga was struck by one of Furukawa's dancers, Yuko Kaseki. Iova-Koga and Kaseki began collaborating the following year in Berlin and went on to create several acclaimed touring works.

After four years of developing Harupin-Ha in Japan and performing in cabarets throughout Japan, Tamano had begun to solidify his company's identity and gathered enough funds to travel. During their 1976 tour, Tamano and his dancers shot a series of photos in Death Valley (see Figure 2.1) that is reminiscent of Hosoe's famous "Kamaitachi" series, American style. The dancers run through the bleached desert landscape trailing shockingly red fabric, pose precariously with naked flesh over unforgiving craggy rocks, and wrap their bodies around one another as an oasis of comfort in the harsh landscape. They are virile and irreverent. The only thing missing is the toothless grins of locals (from the Kamaitachi series), but one can almost image them as Tamano crouches as if defecating on a tourist sign.

Figure 2.1 Death Valley (1976). Dancers Left to Right: Hiroshi Kasai, Koichi Tamano, Mariko Ohno.

Source: Courtesy Harupin-Ha, reprinted with permission from Harupin-Ha

Following the West Coast foray, Tamano returned to Japan to rehearse *Rito* (*Pear Head*) a piece Hijikata had choreographed for Tamano's newly formed then Tokyo-based Harupin-Ha dance company. Perhaps in an effort to build his legacy and encourage select students to branch out, Hijikata was also choreographing for Nakajima's Muteki-sha at this point, in addition to Hakutobo (with Yoko Ashikawa). Nakajima also choreographed a dance on Harupin-Ha. All of these companies were performing at the Hangidaitokan Performance Series at Asbestos-kan in Tokyo in 1976, until the performance space was closed down in December following complaints from neighbors (Kurihara and Ruyak 2000, 32).

During this period, Tamano also made the foray that DanceLoveMachine and other butoh artists had made to Berlin, creating a collaboration there with Mitsutaka. He would return to Berlin several times over his career to work with Ishii.

In 1977, Tamano was one of three disciples for whom Hijikata choreographed solos. The other two were Saga Kobayashi and Moe Yamamoto. Tamano's piece was *Nagasu kujira* (*Fin Back Whale*), the solo version of the original Harupin-Ha piece that Hijikata had choreographed in 1972. *Fin Back Whale* was Tamano's first performance when he relocated to Berkeley, California in 1979, with his wife Hiroko and their first daughter.

Nagasu kujira (Fin Back Whale)

Tamano is wearing a white lace sheer shift dress with intricate pleats and embroidery, body painted white, and hair teased up into a point about a foot above his head and brushed in white paint—presumably this is the fin of the whale? The sound score is water dripping and high-pitched electronic tones that sound remotely like snippets of whale songs. Knees bent and balanced on the outer edges of his feet; he rotates and takes small steps. His arms float a little outward from the sides of his hips, and his mouth works as if a whale taking in water and filtering out krill. A melodic electronic music score by Kitaro (a frequent collaborator with Tamano) plays, and Tamano teeters across the stage. He settles down into a crouch like a whale resting at the bottom of the ocean, and hovers there, arms/fins floating.

Waves lap on the shore, and eventually he rises as a different being, tall and thin, taking quick, mincing steps. Eventually, he bends his knees again and settles down to a crouching hover, this time with arms floating overhead, accenting the currents of the water as they ripple through his seaweed-like limbs. He fully crouches again, and Hiroko appears behind him to unbutton his dress, which he stands up and shimmies out of, pulls it in front of his body, and crouches again, holding the dress in his lap. He stands up, drops his shed lace dress which in this posture resembles a shed whale skin, dances around a bit in just a gold g-string, and then crouches again to be dressed by Hiroko, this time in a red kimono with long hanging sleeves. His hands and mouth move as if they were a sea anemone, reaching and sucking in plankton, shuttling it toward his mouth. Bagpipes play *Amazing Grace*; he rises triumphantly with a dried flower in his right hand. He makes his body angular and flat, folding it to the side in the Maya pose (a la Nijinsky in *Rite of Spring*), extends a leg hip-height in front of him, lifts the heel of the standing foot, and, in a somewhat comic gesture like a cartoon character taking off on a run, begins a zip zag walk. It is a move seen in Hijikata's *Nikutai no hanran*, with a similar impish facial expression. This crisscrossing angled walk continues until the music ends and he bows deeply, still in the remote state of his performance.

The movements in *Fin Back Whale* mark a moment in time when Hijikata was developing a movement vocabulary and methodology in *27 Nights*. These same movements are replicated by Tamano in numerous other pieces and become a sort of codices of Bay Area butoh. One can see them in the dancers of many Harupin-Ha students, including early works of Shinichi Iova-Koga. The crouched position reminiscent of Nijinsky, elbows bent, body flattened as if pressed into a wall (or a frieze) echoes throughout the works. The Tamanos took this two-dimensional figure down to the floor in a movement referred to as "crocodile," a sequence that was employed in several works over the years.

Building on a growing network in the Bay Area, Harupin-Ha secured performances at San Francisco Museum of Modern Art (SFMOMA), Mills College, and the Exploratorium Museum. They toured up to Vancouver, Canada through the connections they had made at the 1976 Japan Now Festival. They also performed in many small experimental galleries (see Figure 2.2).

Figure 2.2 San Francisco Gallery Performance (1979). Dancer: Koichi Tamano.

Source: Courtesy Harupin-Ha, reprinted with permission from Harupin-Ha

The Tamanos remained connected to the butoh community in Japan as well, so when visa time constraints brought the Tamanos back to Japan in 1980, Koichi performed in Dairakudakan's *Betsu no hikari* (*Another Light*) under the direction of Akaji Maro. The relationship with Dairakudakan and presenters at the theaters where they performed would later help the Tamanos return to Japan on tour with the American-based Harupin-Ha company.

Canadian producer Myra Davies had seen Harupin-Ha's work in Vancouver the previous year and tracked them down in Tokyo. Says Hiroko, it was Davies' skilled administration that brought them back to North America in the Fall of 1980 for a Canadian tour with their 1979 piece *Swamp*. From there, their passage back into the United States was relatively simple (Hiroko Tamano pers. comm., December 14, 2017).

Esmerelda Kay, lead singer of the punk rock group Noh Mercy, invited the Tamanos to hold class at her 922 Valencia Street studio, which Hiroko credits as the beginning of building a local scene in the San Francisco Bay Area. Kay wrote glowingly about the experience:

> Koichi Tamano (the world famous student of the Great Butoh Dancer Hijikata) and his incredible wife Hiroko Tamano came to the US and taught the first BUTOH classes in America in our storefront where I lived with Tommy Pace and Magenta Mason. The classes were beyond amazing. Our dear friend Nobuo translated for us . . . instructions like: "You are knee deep in a swamp of sewage, holding an egg in your mouth and a bee is circling your head. You must cross this swamp to the other side keeping one eye closed and the other eye on the bee and without breaking the egg."
> (Kay 2021)

Noh Mercy's aesthetic[6] was clearly drawn from Japanese culture: Esmerelda's makeup borrowed Kabuki stylization and precision, with angular red eyebrows and cheekbones. The "American style" to which Hiroko refers was their unique twist that referenced David Bowie and Prince, and the San Francisco drag culture. Esmerelda's costume was frequently a mélange of fishnets, a corset, lace-up boots, and a kimono draped loosely around the whole ensemble. Her wild hair was teased up to look like a Kabuki demon (or maybe that was just eighties hair). In a 1977 performance at the Eureka Theater (see Figure 2.3), she wore *geta*, the platform Japanese rice field sandals. The retelling of that performance sounds like a butoh performance: "Esmerelda came out, spoke something in Japanese, went into labor screaming, squatted, gave birth to a bloody cow bone and started the set" (Kay, 2018). Their self-titled album cover featured Kay and her bandmate Tony Hotel in red and pink suits, white face makeup with red Kabuki eye accents and baby doll lips, a red and a black wig, and red telephone cords wrapped around their bodies. Says Kay, "Hiroko and Koichi heavily influenced Noh Mercy" (Esmerelda Kay pers. comm. September 29, 2021). In a Facebook post from decades after their collaborations/interactions, which featured the Tamanos and their young dancers in disheveled white and

Figure 2.3 Noh Mercy at Eureka Theater, San Francisco (1977). Pictured left to right:
  Esmerelda Kay, Tony Hotel.

Source: Reprinted with permission from Esmerelda Kay

red kimonos, faces painted white with red accents, and dried flowers sticking out of the women's hairdos, Esmerelda wrote the caption: "My butoh friendos and the visual inspiration for NOH MERCY" (Kay 2013).

Says Hiroko of the Valencia Street studio, "all the kids looked so crazy, [there was a] big influence of drag queen and kabuki style, [they had a] strange way of wearing kimono, very American style, but [they were] seriously looking for something vivid to them for performance" (Hiroko Tamano, pers. comm., December 14, 2017). She recalls the vibrant energy of this "community zone" for Valencia neighborhood, bedecked with many photos of "big makeup and spaghetti in hands—I like it!" says Hiroko (Hiroko Tamano, pers. comm., December 14, 2017). Another all-female band, Pink Section, rehearsed in Noh

Mercy's basement, where the Tamanos also taught classes. Pink Section's lead singer Carol Dietwaler was one of the dancers on the Tamanos' first tour to Canada with *Swamp*.

Grafting on to the existing avant-garde in San Francisco, Harupin-Ha built a company, and then a community. By the 1980s, they had a home studio where they rehearsed and taught regular classes, built an established following, and established a touring network up and down the West Coast into Canada.

1980s: US and Mexican Presenters Begin to Program Butoh Performers

A shift came when high-profile presenters began to seek out and commission butoh performances. Ellen Stewart was the first theater to bring butoh to the United States with Kazuo Ohno's 1981 tour of *Water Lilies*.[7] The section that follows is a dizzying compilation of Japanese butoh artists crisscrossing the North American continent. I have tried to discuss their forays in roughly chronological order; however, in some cases I opted to complete a short profile on an artist or presenter that will overlap with the subsequent section in terms of dates and locations.

The same year that Ohno performed in New York (1981), Sankai Juku premiered in Mexico the internationally prestigious FIC in Guanajuato, Mexico. Their notoriety had been bolstered by their success at the Nancy and Avignon Festivals in 1980, which is likely where international presenters began to take notice of their work. On Sankai Juku's Mexican tour, the troupe left a profound image for Mexican audiences in the form of a photoshoot with renowned Mexican photographer Paulina Lavista on the sacred Aztec temples of Teotihuacán. The photos likely circulated among those involved in that first tour but would not be seen widely until Lavista's 2004 exhibition entitled *Danza Sacra . . . o Profana* (*Sacred Dance . . . or Profane*) at la Galería Fotográfica del Centro Cultural Casa Lamm (Mac Masters 2004).

American Dance Festival joined the trend, bringing Dairakurakan's *Sea Dappled Horse* in 1982. Dairakudakan also appeared at the Pepsico Summerfare Festival on that same tour. They were the first butoh company to perform at both of these important arts festivals.[8]

Stewart then presented Min Tanaka in 1983 in his own production of *Emotion*, in its US premiere.[9] In *Emotion*, Tanaka wears a hooded raincoat and carries a shovel, which appears to become a weapon against him as he collapses under it in one production shot. On that same tour, La MaMa hosted a workshop with Tanaka, marketed as "Body Weather Laboratory of Tokyo" with the tagline "Japanese modern dance techniques" (Zukof 1983). In collaboration with La MaMa, Western Mind produced a performance of *Light Opera*, directed by Tom O'Horgan (famed Broadway director of *Hair!* and *Jesus Christ Superstar*) and choreographed by Tanaka. Tanaka remained in New York for the two months of this collaboration and performance, working closely with New York-based dancers and actors.

La MaMa also hosted the "Terayama Shuji Memorial" performance in 1983 to honor the artist's life, work and impact on American artists. La MaMa claimed its place as the epicenter of Japanese contemporary performance in New York.

US-based Japanese artist Kei Takei crisscrossed the country in 1984, performing multiple pieces at La MaMa in New York and Herbst Theater in San Francisco. Dance critic Allan Ulrich reviewed her performance in the *San Francisco Examiner*, though there is no mention of the Tamanos or of butoh, so it seems he had not drawn the connections yet. However, other Bay Area dance critics *had* begun to write about butoh. Rita Felciano of the *San Francisco Bay Guardian* reviewed the Tamanos 1981 performance of *Swamp* at the San Francisco Ethnic Dance Festival. It was the first time she had seen butoh, and she was struck by the images and mesmerizing movement. Kate Regan had also reviewed the Tamanos in 1979 (a piece called *Silent Geisha*) and 1982 at the Natoma Gallery. Critical attention was slowly building for this new art form taking hold in the United States.

1984 also marked the beginning of fascination with Sankai Juku in the United States, when they first performed at the 1984 Olympic Arts Festival in Los Angeles. They have since performed in more cities and for more performances in the United States more than any other Japanese butoh artist or company. Between 1984 and 2020, they performed in more than 50 US cities, many of them multiple times including five times each in Boston, Pittsburgh, six times in Ann Arbor and Washington, DC, nine times in Seattle and the San Francisco Bay Area, 11 times in Los Angeles, and 13 times in New York (Sankai Juku, n.d.). There is a reason why Sankai Juki is most often the introduction to this art form for many dancers in the United States. By contrast in Mexico, Sankai Juku has performed only four times to date, 1981, 2006, 2008 at FIC, and in 2013 at Palacio de Bellas Artes.

Sankai Juku wowed audiences in the first ever Olympic Arts Festival with *Jomon Sho* (*Homage to Prehistory*). LA Times critic Dan Sullivan called them "crazy Japanese acrobat-dancers . . . dangling head down from the Dorothy Chandler Pavilion . . . an apt symbol for what's at stake when an actor undertakes to do theater in the film capital of the world" (Sullivan 1984). The butoh company performed on an incredible lineup, including Pina Bausch, Ariane Mnouchkine, Tadashi Suzuki, and Robert Wilson.

Kazuo Ohno returned to New York, this time at the Joyce Theater, with his 1985 tour of *La Argentina*. The Joyce is known for contemporary dance, and Ohno's presence there signals an acceptance of butoh *as* Japanese contemporary dance. Dance critic Jack Anderson commented on the puzzling ways in which Ohno played with gender: at one point the dancer shed his dress yet remained in his female wig and high-heeled shoes, now stripped down to his men's athletic shorts. "Simultaneously a man and a woman, he transcends sexual distinctions" (Anderson 1985). Anderson called the piece "an eloquent tribute" to the famous Argentine dancer that is neither a reconstruction nor an imitation, but an evocation of her energy and spirit (Anderson 1985). It left an "indelible impression" (Anderson 1985), and Anderson reviewed subsequent performance by Ohno in New York in 1986 and 1996.

Tanaka returned in 1985 to present another solo, *Form of the Sky*. The piece was noted in *The Villager* alongside a longer review of the Bill T. Jones/Arnie Zane Dance Company. Tanaka's dance was likened to that of Kazuo Ohno who had performed just weeks earlier at The Joyce Theater. Though the review by Doris Diether (1985) was mostly description of actions and not really a critique, Tanaka was gaining traction in the New York performing arts community.

Dance critic Anna Kisselgoff suggests that by mid-1980, grotesque imagery and dark humor was an increasing trend within New York-based dance performances. She cites Pilobolus' *Stabat Matter* and Martha Clarke's *Garden of Earthly Delights*, which was inspired by the Hieronymus Bosch painting of the same name. Both pieces are erotic and irreverent in the same breath, Clarke's featuring dancers in tights with anatomical parts painted on their bodies and both invoking lewd and scatological references. Says Kisselgoff, prophetically:

> It is too soon to make firm connections within an evolving trend that is a form of movement theater. But some links are clear. Pilobolus and Miss Clarke have a streak of black humor that could be related to the dark humor in Dai Rakuda Kan. And perhaps these Americans and the Butoh groups, all of whom perform regularly in Paris, have some common ground.
>
> (1984b)

Indeed many cultural shifts supported this return to dark humor and grotesque. The Culture Wars of the 1980s polarized US public opinion, and political satire made its way into every corner of popular culture. As much as butoh might have influenced a resurgence of interest in the grotesque, it might equally have just been an apt expression for the zeitgeist.

Butoh continued to draw increasing attention and even became a more mainstream attraction with Sankai Juku's excerpt of piece *Jomon Sho*, dangling over the Mutual Life Building in Pioneer Square, a popular tourist and downtown lunch spot. Tragically, one of the dancers' ropes frayed and Yoshiyuki Takada plunged six stories to his death. There were more than 1,000 onlookers including children who witnessed the event in shock, thinking it had been part of the act since the dancers did not scream or show any sign of distress as he fell (Van Biema 1985).

The death of Sankai Juku dancer Yoshiyuki Takada, for better or worse, garnered more attention for butoh in the United States. The accident was covered by *The New York Times*, the *Los Angeles Times*, and caught live by local TV reporter Greg Palmer, broadcasting for King Five News. There is even a clip of the accident on YouTube, minus the actual impact.[10] Sankai Juku canceled its remaining US engagements that year. When the company returned the following year, they began their 1986 tour in Seattle as a tribute to their fallen dancer as well as to the audiences who remained haunted by the tragic event. They still performed *Jomon Sho* on this US tour; however, the hanging scene was now replaced with four dancers crouched in a fetal position, moving into a "plant-like cluster while lying on their backs like infants learning to move their limbs" (Kisselgoff 1986). Kisselgoff's review called the dancer's death back to public attention, signaling the avant-garde content of the group, even as it started to become more mainstream. The choreographic change, and the public comment before the first performance in Seattle, helped audiences feel cared for by the company, something that would not have likely been a consideration of butoh pioneer Hijikata. Though no dancers died in any of Hijikata's performances, a few chickens were at least abused and the taunting-death attitude was part of the appeal. Sankai Juku perhaps garnered such broad appeal by attending to their audience in a different way.

The New York Times coverage of Sankai Juku's Fall 1986 US tour is significant for two other reasons as well. First, Kisselgoff links butoh to the Chernobyl nuclear disaster which had occurred earlier that year (1986). In doing so, she continues the narrative of butoh as connected to tragedy and makes it relevant to global current events (albeit a continued misunderstanding of butoh as a response to Hiroshima). Second, Kisselgoff notes that "Sankai Juku's sensational success story has aided receptivity toward other Butoh performers in New York" (1986). I would add that it aided critical attention and funder support for butoh on both the East and West Coasts of the United States, as well as in Mexico through the imprimatur of the FIC. Kisselgoff herself began reviewing Eiko and Koma in 1978 but did not explicitly draw the connection to butoh until the duo's 1984 American Dance Festival performance after having seen Sankai Juku in Toronto (Kisselgoff 1984a). Of course, Eiko and Koma were careful to cast their work as "avant-garde" and draw the distinction from butoh, and Hijikata and Ohno's influence on their work (see Candelario 2016). Kisselgoff no doubt respected their genre designation; however, beginning in 1984 she starts to map Eiko and Koma within the growing butoh diaspora in the United States, popularized by Sankai Juku. In her review of Sankai Juku at the Pepsico Summerfare Festival (Kisselgoff 1984a), Kisselgoff begins to lump Eiko and Koma in with butoh performers: "philosophically," she writes, "butoh concentrates on metamorphosis and transcendence" (Kisselgoff 1984a). She then describes the slowly "changing shapes" and "extraordinary flow" with which both Eiko and Koma, and Sankai Juku, "remold" and "mutate" their bodies in *Grain* and *Jomon Sho,* respectively.[11]

From this point on, *The New York Times* has extensive coverage of butoh, partially because such notable performers as Kazuo Ohno, Sankai Juku, Dairakudakan, Min Tanaka, and Natsu Nakajima are frequent New York visitors, but also because critics have begun to pay attention to the genre. In San Francisco, reviews of the Tamanos work began to appear regularly in the *San Francisco Chronicle*, the *Examiner*, and the *SF Bay Guardian*. Rita Felciano, critic for the *Guardian*, championed butoh for many years and helped educate audiences. Her thoughtful and informed critiques supported the success of the San Francisco Butoh Festival throughout its nearly decade-long run from 1994 to 2002.

In New York, several important presenters regularly began to feature butoh performers from Japan in their seasons. La MaMa presented Takei's Moving Earth in 1984 and 1985. Asia Society, which had long presented Japanese traditional performing arts including Kabuki, brought Natsu Nakajima to New York in 1985 for her US premiere, with *Niwa* (*The Garden*) (Kisselgoff 1985). Dance Theater Workshop (currently New York Live Arts) sponsored Kazuo Ohno's return to New York in November 1985, this time in a performance with his son Yoshito, performing both *La Argentina* and *The Dead Sea* (Dunning 1985).

Ko Murobushi first performed in Mexico in 1985, invited by José Luis Cruz of UNAM, the theater school most known for experimentation. Murobushi performed the duet *Ephémère* with Urara Kusanagi at the Sala Miguel Covarrubias. The pair were the only Japanese artists included in the festival, Tercer Gran Festival Ciudad de México. The festival featured artists from Spain as the principal guests, as well as artists from Russia, the United States, Venezuela, India, and Switzerland, among others. Though the aesthetic and genre represented varied from opera to minimalist contemporary dance, there seems to be a preponderance of photos and descriptions of a similar ilk. The Martha Graham Company represented the United States with *Cave of the Heart*. The program notes characterized Graham, who was still alive at the time,[12] as "a temperamental woman, a witch, a demon, an angel"[13] (Ko Murobushi Archive 1985).

The program billed Murobushi as

> belonging to the generation of Japanese artists that had emigrated to Europe to say what was unacceptable in their own country, because Butoh signified equally breaking all the rules of traditional Japanese aesthetics and a rejection of all the vestiges of civilization.[14]
>
> (Ko Murobushi Archive 1985)

Archive images show Murobushi in thigh-high tights and tuxedo tails, with his face covered in lace. In another image, he wears a tiered pink lace dress, and in a third image, he and Kusanagi are naked save for g-strings. The program image featured Murobushi's naked torso, with his hands in claws and arms crossed in front of his chest.

Murobushi was among like-minded Mexican artists, who were investigating similar approaches of performativity between dance and theater, and questions of human form and consciousness. Mexican-born and Russian-trained avant-garde ballerina Farahilda Sevilla performed *Natura Danza* (*Nature Dance*) with her group, Teatro del Cuerpo (Theater of the Body). Sevilla was fascinated by theatricality, notably Antonin Artaud, and trained her company with several experimental theater artists (Stephens 2010).

Farahilda and the first generation of Teatro del Cuerpo dancers[15] met in a workshop given by Abraham Oceransky in 1983 (Rosales 2011). Sevilla was a progressive and curious performance researcher, and this coupled with her language abilities in Russian, Spanish, and English led her to translate and publish texts by important European directors including Peter Brook and Jerzy Grotowski (Danzjáfora 2017).

A number of featured guests on the Tercer Gran Festival program performed at the prestigious Palacio de Bellas Artes. Many others were presented at the Instituto Nacional de Bellas Artes (INBA) satellite theater, Teatro de la Danza, a theater dedicated to contemporary and experimental dance that opened at Centro Cultural del Bosque in 1981. The opening of this venue was a significant moment for experimental dance in Mexico, bringing the avant-garde into the state-funded system. Incidentally, Centro del Bosque was the primary venue for the 2019 Cuerpos en Revuelta butoh festival.

In inviting Murobushi to perform in 1985, Cruz was tapping into a larger fascination with Japanese performing arts. Cruz himself had been influenced by Japanese emigre artist cum Mexican national Seki Sano (Cruz 2017). Cruz also invited Jose Luís Paredes Pacheco to accompany him on a tour of Japan to view contemporary theater. Paredes was in a Mexican rock band and later became the director of UNAM's Museo El Chopo, and a leading advocate of butoh in Mexico City (Espartaco Martínez, email message to author, September 19, 2019).

Through UNAM, Murobushi encountered experimental theater director Abraham Oceransky and began an artistic dialog and presenting relationship that (as mentioned earlier in this chapter) would last from 1985 until Murobushi's death in Mexico in 2015. Murobushi would premiere in the United States much later, in 2002.

Murobushi had numerous tours in Mexico between 1985 and 2015, teaching 12 intensive workshops and presenting 19 major performances in Mexico, as well as participating in an academic conference hosted by Oceransky at Centro Nacional de las Artes in Mexico City in 2001. Murobushi performed many of his iconic works, including *Quick Silver* and *Ritournelle*. He also collaborated with several Mexican artists, including on *Vera: A Road Movie for a Soul* (1999, Directed by Francisco Athie, Choreography by Murobushi for Urara Kusanagi, who plays the android Vera), *Murmullos de Paramo* (2006), an experimental opera written and directed by Julio Estrada with performance by Murobushi, and a piece he made specifically for Mexico, *Murobushi y el Popol Vuh* (2015). INBA commissioned Murobushi to work with its students in the creation of the work, which was, according to the program notes, "a fusion between Asian and indigenous cultures as living symbols of creation myths"[16] (Ko Murobushi Archive 2015). The project was conceived as a "moving mural" with images from the Mayan codices, told in four main sections: "air, which represents memory, earth, which is life, fire, which are dreams, and water which represents time"[17] (Ko Murobushi Archive 2015). The piece played out in the framework of a ball game, in which the losers were often subject to human sacrifice in the narrative of the Popol Vuh.

Nakajima was the second Japanese butoh performer to be presented in Mexico and FIC in 1987. On that same 1987 tour, the Asia Society in New York brought Nakajima back a second time with a new version of *Niwa*, this time accompanied by her dancer Yuriko Maezawa (Kisselgoff 1987a). New York's City Center Theater hosted Dairakudakan's second US appearance in April 1987 with *The Five Rings* (Kisselgoff 1987b, H8.). There were not many other engagements as the large 30-plus-person cast was difficult to tour to other locations.

Also in 1987, Stewart embarked on a year-long creative process and touring project with Tanaka inspired by *Oedipus*. Maureen Fleming was invited to join Tanaka in this production and then, with support from Stewart, went on to study and perform with Tanaka's company Maijuku and also with the Ohnos at their studio in Kamihoshikawa (Fleming, pers. comm., April 17, 2019). Asia Society next invited Kazuo Ohno in June 1988, presenting the piece Stewart had presented in 1981, *Water Lilies* (Dunning 1988).

Stewart next presented Nakajima's company Muteki-sha in 1989 in a collaboration with Yukio Waguri and a cast of 14 dancers in *Sleep and Reincarnation from Empty Land*, at La MaMa Annex Theater (Dunning 1989). This was Waguri's first performance in the United States and would begin a lasting connection with New York-based dancers. This same year, Kei Takei performed for a third time at La MaMa. Dunning was considerably less moved by *Sleep and Reincarnation* than be previous performances of Nakajima, calling it "generic" and "derivative," likening it to "many other dances performed in New York this week." Dunning does have strong praise for Nakajima as a performer on her own though but remains unconvinced about her choreographic skill with an ensemble (Dunning 1989). In 1989, the Cervantino invited Kazuo Ohno to perform, for which he danced *Dead Sea* and *Water Lilies* on October 27, his 83rd Birthday (Kazuo Ohno Dance Studio, n.d.).

Physical Theater: Grotowski and Barba

Equally important to the American performance landscape of this time is Polish theatre artist Jerzy Grotowski and the impact of his methods for training actors. Grotowski influenced an entire generation of artists in the United States, including The Living Theater, Ellen Stewart's La MaMa, Performance Group, The Wooster Group, and Mabou Mines. Brought to the United States initially by the Brooklyn Academy of Music (BAM) in 1969, Grotowski impacted theater practices throughout the country. Theater director and scholar Richard Schechner (Performance Group, Wooster Group) and UC Irvine professor Robert Cohen were instrumental in Grotowski's influence in New York and Los Angeles in particular.

Grotowski had worked with butoh artists and been influenced by their methods. Natsu Nakajima confirms that he and Kazuo Ohno had shared mutual investigation both in and out of the studio. Nakajima was herself interested in the work of Grotowski and of his protégé Eugenio Barba. After a period of exploration and dialogue, Nakajima translated Barba's book *The Secret Art of the Performer* into Japanese. These artists crossed paths many times, including at the 30th Anniversary of Odin Theater (see Figure 2.4), to which Kazuo and Yoshito Ohno, and Nakajima had all been invited. Kazuo Ohno and Sanjukuta Panigrahi danced a duet as a special performance at the event (Natsu Nakajima pers. comm. August 4, 2019).

Grotowski had visited Mexico in 1968 as part of his own theatrical research of indigenous forms. He then returned in 1981 and 1985 to create work with Mexican artists and international followers to create a site-specific project at the base of the Iztaccíhuatl volcano, in the territories of the Huichol and Amecameca communities (Esparza et al. 2015, 5). In the United States, Grotowski first visited New York in 1969 and then taught at Columbia University in the 1980s. He influenced a number of theater groups and directors, including Peter Brook, Joseph Chaiken, Andre Gregory, Mabou Mines, and Richard Schechner's Living Theater (Gussow 1999). Grotowski's *Toward a Poor Theatre* was translated into English in 1968 and Spanish in 1970 (Grotowski Encyclopedia 2020).

Figure 2.4 Odin Teatret 30th Anniversary (1994). Pictured left to right: Kazuo Ohno, Sanjukta Panigrahi, Eugenio Barba, Jerzy Grotowski.

Source: Photo by Fiorenza Elda Sandra Bemporad, reprinted with permission from Fiorenza Elda Sandra Bemporad

Grotowski's influence is felt in Latin American perhaps most acutely through the efforts of his disciple Eugenio Barba, whose work on "pre-expressivity" echoes throughout university training programs and experimental theater companies' mission statements. Barba's book, *The Floating Islands: Reflections with Odin Teatret,* was translated into Spanish and published by UNAM in 1983, and the following year Barba himself came to give his first workshops in Mexico. Barba was invited to direct through a joint effort of Mexico's Teatral Itaca and INBA in May of 1984, and that same year, returned with Odin Teatret to give a performance, which won the Mexican Theater Critic's Award for most important foreign production that year (Bert 1986, 31). The vast majority of Barbe's texts have been translated into Spanish and released in Mexico even before other locations in Latin America, including *Beyond the Floating Island* (1986 released in Mexico), *Anatomy of the Actor* (1988), *The Secret Art of the Performer* (1990), *The Paper Canoe* (1992), *Theater: Solitude, Craft, Revolt* (1998), *Land of Ashes and Diamonds* (2008), *Burning the House: On Directing and Dramaturgy* (2012), and *The Moon Rises from the Ganges: My Journey through Asian Acting Techniques* (2017). The relationship continues until this day, with the recent symposium given in January 2020 with Barba and actress Julia Varley, both speaking in Spanish, in a hybrid live and online course called "Thinking about Actions" at Teatro Helénico in Mexico City.

One Mexican butoh artist, a former Dairakudakan dancer and graduate of experimental theater school La Casa del Teatro, jokes that Barba is under every stone that one lifts in the Latin American theater world (Espartaco Martínez, pers. comm., April 15, 2018). Through the practices of these companies and schools, acting became a decidedly more physical endeavor. Training underscored full-body engagement and imaginative play, and "authenticity" became the hallmark of successful performance.

The 1990s: A Local Butoh Community Coalesces in San Francisco

Now established in the Bay Area, the Tamanos taught classes and developed their company with a consistent group of dancers. They performed at several art exhibition spaces including Natoma and Kala Galleries and the Luggage Store. They opened Country Station[18] sushi restaurant, which became a famous landmark in and of itself, its walls covered in avant-garde art, Beatles songs regularly blasting, and Hiroko dancing and singing around the joint. Local performers gathered there after shows.

The Tamanos kept up their contacts in Japan, which facilitated continued touring. In 1986 when Hijikata died, Koichi returned to perform in the memorial and then returned one year later to perform in Dairakudakan's *Roshomon* and *Romanoff's Sea* with Hijikata's widow Akiko Motofuji and Ishii Mitsutaka, one of the original performers from Asbestos-kan who appeared alongside Kasai and the Ohnos in the 1965 *Rose Colored Dance* among other early dances. Tamano also performed in these early works, and by 1970 had a major role in *Gibasan*. These relationships helped set up Japanese tours for Harupin-Ha's *Fetus of Nature* in 1987 and for *Piece on Earth* in 1990 and 1991.

The American-based dancers who formed Harupin-Ha at this point were Hannah Sim, Kinji Hayashi, and Ellie Herman. All three dancers had strong physical practices and were highly skilled performers. Herman became a successful Pilates instructor. Sim, together with Mark Stenger (*Stranger Things*), also directed Osseus Labyrinth and performed in music videos for the band Tool. Hayashi would become an important figure in Bay Area butoh, collaborating with many young butoh artists and also with established artists in other disciplines, such as Pamela Z.

Hiroko comments that Hayashi's talent in particular was a unique and specific ability to express the "depth of the body," or inner experience (Hiroko Tamano pers. comm. June 23, 2010). Originally trained in electrical engineering, Hayashi worked near the United States Air Force Base in Yokota, Japan. He emigrated to California in 1975 with an American lover and studied theater, film, and photography at Oakland's Laney College. He then received his Bachelor of Arts degree in Conceptual Art from San Francisco State University. Like many of the early Japanese dancers who worked with Hijikata, Hayashi brought a multi-disciplinary background outside of dance to his butoh investigation (Buskirk 2018).

Watching Harupin-Ha's *Fetus of Nature* (see Figure 2.5), it is evident that the trio of Hayashi, Sim, and Herman are well-rehearsed. The costumes are odd but cleanly designed, with white rake heads and shoes as hats, neatly folded

Figure 2.5 Harupin-Ha Company in *Fetus of Nature* (1988). Dancers left to right: Hiroko Tamano, Hannah Sim, Kinji Hayashi, Ellie Herman.

Source: Courtesy Harupin-Ha, reprinted with permission from Harupin-Ha

white draping, and white makeup. The dancers are fluid, in control, precise, and inky. The Tamanos had begun to build a group of grammar through these new dancers and to solidify their style.

Following the costly and grueling 1991 tours, the Tamanos focused more energy on building their Western US base, with performances and workshops in Oakland, San Francisco Art Institute, Mendocino Arts, Naropa Institute in Colorado, and Nevada Theater in Nevada City. Koichi also began cultivating a relationship with Japanese ex-patriot Nagoyo Tada in Paris, France, creating several solo and duet works, and by 1994 had built enough contacts and audience in France to bring the American company to Marseille, France with *Goblins*. Costume designer Alenka Mullin and dancer/yogini Leigh Evans joined the company during this time, both of whom would later collaborate with future Harupin-Ha dancer Shinichi Iova-Koga in his company inkBoat. Mullins and Iova-Koga met during this production, and later married and formed their own company, Uro Teatro Koku, which ran for several years before the couple split up and Iova-Koga formed inkBoat (see profile in Chapter 4). Molly Barrons joined the company when they returned from France to perform in *Goblins* at Theater Artaud in San Francisco; Barrons became one of the most enduring supporters of the Tamanos work and was also an indispensable assistant to Brechin Flournoy in the later years of the San Francisco Butoh Festival.

Watershed Moment in Mexico

Byakko Sha was invited by José Luis Cruz in 1993 to present *Hibari to nejaka* (*The Lark and the Reclining Buddha*) at the Museo Nacional de Antropología in Mexico City. The performance was in the evening in a spectacular courtyard, where temple gates and giant head statues rose out of trees and brush, approximating a sense of discovery of the ancient ruins. Dance writer Gustavo Emilio Rosales provides a first person account of the experience:

> It was night. Spring had past, and the atmosphere was overloaded with electricity. . . . During the two hours in which the performance took place, the predominant sound in the public area was a profound silence: it seemed that observers did not exist. At the end of the function, the paralysis of those who watched was aggravated, but for a mere few seconds, when suddenly an irrepressible urgency compelled us to rise up at once and *en masse*. We ran to the astonished dancers to embrace them, to carry them, to squeeze them, to weep in their hands, among the clothes or the skin of those who were at our side: we howled. I have not witnessed anything like this again: a catharsis.
>
> (Rosales 2019, 311–312)

Diego Piñón was recruited by the Japanese company to participate in the performance as some sort of "gatekeeper" whose job was to remain statuesquely still for prolonged periods and then at some point to cut an infant's hair (Piñón 2018, 14). He describes the intensity of maintaining that stillness amid the unfolding spectacle, saying "it required a level of concentration I had not yet experimented with" (Piñón 2018). From that moment on, Piñón sought out butoh training, eventually traveling to Min Tanaka's Body Weather Farm in Hakushu-sho.

Espartaco Martínez notes that most of the Mexican dancers who pioneered butoh in Mexico were in attendance at this significant event. He writes: "it left such an incredible impression, they transformed the idea of dance in Mexico with that performance" (Espartaco Martínez, email message to author, September 20, 2019).

Similar to Grotowski's fascination with Mexico, many Japanese butoh artists have cited an affinity for Mexico's indigenous culture. Vargas recounts stories of Natsu Nakajima, Akira Kasai, Ko Murobushi, and Yukio Waguri, all separately visiting the Museo Nacional de Antropología and being in awe of the Aztec, Mayan, and Olmec artifacts, and each in one form or another remarking "*this* is butoh" (Eugenia Vargas, pers. comm., March 13, 2018).

Indeed, many Mexican butoh artists have made these connections with indigenous culture in their work. Some have incorporated indigenous rituals in their performance research, namely, Diego Piñón and Eugenia Vargas. Others have adopted iconography and deities, particularly Tania Galindo whose company Butoh Chilango has referenced many Aztec deities in its work. In many ways, the connections between ritual sites, communal performance, and animistic presence of deities aligned through the encounter with butoh.

Returning briefly to the theme of violence, perhaps that 1993 Byakko Sha performance on the curated arrangement of ancient ruins plucked layers of generational trauma that has spanned centuries. The alienation of globalization is real, as modern Mexico City begins to look like every other contemporary colonial city with European architecture, manicured boulevards, and shiny glass additions bringing a layer of sparkle to the stone facades. US, European, and Japanese brands increasingly dominate the thoroughfares. Add to that the double affront of a museum exhibition of ancient ruins, the curation of the conquered by the conqueror. It is no wonder the audience that night witnessed a shock as the stone carvings of serpent gods and warrior heads were activated by ghost-like alien creatures moving in liminal time. It must have felt like reaching through a rip in time, with ancient and contemporary witnessing one another and the long trail of destruction humans have wrought. Butoh may have resonated so deeply in Mexico (but also in the United States, which has its own generational trauma) because butoh is an effective conduit for touching that darkness and dancing with it.

Notes

1 Decker refers to a speech made by Luis Urías in a closed-door session at the Primer Seminario de Investigación y Curaduría: Tecnología, medios audiovisuales y experimentación artística, Centro de la Imagen, Mexico City, October 29, 2014.

2 Decker points out that the scene invoked other destructive art acts, specifically piano demolitions staged by George Maciunus and the Fluxists in 1962 and Rafael Montañez Ortiz at the 1966 DIAS Symposium held in London. Jodorowsky had also destroyed a

piano in the *efimeral* October 1963 performance at the Academy of San Carlos. While he was not the first artist to perform this act, he certainly brought it to a new level with the venues and media outlets through which he presented his events.

3 "Me di cuenta que había un trabajo de conciencia, el arte no es una cosa superflua, no es una materia vulgar, no es una forma de trabajo económico, es un monasterio" (Milenio 2020).

4 Thornbury notes this concept in relation to Japanese language theater productions in the 2000s that receive previews and not reviews, implying that they are "culturally interesting but not necessarily artistically compelling" (98), but the same concept applies in the case of the 1970s avant-garde work, which did receive critical reviews on par with their American contemporaries.

5 So significant was the presenter/artist relationship that LaMama held the primary American memorial service for Terayama upon his untimely death of nephritis in 1983 (Zukof 1983).

6 After the band's breakup, Esmerelda went on to costume many performance acts, including hip-hop artists Busta Rhymes, ODB, E-40, Faith Evans, Timbaland, Digital Underground, and 1980s Japanese pop-punk girl band, Shonen Knife (Last.fm 2021).

7 Although museums had previously invited butoh artists to participate in Japanese-themed exhibitions, such as the Japan Now Exhibition in LA and San Francisco, it was significant that La Mama was the first theater presenter to host butoh artists from abroad because it ushered in the Japanese avant-garde performance on par with American experimental theater.

8 Kei Takei's company followed this trajectory as well, performing at ADF in 1983 and Pepsico in 1986 (Kei Takei's Moving Earth, n.d.).

9 Kei Takei's company followed this trajectory as well, performing at ADF in 1983 and Pepsico in 1986 (Kei Takei's Moving Earth, n.d.).

10 See YouTube: www.youtube.com/watch?v=sDtnSge-mjU.

11 Kisselgoff does note a distinction for Eiko and Koma: "Oddly, there is a delicacy about Eiko's and Koma's performance that makes the other Butoh groups seem coarse" (NYT July 15, 1984, p. 54).

12 Martha Graham died April 1, 1991, at the age of 96.

13 "Esta temperamental mujer, bruja, demonio y ángel . . ." (Ko Murobushi Archive 1985).

14 "Murobushi pertenece a la generación de las artistas japoneses que emigrant a Europa para decir lo que en su propio país resulta una acusación imperdonable, porque Danza Butoh significa igualmente el rompimiento con todas las reglas estéticas japonesa tradicional y tambien la negación de todo vestigio de civilización" (Ko Murobushi Archive 1985).

15 The dancers of Teatro del Cuerpo were Rosario Armenta, Rocio Flores, Marta Galván, Graciela González, and Farahilda Sevilla (Rosales 2011).

16 "Una fusión entra las culturas orientales e indígenas como signos vivos para la representación con los mitos de creacción" (Ko Murobushi Archive 2015).

17 "Los cuatro movimientos estarán relacionado con los cuatro elementos de la vida: el aire, que es el recuerdo; la tierra, que es la vida; el fuego, que son los sueños; y el agua, que es el tiempo" (Ko Murobushi Archive 2015).

18 Country Station closed in 2004, when the duo returned to Japan for a spate, but they reopened restaurant Tamasei in Noe Valley in 2006 and ran it until 2009.

Works Cited

Anderson, Jack. 1985. "Dance: Kazuo Ohno." *New York Times*, Nov. 24, 1985.

Asher-Perrin, Emily. 2017. "Rereading Frank Herbert's Dune: Alexander Jodorowsky's Dune Didn't Get Made for a Reason . . . And We Should All Be Grateful for That." *Tor. com*, May 2, 2017, www.tor.com/2017/05/02/jodorowskys-dune-didnt-get-made-for-a-reason-and-we-should-all-be-grateful/. Accessed Aug. 26, 2019.

Banes, Sally. 1991. "American Dance and Performance Art: The Sixties and Seventies." In *Breakthroughs: Avant-Garde Artists in Europe and America 1950–1990*, edited by John Howell, 157–163. Columbus: Rizzoli in association with Wexner Center for the Arts, Ohio State University.

Bert, Bruno. 1986. "Teoría y dramaturgia. Eugenio Barba. Más allá," *Tiempo Libre* 345 (December): 31.

Buskirk, James (Diego). 2018. *Kinji Hayashi, Unpublished Obituary*. July 2018.

Carter, Curtis L. 2013. "Carroll, Noël. Living in an Art World: Reviews and Essays on Dance, Performance, Theater, and the Fine Arts in the 1970s and 1980s. Louisville, KY: Chicago Spectrum Press, 2012." *The Journal of Aesthetics and Art Criticism* 71, no. 3 (Summer): 291–94.

Candelario, Rosemary. 2016. *Flowers Cracking Concrete: Eiko & Koma's Asian/American Choreographies*. Middletown: Wesleyan University Press.

Carroll, Noël. 2012. *Living in an Artworld: Reviews and Essays on Dance, Performance, Theater, and the Fine Arts in the 1970s and 1980s*. Louisville: Chicago Spectrum Press.

Castillo, Juan Camilo, and Dorothy Kronick. 2020. "The Logic of Violence in Drug War." *American Political Science Review* 114, no. 3 (August): 874–887.

Corry, John. 1980. "Stage: 'Directions to Servants' of Shuji Terayama at La Mama; The Cast." *New York Times*, June 21, 1980.

Cruz, José Luis. 2017. "Teatro" ABCDMX Canal oficial del Grupo Parlamentario de Morena en la Asamblea Legislativa del Distrito Federal, youtube video, 6:55, www.you tube.com/watch?v=ddolsEN_fZU. Sept 7, 2017. Accessed Feb. 2019.

Danzjáfora. 2017. "Farahilda Seville." https://danzjafora0.wixsite.com/danzjafora/directora. Accessed Oct. 15, 2019.

Deak, Frantisek. 2006. "Allan Kaprow 1927–2006." *TDR (1988–)* 50, no. 4 (Winter): 9–12.

Decker, Arden. 2015. "Los Grupos and the Art of Intervention in the 1960s and 1970s in Mexico." PhD diss., City University of New York.

Diether, Doris. 1985. "More Butoh at La MaMa." *The Villager*, Dec. 19, 1985.

Dillon, Sam. 1998. "Mexico City Journal; Anniversary of '68 Massacre Brings Facts to Light." *New York Times*, Sept. 14, 1998. www.nytimes.com/1998/09/14/world/mexico-city-journal-anniversary-of-68-massacre-brings-facts-to-light.html

Dunning, Jennifer. 1989 "Death-Life Celebration by Muteki-sha Troupe." *New York Times*, Oct. 29, 1989.

Dunning, Jennifer. 1988. "Japanese Images of Water Lillies." *New York Times*, Jun. 30, 1988.

Dunning, Jennifer. 1985. "It's a Great Way to Start a New Dance Season." *New York Times*, Nov. 22, 1985.

Escoto, Daniel. 2021. "1, 2, 3, 4, 5 a gogó: Pop, Avant-Garde, and TV in Late-Sixties Mexico." *The Journal of Popular Culture* 54, no. 1 (March): 27–46.

Esparza, José, Chong Cuy, Rodrigo Ortiz Monestario, Natalia Espinosa. Trans. José Esparza Chong Cuy, Víctor Altamirano. 2015. *Pasajeros No. 1: Jerzy Grotowski*. Fundación Jumex Arte Contemporáneo.

Fowler, Glenn. 1983. "Shuji Terayama, Playwright, Dies." *New York Times*, May 14, 1983. www.nytimes.com/1983/05/14/obituaries/shuji-terayama-playwright-dies.html.

Gomez, Eirinet. 2015. "Falleció Rocío Sagaón, destacada bailarina, coreógrafa, escultora y actriz." *La Jornada* (August): 6.

Grotowski Encyclopedia. 2020. "Towards a Poor Theatre." Last modified Dec. 22, 2020. https://grotowski.net/en/encyclopedia/towards-poor-theatre. Accessed Jul. 9, 2020.

Gussow, Mel. 1999. "Jerzy Grotowski, Director, Is Dead at 65." *New York Times*, Jan. 15, 1999.

INBA. 2019. "Teatro El Galeón *Abraham Oceransky* cumple 47 años de ser el recinto por excelencia para la vanguardia y la experimentación del arte escénico." Boletín No. 1797, Nov. 20, 2019. https://inba.gob.mx/prensa/13362/teatro-el-gale-oacuten-abraham-oceransky-cumple-47-a-ntildeos-de-ser-el-recinto-por-excelencia-para-la-vanguardia-y-la-experimentaci-oacuten-del-arte-esc-eacutenico. Accessed Jun. 29, 2021.

Kay, Esmerelda. 2021. https://facebook.com/nohmercy Facebook post, June 18, 2021.

Kay, Esmerelda. 2018. "1977 NOH MERCY SHOW AT THE EUREKA THEATER SF." https://facebook.com/nohmercy Facebook post, October 20, 2018.

Kay, Esmerelda. 2013. www.facebook.com/esmereldak Facebook post, November 5, 2013.

Kazuo Ohno Dance Studio. n.d. "Archives." www.kazuoohnodancestudio.com/english/archives/poster/poster_014.html. Accessed Sept. 23, 2019.

Kei Takei's Moving Earth. n.d. "Kei Takei." https://keitakei.org/kei.html. Accessed Sept. 15, 2020.

Kisselgoff, Anna. 1987a. "Dance: Butoh by Natsu Nakajima." *New York Times*, Oct. 1, 1987.

Kisselgoff, Anna. 1987b. "Dai Rakuda Kan's Theater of Raw Images." *New York Times*, Apr 19, 1987, H8

Kisselgoff, Anna. 1986. "The Dance: Sankai Juku Opens." *New York Times*, May 1, 1986. www.nytimes.com/1986/05/01/arts/the-dance-sankai-juku-opens.html.

Kisselgoff, Anna. 1985. "Dance that Startles and Challenges is Coming from Abroad." *New York Times*, Oct. 13, 1985.

Kisselgoff, Anna. 1984a. "Dance: Eiko and Koma in a Durham Premiere." *New York Times*, Jun. 24, 1984.

Kisselgoff, Anna. 1984b. "Dance View: Grotesque Imagery Has Come to Dance." *New York Times*, April 15, 1984.

Ko Murobushi Archive. 2015. "Document 001: Program, *Ko Murobushi y el Popol Vuh.*" Academia de la Danza Mexicana Auditorio Josefina Lavalle, May 18–24, 2015.

Ko Murobushi Archive. 2006. "Document 001: Program, *Murmullos del Paramo.*" VIII Festival Internacional Música y Escena, Sept. 8–9, 2006. https://ko-murobushi.com/eng/works/view/428.

Ko Murobushi Archive. 1999. "Document 001: Description, *Vera: A Road Movie for the Soul.*" https://ko-murobushi.com/eng/works/view/309.

Ko Murobushi Archive. 1985. "Document 001: Program for *Ephémère.*" Tercer Gran Festival Ciudad de México, Aug. 1–4, 1985. www.ko-murobushi.com/eng/works/view/131.

Kurihara, Nanako. "Hijikata Tatsumi: The Words of Butoh: [Introduction]." *TDR (1988–)* 44, no. 1 (2000): 12–28.

Kurihara, Nanako and Jacqueline S. Ruyak. 2000. "Hijikata Tatsumi Chronology." *TDR (1988)* 44, no. 1 (Spring): 29–35.

Last.fm. 2021. "Noh Mercy: Biography." www.last.fm/music/Noh+Mercy/+wiki. Accessed Nov. 6, 2019.

Mac Masters, Merry. 2004. "La fotógrafa Paulina Lavista inaugura en Casa Lamm su exposición Danza sacra . . . o profana: El Butoh y la magia de Teotihuacán en imágenes." *La Jornada*. Nov. 4, 2004.

Malkin, Elisabeth. 2018. "50 Years After a Student Massacre, Mexico Reflects on Democracy." *New York Times*, Oct. 1, 2018. www.nytimes.com/2018/10/01/world/americas/mexico-tlatelolco-massacre.html

Martin, Ken. 2018. "Mexico City, Koans, and the Zen Buddhist Master: Alejandro Jodorowsky, Ejo Takata and the Fundamental Lesson of the Death of the Intellect." *TRANS-MODERNITY: Journal of Peripheral Cultural Production of the Luso-Hispanic World* 8, no. 3 (Fall): 114–126.

Maya, Laura Navarrete. 2002. "Abraham Oceransky." Centro de Estudios Literarios CEL (IIFL-UNAM). www.elem.mx/autor/datos/130622. Accessed Dec. 9, 2019.

Milenio. 2020. "'El arte es un monasterio': Abraham Oceransky habla de su trabajo como dramaturgo." *Milenio*, Jan. 28, 2020, www.milenio.com/cultura/escenario/abraham-oceransky-constructor-teatros-glorifica-arte. Accessed Jul. 29, 2021.

New Yorker. 2021. "Kei Takei/Moving Earth Orient Sphere." www.newyorker.com/goings-on-about-town/dance/kei-takei-moving-earth-orient-sphere. *New Yorker*. January 25, 2021. Accessed Sept. 11, 2021.

Piñón, Diego. 2018. Trans. Indira Percek, Ed. Christopher Mankowski "Mi Paso Por Butoh" [My Passage through Butoh]. INBA *Danzaria Magazine* #54. July 2018.

Richard, Frances. 2009. "Carolee Schneemann." *Artforum International* 47, no. 9 (May): 236–237.

Rodríguez, Patricia. 2020. "Veracruz, la inspiración de Oceransky," Identidad Veracruz, Feb. 2, 2020. www.identidadveracruz.com/2020/02/02/veracruz-la-inspiracion-de-ocer ansky/. Accessed Jun. 29, 2021.

Rosales, Gustavo Emilio. 2019. "A Sun More Alive." In *The Routledge Companion to Butoh Performance*, edited by Bruce Baird and Rosemary Candelario, 312–313. New York: Routledge.

Rosales, Gustavo Emilio. 2011. "La Danza Autónoma," *Cuerpo a Cuerpo* (blog), Bitácora de reflexiones 2011. https://cuerpoacuerpo10.blogspot.com/. Accessed Oct. 15, 2019

Sankai Juku. n.d. "Schedule." www.sankaijuku.com/2010-5?lang=en. Accessed Nov. 29, 2018.

Steinberg, Samuel. 2016. *Photopoetics at Tlatelolco: Afterimages of Mexico 1968*. New York: University of Texas Press.

Stephens, Manuel. 2010. "Arte y Pensamiento." *La Jornada*, Jun. 13, 2010. www.jornada.com.mx/2010/06/13/sem-manuel.html. Accessed Oct. 14, 2019.

Sullivan, Dan. 1984. "Stage: Olympic Arts Festival It Dared to Be Arrogant." *Los Angeles Times*, Aug. 12, 1984.

Tanaka, Michiko. 1994. "Seki Sano and Popular Political and Social Theater in Latin America" in *Latin America Theater Review* 27, no. 2 (Spring): 53–69.

The Village Voice. "The Village Years: The Birth of the Village Voice: 1955–1965." 2005. *The Village Voice*, Oct, 8–23, 30.

Thornbury, Barbara E. 2016. *American's Japan and Japan's Performing Arts: Cultural Mobility and Exchange in New York 1952–2011*. Ann Arbor: University of Michigan Press.

Van Biema, David. 1985. "Drama Turns to Tragedy as a Japanese Avant-Garde Dancer Plunges to his Death in Seattle." *People*. September 30, 1985.

Vega, Patricia. 2019. "El Galeón también se llama Oceransky." *Letras Libres*, Jan. 30, 2019. www.letraslibres.com/mexico/revista/el-galeon-tambien-se-llama-oceransky. Accessed Sept. 15, 2019.

Wochi Kochi. 2013. "Dairakudakan Meets Brazil, the World Meets Butoh." *Web Magazine Wochi Kochi*, Japan Foundation. www.wochikochi.jp/english/topstory/2011/03/butoh.php Accessed Dec. 28, 2018.

Yoo, Mia. 2019. "La MaMa Experimental Theater Club Artistic Director Mia Yoo." Interview by Kyoko Iwaki. *Presenter Interview*, The Japan Foundation Performing Arts Network, March 12, 2019. https://performingarts.jp/E/pre_interview/1804/1.html. Accessed Jul. 15, 2020.

Zukof, William. 1983. Communication to Kazue Kobata on behalf of Min Tanaka, March 29, 1983, La MaMa Archive, New York, New York.

3 American Anchor Artists and Festivals

Introduction

In the United States, two artists developed their practice on opposite sides of the country: Joan Laage and Maureen Fleming. Both intersected significantly with the Ohnos: Laage through Kazuo as the doppelganger of her dying mother and Fleming through both Kazuo and Yoshito but perhaps most significantly through Yoshito when he created and performed a duet with her in New York in 1991 (see Figure 3.1). These two American artists developed at almost the same time, although in seemingly separate circles. Laage is the senior artist by six years and was active in cultural studies and numerous other dance forms including Bharatanatyam before coming to butoh as her primary study in 1988 with Kazuo Ohno and then in 1989 with Yoko Ashikawa in the company Gnome. Fleming's path is etched in injury which led her to movement as therapy, as well as through myth and archetype, factors which lay a foundation of her initial connection with butoh. Further, Fleming was at the epicenter of the New York experimental performance scene—Ellen Stewart's La MaMa—and was swept into butoh in 1985 in Stewart's *Oedipus*, choreographed by and featuring Min Tanaka.

Fleming and Mexican artist Diego Piñón share a connection to Min Tanaka, and all three artists share a strong bond to the Ohnos. I chose to profile these three artists because they have had such a significant impact through their touring and/or teaching, each in their own way strongly defining butoh in the Americas.

The closing section of this chapter highlights the San Francisco Butoh Festival, which featured Fleming, Laage, and Piñón at different points in its eight-year run. This festival is critical to the growth of butoh in the Americas, as it did much to build touring networks, educated audiences, critics, and funders, and coalesced a global student community in festival format, a model that would be replicated by other festivals to come.

Maureen Fleming (b. 1954, Yokohama, Japan) Based in New York City

A 2004 New Yorker review of Maureen Fleming's *Decay of the Angel* calls her "perhaps the foremost American practitioner of butoh" (New Yorker 2004).

DOI: 10.4324/9780429028472-3

Figure 3.1 Eros (1991). Dancers left to right: Yoshito Ohno, Maureen Fleming. (c) Lois
    Greenfield 1991.

Source: Photo courtesy Lois Greenfield, reprinted with permission from Lois Greenfield

Her hallmarks are "metamorphosis" and "transforming her body with agoniz-
ing slowness" (New Yorker 2004).

Fleming, the daughter of a Navy Lieutenant Commander, was born in Japan
following the American Occupation. When she was a small child, she was
involved in a violent accident that framed her questions of identity from an
early age. She and her sister were launched through the car windshield when
her mother stopped short to avoid a cyclist. According to Fleming's retelling
of her mother's description, the Japanese man on the bicycle laughed before
riding away as her distraught mother held her two screaming and bloodied
daughters. Both the physical and psychological pains from that incident have
marked her creative work and focus on healing, both cultural and corporeal.
Being confronted with racial tension early on in life pushed her to want to
understand the Japanese man's perspective.

As a result, a driving force in Fleming's artistic work is "a deeper understanding of human potential," which she has sought to engender through "dynamic in-depth collaborations where new boundaries between cultures and art forms are crossed" (Maureen Fleming, pers. comm., April 17, 2019). Herself of mixed race, "Black Irish"[1] as it were, Fleming sees her work as offering an end to painful cycles of racial and ethnic violence and instead, seeking regeneration (Maureen Fleming, pers. comm., April 17, 2019).

Fleming found a kindred spirit in author and anthropologist Joseph Campbell who was influenced by Adolf Bastian's concept of "elementary ideas," which is a term for the source of myths and archetypal images that appear across cultures. Says Fleming of one of her signature images—a nearly naked female body carrying an equally naked tree branch— "a woman becoming a tree is an elementary idea with different folk traditions in many places, such as the Greek story of Daphne" (Maureen Fleming, pers. comm., February 7, 2020). Human and nature merged into metaphor.

The flower is another elementary idea that pervades Fleming's work. Reinforced by Kazuo Ohno's lessons—for example, dance from the instruction "a flower opens in your face"—Fleming has continued to explore her connection to nature throughout her career. In *WILDFLOWERS, A Feminine Genesis*, developed in Ireland where Fleming also holds an Irish passport through her maternal grandmother, Fleming depicts feminine Irish creation mythology through the images of wildflowers, which Fleming evokes with her body and fabric. Drawing on the ephemeral beauty of flowers, Fleming probes human understanding of the cosmos: "Is immortality a paradigm we await or is it present in the here and now?" (Fleming 2018). She was inspired by the Irish poet W.B. Yeats' writings in which there is often a blur between the temporal and the eternal moment: "Birth hour and death hour meet . . . Men dance on deathless feet" (Yeats 2002, 115–116) and from Rumi, "the flower of what's true opens in the face" (quoted in Barks 1995, p. 38). Flowers in Fleming's work have become a metaphor for the self and soul (Maureen Fleming, pers. comm., February 7, 2020).

Dance training was Fleming's vehicle for healing. Due to the accident, she has experienced low-grade pain in her body since a young age and notes that her initial movement drive was to find a comfortable place to simply exist in everyday life. She remembers giving dance classes to her sisters at the age of 5, asking them to fall asleep in different positions. She eventually enrolled in classical dance as well, becoming "religious" about ballet training from the age of 7 (Maureen Fleming, pers. comm., April 7, 2019). Eventually, she committed to the Cecchetti Method, training with British-born Cecchetti disciple Margaret Craske who invited her to audition for the Manhattan School of Dance in New York City, where she studied on scholarship for seven years. She trained with some rather elite dancers; New York Ballet Theater director Diana Byer was among her classmates. For Fleming, however, ballet was a means to an end rather than an aesthetic pursuit unto itself. Her movement exploration went beyond any prescribed technique to a larger quest for ease in her body and also a sense of connection with others through movement.

In her journey to develop her own work, Fleming encountered several critical artists and thinkers that confirmed and enhanced her vision. As noted earlier, she recalls discovering comparative mythology through Joseph Campbell's writing, which greatly impacted the ways in which she describes her art. Campbell and other progressively minded people were a part of her community in New York City in the 1980s. Following one of her performances, Campbell said to her: "your dance is your transcendence," which Fleming credits with "heightening her awareness of her calling" (Maureen Fleming, pers. comm., April 17, 2019).

Fleming was further influenced by the creative practice of Campbell's wife, Jean Erdman. Erdman had studied hula and Isadora Duncan technique in Hawaii before training with Martha Graham at Sarah Lawrence College in 1934–5. Erdman quickly became a principal dancer in the Graham company and eventually struck out on her own (Fox 2020). Erdman collaborated with avant-garde composers Teiji Ito, Guy Klucevsek, and John Cage, among others, and experimental filmmaker Maya Deren.[2] Writes Fox, Erdman's work "was suffused with the dreamlike aura of myth and legend" (Fox 2020). Fleming created her original work *Spirit Walk*, for which Erdman's frequent collaborator Teiji Ito had composed the music in 1982 before his untimely death of a heart attack in Haiti. Teiji's brother Genji played in his stead in the 1985 performance at Riverside Dance Festival. Erdman was in attendance, and following the performance, she asked Fleming to collaborate and perform in a Philip Gotanda play *Dream of Kitamura*, presented in 1987 at St. Ann's Warehouse in Brooklyn.

Throughout the 1980s, Fleming presented dances in a variety of Downtown New York venues, including La MaMa, which was a space particularly known for artists who blurred artistic disciplines. She felt right at home. Legendary La MaMa Artistic Director Ellen Stewart drew an incredible community of artists. Says Fleming, one of Stewart's inspirations was theater director Peter Brook, who was combining a heady array of theatrical concepts and practices from around the world. Genji Ito asked Fleming to create a memorial dance for a La MaMa event. Her response to his music and the theme was to move extremely slowly which, she realized in hindsight, bridged her previous interest in ritual to her eventual study of butoh.

Fleming's relationship with Stewart and La MaMa grew quickly intertwined. As she recalls that period of her life, Fleming says:

> I remember performing in La MaMa's "La Galleria" and suddenly I was painting studio walls in La MaMa's 1st Street basement. And then Ellen said "ok baby, here's the keys" and after Fleming had a following of students, "ok baby now we're doing '*Orphei*.'"
>
> (Maureen Fleming, pers. comm., April 17, 2019)

Fleming gratefully acknowledges that Stewart took her under her wing and helped build her early career.

Stewart cast Fleming in the production of *Mythos Oedipus* starring Japanese butoh artist and film actor Min Tanaka for its 1985 premiere in the Greek ruins of *Delphi*. At this point, Fleming had seen only a video of Sankai Juku before she found herself wearing a nine-foot wig and riding atop the shoulders of four men in this butoh/avant-garde Greek theater production.[3]

Though butoh was new territory, to Fleming the work felt like a continuation of her own research. She became fascinated with possession states and goddess cultural rites. She felt echoes of previous work: the *Solaris/Lakota Project* (1980–1983, directed by Henry Smith) involving Lakota from the Pine Ridge and Rosebud reservations, and touring to Africa, France, and Sweden, as well as her encounters with Erdman, Campbell, and Teiji and Genji Ito. Additionally, Fleming notes that growing up with four uncles who were all Catholic priests ensured that ritual was an integral part of her worldview, even though she took the practice in a different direction. From her personal research in improvisation and dances from around the world, she was familiar with the idea of using images to enter into an altered state, which is a method that Tanaka also employed in his work. Says Fleming, "Min opened a door as to how to get there," in a way that would influence her own creative research for many years to come (Maureen Fleming, pers. comm., April 17, 2019).

Following the June 1985 *Mythos Oedipus* production in Greece, Tanaka invited Fleming to perform with his company in the *Fool's Festival* in Copenhagen, Denmark, and to study with him in Japan when he was first establishing the Hakushu farm. Stewart supported Fleming to stay in Japan for several months, during which time Los Angeles-based Japanese butoh artist Oguri and Dutch dancer Frank van de Ven were also there.[4] Says Fleming,

> Tanaka knew how to channel spirits and other entities. He was shamanic and very violent . . . he would say "my center is on the wall" and I could feel that . . . he would inhale and dance a space and become a deeper self.
> (Maureen Fleming, pers. comm., April 17, 2019)

She recalls fondly that Tanaka "repeatedly pushed the students to their extreme, and helped people develop their own teaching" (Maureen Fleming, pers. comm., April 17, 2019). She thrived with the challenge. In her artist bio for the 1988 production of *Mythos Oedipus*, she wrote, "In 1985 she was captured by Min Tanaka and taken to Japan where she learned to stand under an icy waterfall in November" (The Great Jones Repertory Company 1988). When Fleming eventually became injured with the Body Weather training in Tanaka's company, Maijuku, this forced her to find her own way and eventually lead to her unique approach to movement and original choreography.

When Fleming returned to New York City from Japan in 1985, she became an official artist in residence at La MaMa. Avidly researching exercises that healed her own body, she conducted ongoing workshops under the title "Body Structure" at La MaMa's 1st Street studio. It was during this period that Fleming connected the injury she experienced during the intensive training with

Maijuku in Japan, with the accident she had as a child in Japan. The initial trauma had left a bone spur that had grown throughout her life and the loss of a disc between the fourth and fifth vertebra, confirmed by an X-ray, was now causing nerve damage in her neck from all of the full body pounding into the earth from the training in Japan. Surgery was recommended; however, Fleming insisted on discovering her own healing through movement. After all, she had been doing this intuitively since childhood. Little by little, in the literal process of healing, Fleming developed both a codified physical practice and a large following of students. Beginning with workshops at La MaMa studio, she was eventually invited to teach at New York University, where she was on faculty in the Experimental Theater Wing for many years, as well as Trinity and the Juilliard School.

In 1988, Fleming returned to Japan to study with Kazuo Ohno, during which time she met Susan Blakely Klein, author of one of the first English scholarly documents on butoh: *Ankoku Buto: The Premodern and Postmodern Influences on the Dance of Utter Darkness* (Klein 1985). Arranged by Klein, Fleming initially stayed at the Ohno's summer home in Kamakura. During this time, Yoshito Ohno became invested in her growth as a student and artist. In 1990, she returned to Japan on an Asian Cultural Council Fellowship, where she stayed in the Ohno studio in Kamihoshikawa, studying with Kazuo and Yoshito Ohno, preparing for the premiere of her work *After Eros* in 1991 at La MaMa. While in Japan, she was invited to perform her signature work *Axis Mundi* in the event "Butō Festival" organized by Akiko Motofuji to honor Tatsumi Hijikata. Kazuo Ohno, Yoshito Ohno, and Min Tanaka all performed in this festival, which took place at Asbestos-kan in Tokyo, Hijikata's studio performance space.

She returned to New York and a year later in 1991, she performed *Eros* with Yoshito Ohno at La MaMa. It was an evening of interlocking solos, some new and others mined from previous work. Dance critic Deborah Jowitt's analysis deems the partnership successful: "The solos work together quite beautifully . . . Fleming seems to incarnate the primal stages he [Ohno] is confronting or remembering. Woman become rock. Becoming flesh. Turning into a tree. Dying. Being born. The images are beautiful, cruel" (Jowitt 1991). The following is a description of the evening length work, viewed by the author on video at the La MaMa archive.

Eros

Eros opens with Fleming folding into an incredibly slow backbend, to the sound of percussionist Mickey Hart chanting. As she approaches the end of her descent, her head turns eerily toward the audience. She's naked except for a small patch covering her genitals. She continues her arch backward, then crumples down and contorts her body into knots, curls around her foundation, and gets her feet under herself, and then slowly unfurls her spine and stands up facing the opposite direction. Her white powdered body looks like a chiseled, moving marble sculpture as it is exquisitely side-lit against the black curtain. As she curls back down into squatting weeping Buddha position, thunder strikes and lights fade to black.

In the second scene, a blue light slowly fades up, revealing Yoshito in a crouched position. As he rises his arms stiffen into blades, which gesture as if dousing for water. He is dressed in white sailor pants and a collared shirt, a costume he wore for the duet Dead Sea with his father, Kazuo. Facing upstage, he curls his arms in front of him and then turns back toward the audience, indicating up and down with alternate hands, heaven and hell, then both to heaven, and both to hell. Between each gesture he stirs his hands, like in the children's song wheels on the bus. He steps into a pool of water and we see his reflection. At one point he traces one finger across his neck, and his head drops forward. Immediately, he is reborn and continues the gestures.

Arms outstretched he turns and walks upstage. A soulful version of silent night begins, gestures of folded hands as if sleeping flit in and out of his slow arm dance. He slowly walks off upstage, like a fading spirit leaving this world. Soft thunder as he exits, and then he re-enters with a silver bucket above his head, walks a semi-circle around the front of the stage, and then pours more water into the pool. He puts the bucket back on his head and exits upstage right. He re-enters from stage left with the bucket and we hear light thunder again.

The next section is Maureen's infamous staircase dance. "The Stairs" premiered in 1989 in "Water on the Moon" at La MaMa (Small 1989). She descends in excruciatingly slow motion, upside down demonstrating her exquisite control. It doesn't seem like it should be possible as she slowly unfurls and rolls, upside down, down the staircase. Yoshito returns bare chested this time, slow turns with a series of gestures, beast claw hands, stiff arms, and stiff-legged jumping like in Eiko Hosoe's film Navel and A bomb. He punches and jabs around his chest, which he puffs up so that his ribs protrude. His body is painted white. We hear classical music drowned out by wind.

The next scene is Maureen with fabric across her face, seated in a Graham-esque z-sit, arms outstretched, chest arched back, wind blowing the fabric back, and light is red tinted. She slowly rises and arches back, with the fabric fluttering the entire time like a flag across her body. Suddenly, her limbs whip as if blown by strong wind, wildly tossing her upper body about as her legs stay rooted. Yoshito returns in a white suit and hat with flowers, similar to the one worn by Kazuo in *Dead Sea*.

Lights come up for the final scene, illuminating Fleming in the water with branches. She slowly rises and walks a few piercing steps, bent over, and walking on tiptoes with her arms outstretched behind her, birdlike. Yoshito appears with a picture frame around his face. She continues to wield the branches, raising them over her head. She slowly returns to a crouch and then drops the branches and slides out to an elongated position, stopping just at the point before she touches the ground with her whole body. She has mastered an incredible physicality that makes the audience catch their breath. It's as if she stops just before the moment of resolution, suspending weight against gravity. Her physical control is just exquisite to watch, and she never stays in a recognizable shape for very long.

The 1991 performance with Yoshito marked a new chapter in Fleming's career, one in which she grew to increasing international prominence as a solo artist who had truly established her own voice. John Gillespie, former director of Japan Society, aptly described Fleming's unique approach to performance: "She is neither Eastern nor Western, belonging neither to butoh nor ballet. She is herself, *sui generis*, made of many diverse elements into one of a kind" (Gillespie 2018). Gillespie's commentary reinforces the assertion that Fleming has an artistic voice unto herself.

Following Stewart's initial effort to produce Fleming in France, Fleming vigorously pursued an international career, with much success. She performed in the Milanoltre [Beyond Milan] Festival, where dance critic Ugo Volli declared: "Fleming is a sensational discovery, one of the rare, esthetic emotions in recent years" (Volli 1993). Of her 1996 performance in Paris, *Le Figaro* proclaimed: "Not only is Maureen Fleming a phenomenon, but also a sensitive artist who uses the butoh technique for original creations of great aesthetic harmony" (*Le Figaro* 1996). This is a notable feat in Paris, where butoh first ventured beyond Japan and informed audiences were harsh critics. She returned to New York later that same year with *After Eros*, a series of solos which included her breathtaking descent down a staircase headfirst. Jack Anderson of *The New York Times* proclaimed: "She appeared to transform into stone. She also appeared to transcend the material world and enter the realm of pure spirit . . . it involved more than virtuosity . . . [the performance] became a sacred journey" (Anderson 1996). She became recognized worldwide as an original artist on her own terms, with her own truly unique expression.

Among her many international commissions, she was a Fulbright Scholar in Colombia (2005), South Korea (2006, 2007), Ireland (2016, 2017), and Latvia (2019). Between 2006 and 2011, she was an artist in residence at the Seoul Institute for the Arts, where she developed her groundbreaking Fleming Technique and "regenerative" training methods with Fleming Elastxx, a patented device of her own invention (US Patent 2020). She has also been a frequent guest at international festivals in Italy, France, Germany, Colombia, Brazil, Argentina, Japan, South Korea, and Latvia, where dance movement therapy practitioner Simona Orinska has been developing a butoh community since 2005. Orinska has created a large following of welcoming students spreading the butoh diaspora and creating many opportunities for cultural exchange.[5] During Fleming's 2019 Fulbright in Riga, Latvia, she presented her work *Mother and Child*, set to Gorecki's *Symphony of Sorrowful Songs* and featuring 12 dancers including Orinska as a memorial to the 90,000 Jewish Latvian people who perished under the German occupation during World War II. The piece was performed at the STARTELPA Festival at the Latvian Performance Art Center, where she also presented her work *B. Madonna*.

Major works by Fleming include *Eros* (with Yoshito Ohno, 1991), *Axis Mundi* (1988 Commission for Creative Time NYC and later presented in the 1995 San Francisco Butoh Festival on a shared program with Akira Kasai), *After Eros* (1996), *Decay of the Angel* (2004), *Waters of Immortality* (2007), *B. Madonna* (2013), and *WILDFLOWERS, A Feminine Genesis* (2018). Many of the dances feature Fleming surrounded by a billowing, gauzy fabric, of iconic red, black, orange, or white. She is frequently nude, or nearly so, and unpainted. She has a host of frequent collaborators, including multi-disciplinary artist Chris Odo; musician Bruce Brubaker; composers Philip Glass, Guy Klucevsek, and Colm Mac Con Iomaire; and author David Henry Hwang. When Lois Greenfield was working for the Village Voice, she photographed Maureen Fleming and Yoshito Ohno during the 1991 performance of *Eros*. Following this first encounter, Lois Greenfield continued to photograph Fleming in her studio. Fleming's choreography and costume designs became the subject of many of Greenfield's most famous photographic images. After studying photography at the Seoul Institute of the Arts while a Fulbright Scholar there in 2006, Fleming began to create her own photography of her choreography and presented her first photography installation "Dances from Home" at La Galleria in 2009 in conjunction with photographers who had also captured her original images including Lois Greenfield, Philip Trager, Spencer Tunic, Christopher Odo, and Ethan Hoffman.

Among her significant students, Fleming cites Dana Iova-Koga (also a student of Min Tanaka at Hakushu, and the life and creative partner of Shinichi Iova-Koga, profiled in Chapter 4), Ximena Garnica (profiled in Chapter 4), Venezuelan-based Juan Carlos Linares (teacher at La Universidad Nacional Experimental de las Artes (Unearte)), and Antony and the Johnsons (Maureen Fleming, pers. comm., April 17, 2019). Anohni, the transgender lead vocalist of Antony and the Johnsons, was a student at NYU in the early 1990s, when Fleming was a regular professor in the Experimental Theater Wing (ETW). Says Anohni of the impact butoh had on her own art:

> Especially on stage for me, I'm always applying the vocabulary I studied in butoh, as a singer. Rarely am I mining my personal life for motivation to sing. Usually, I'm engaged in seeking a creative impulse, or a set of imagery that can propel me through the song or the moment, to unveil the present for me in a different way.
>
> Maybe as I'm singing, a flock of flamingos are bursting out of my heart, and I ride the momentum of those birds as I sing forward. Maybe when the audience exhales it creates a green mist that collects before them, as a momentum, and it dances in a circle that resolves in a huge glowing pool in the middle of the room, and we all look at it and I sing into that place.
>
> (Barclay 2009)

In particular, Fleming's technique of using image to access states was the key for Anohni.

> I studied with this teacher named Maureen Fleming, who was amazing. Before that I went to a performing arts school, which was so focused on technique and things that were too abstract to me. Maureen would just plug me right in with a crazy image that really worked for me.
>
> (Barclay 2009)

Anohni became fascinated with Kazuo Ohno and as a band, Antony and the Johnsons eventually met the Ohnos in Japan. They performed with Yoshito at the Sogetsu Hall in Tokyo in 2010. A black and white image of Kazuo Ohno's 1977 *La Argentina* graces the cover of Antony and the Johnsons' 2009 album *The Crying Light*.[6] Says Anohni, "The album is dedicated to him, because he is my art hero and art parent, in a way" (Barclay 2009).

Another notable student of Fleming is Dimitris Pappaionnou, who rocketed to international fame when he choreographed *Origins* for the 2004 Athens Olympics Opening Ceremony. Pappaionnou was cast as a chorus dancer in Ellen Stewart's 1985 production of *Mythos Oedipus* in Athens, under choreographer Min Tanaka. He subsequently traveled to New York in 1986 to continue his studies in butoh and contemporary dance through connections he had made in the Greek production (Ozzie Rodriquez, pers. comm., September 5, 2020). While enrolled in a program of study with Erick Hawkins, a protégé of Martha Graham, Pappaionnou also took Fleming's workshops at La MaMa. Originally a painter, Pappaionnou went on to found his own Athens-based company Edifos and collaborate with theater director Robert Wilson (Gil 2011). As with Fleming, Ellen Stewart supported and promoted his development, including directing Pappaionnou's 1986 opera *The Monk and the Hangman's Daughter*, which premiered in Baltimore.[7] Many of his dances include seemingly dismembered and multi-limbed humans, emerging from walls and tables. His aesthetic is decidedly dark, though *The New York Times* critic Brian Seibert notes that Pappaionnou delves into Tanztheater's "Bauschian mortal themes with a light tough . . . a comic tone that wards off pretension" (Seibert 2019). Though he does not mention butoh in his website or promotional materials, there are aesthetic connections in his uncanny imagery and temporal pacing.

Fleming continues to teach and influence a new generation of artists and movement educators. Now in her sixties, Fleming is still going strong as a dance artist, creator, and teacher. She credits her rigorous and daily practice with the Elastxx, a part of Fleming Technique, as well as her continued drive toward creative research. Despite injury, her quest has always been the same: "What is the unbreakable, indestructible essence inside each of us that the art of dance seeks to reveal?" Fleming notes that although

> many artists begin creating out of pain, out of a need to escape a particular reality, that need to go somewhere else puts one close to the unconscious

and engenders a reciprocal relationship between life and art that strengthens as we attain higher levels of contact with the beyond we can sometimes reach in the dance.

(Fleming 2013)

Indeed, her body of work is a testament to this quest and has provided a strong foundation for American butoh.

Joan Laage/Kogut (b. 1948, Beloit, Wisconsin, Based in Seattle, Washington Since 1990)

Originally from Beloit, Wisconsin, Joan Laage first studied modern dance in high school. As a student at University of Colorado, Boulder, Laage initially majored in Spanish and French. After she changed her major to dance, a fellow student introduced her to a local Bharata Natyam teacher. In 1974, she relocated to Berkeley, CA, to continue Indian dance studies with the renowned Balasaraswati and her daughter Laksmi. It was here at the Center for World Music, a cultural organization that introduced many prominent Asian artists to the United States through national tours and training programs (Center for World Music, 2020), that Joan was exposed to a variety of dance forms from around the world. These encounters piqued her interest in travel and cultural studies. While in Berkeley, she also studied Indonesian dance forms and modern dance with Laura Dean, and performed her repertoire with live music by Steve Reich (Joan Laage, email message to author, November 14, 2019).

Bolstered by the cultural blending she witnessed at the Center for World Music, Laage continued expanding her training to include Tai Chi. Upon graduation with an MA in dance from Mill College, she secured a teaching position at The University of Otago and left the United States for Dunedin, New Zealand, where she taught for three years from 1978 to 1980. Each summer, she traveled to India to continue studies with Balasaraswati, in dance and also Carnatic singing and language studies. Laage credits the training in classical Indian dance for her highly expressive face and feet and says that this training was later useful when she encountered butoh. She draws the correlation specifically to the use of mask in her training with Ashikawa; they worked with *hannya* (devil) for facial expression with the *kabe* (wall) body posture, though unlike *abhinaya* in classical Indian dance, Ashikawa was not working with mask expression for an emotional goal, but rather an impetus for texture and shape in the face (Joan Laage, pers. comm., January 6, 2020).

At an American Dance Guild/Congress on Research in Dance conference, entitled "Traditional Dance in the Twentieth Century" held in Hawaii in 1978, Laage encountered the "lively debates centered around the questions of modernizing traditional dance and creating modern forms" (Laage 1993, 21). Her initial interest in butoh came from the perception that it was "indigenous Japanese contemporary dance" (Laage 1993, 22). In part, this notion came from the context within which she viewed butoh for the first time. While teaching on the Semester at Sea program, she visited Japan for the first in 1982; Laage witnessed many traditional dance forms, including Noh, Kabuki, Bunraku, and Nihon Buyo (Japanese traditional dance). It was through the lens of her previous experience with Asian traditional performance that she saw Dairakudakan for the first time. While living in Hong Kong, she had seen a photo of the group's director Akaji Maro. She had sought the company out when she arrived in Tokyo and was fortunate that they were performing. She was impressed with the spectacle that she calls "visually . . . striking and mysterious" (Laage 1993, 22). The experience stayed with her and eventually drew her back to Japan as a subject to research.

In 1987–88, Laage pursued her certificate in Laban Movement Analysis at the Laban/Bartenieff Institute for Movement Studies in New York. While there, she met Susan Blakely Klein, who shared her own research in butoh. When Laage decided to pursue Laban's research on "qualitative similarities in butoh" (Joan Laage, pers. comm., January 6, 2020), Klein introduced her at the studios of Kazuo Ohno and Natsu Nakajima in Tokyo. At that time, says Laage, "you still needed a formal introduction to be admitted to these studios" (Joan Laage, pers. comm., January 6, 2020). Her strategy was to use her own body as a research tool for her writing: "I never set out to be a butoh dancer" says Laage, rather she was taking class in order to pursue an embodied understanding.

Laage describes her training in Japan as firmly rooted in both lineages: the choreographed image training and choreographic structures of Hijikata's later work, via Ashikawa, and the improvisational explorations with Kazuo and his son, Yoshito Ohno. She trained with the Ohnos for many years. For her, training with Yoshito was "like experiencing a Zen koan; it was quite a mysterious process, much like understanding how someone believes in god" (Joan Laage, pers. comm., January 6, 2020). With Kazuo, Laage says that the prompts given for class improvisations were more often about

> the mother and fetus relationship, the body as ocean, the body as the fish swimming in the ocean, little fish being swallowed by a bigger fish . . . He wouldn't really tell you what to do, but he would more guide: "*motto chisai*" [do it smaller], bring it inside, don't let it seep out so much.

Kazuo encouraged minimal movement to "allow the *tamashi* [soul] to come up, burst and float up like an earthquake" (Joan Laage, pers. comm., January 6, 2020). Ohno's teachings were particularly special for her:

> At the time Ohno was working with the image of the hungry ghosts [a classic Buddhist archetype of wandering souls], and it was a cathartic experience for me. These images struck me because of my own mother's illnesses; she had multiple sicknesses including cancer of the esophagus. Butoh is not generally cathartic for me, I know it is for some, but for me it's not so personally emotional, but more a deep emotion of the body. But

at the time, he reminded me so much of my mother, who was emaciated toward the end of her life because she couldn't swallow . . . so it was a very personal connection with Kazuo.

(Joan Laage, pers. comm., January 6, 2020)

She says that though in her training methodology she draws more heavily from Ashikawa, she more often senses Kazuo's presence in her performances because that connection was so deeply felt (Joan Laage, pers. comm., January 6, 2020).

In 1989, her first two butoh creations included solos by her and Naofumi Fujitani, a dedicated student of Kazuo's, followed by an improvisational duet (see Figure 3.2). She and Fujitani produced *Dapp'in* (*Shedding*) at Terpsicore in Tokyo, followed by a second performance held in Yokohama's ST Spot. With her *sensei* Kazuo in the audience, Laage remembers feelings of awe and humility (Joan Laage, pers. comm., January 6, 2020). Laage later used Dappin'

Figure 3.2 Joan Laage in *Milky Way* at Terpsichore in Tokyo, Japan (1989).

Source: Photo courtesy Joan Laage, reprinted with permission from Joan Laage (with a change in spelling) for her company name in the United States (Dappin' Butoh). Her first group project was as a guest artist in Taiwan, where she created *Four Seasons in a Rock Garden* with local dancers in 1989.

Imagery training with Ashikawa was what made Laage "captivated with the style" (Joan Laage, pers. comm., January 6, 2020). Ashikawa had been a painter before she worked with Hijikata and would put charcoal drawings on the wall. These drawings spoke to Laage's fascination with graphic images. She also appreciated Ashikawa's ability to make her see things anew: "She [Ashikawa] would also completely disorient us, saying things like 'up is down and down is up' to keep us constantly recalibrating and off balance" (Joan Laage, pers. comm., January 6, 2020). Laage found the challenge quite intriguing.

From Ashikawa, Laage learned the specific use of language employed in butoh. Every month for a year at Terpsichore, Ashikawa would hold a six-hour workshop with live music in which Laage participated. She describes the experience as "super intensive." Onomatopoeia with touch words was common: "like when Ashikawa uttered 'picpicpicpic' while she poked the soles of our feet with a chopstick while we practiced *kujyaku* [peacock]" (Joan Laage, pers. comm., January 6, 2020). Ashikawa and dancers used sweeping gestures to extend and guide the images beyond the body. Laage remembers wondering if they were playing with energy fields or auras and asking herself if butoh is about making energy fields manifest in form. She learned the importance of using internal experience to shape the external form. She describes this in relationship to *ushi*, or bull, one of the most common animal images used in butoh training:

> you feel the spreading of the hips to make the big buttocks of the *ushi* and feel the weight of the horns on the head, and how that makes you move . . . it's not doing, it's allowing, uncovering . . . how you extend your energy changes how you relate to the space.
>
> (Joan Laage, pers. comm., January 6, 2020)

Says Laage, "The other thing is the body in stillness, feeling the packed molecules of the stone, for example feeling the density, and then a dog pees on you, and it changes your state, which can change your shape" (Joan Laage, pers. comm., January 6, 2020). Laage finds that this training is useful for any performer because it teaches fundamental lessons about the body and energy in space.

Even though she was still in research mode, an opportunity came for Laage to further engage in performance. After the year of intensive workshops, Ashikawa formed the apprentice company Gnome so that Hakutobo dancers could train other dancers, among them SU-EN.[8] Laage performed in three or four shows, which was significant exposure to the intensive process of making work. In the beginning, even though she didn't speak Japanese and there was no translation, she had former training in Tai Chi and knew how to bring herself to a beginner's mind, and to make her body available. She describes specific training in weightlessness and awareness of gravity, which she feels "informs butoh [dancers'] ability to direct energy in any dimension—inside, outside, down to the earth, up to the sky. This is how you get to the animal body," or what she refers to as the "available body," the body that is ready to move any direction at any moment. "I would watch Izumi doing the lightening in the body, and then I allowed that energy to permeate my body" (Joan Laage, pers. comm., January 6, 2020). Further, with Ashikawa and with Yoshito, the training was always about the process, or *hoko*, "traveling, not walking . . . moving from one end of the room to the other in a journey." She describes the process of transformation *as* the dance score. At one of Gnome's infamous all-night rehearsals, Laage recalls practicing *hoko* for over an hour, during which time she felt as if she would throw up or pass out, but somehow, she managed to keep going through concentrating on the task of embodying the images. One of the Hakutobo dancers came up to her and scratched her throat to help her find the exposed tendons of the *hannya* mask, a sensation she remembers viscerally (Joan Laage, pers. comm., January 6, 2020).

While in Japan, Laage continued to seek out performances outside of butoh, including Noh, Kabuki, Bunraku, and Matsuri Shinto shrine festivals, which she felt helped her understand critical aspects of Japanese cultural forms. She also witnessed the emergence of the so-called post-butoh movement in Japanese dance, when an increasing number of contemporary dancers were showing signs of butoh influence. Key among these artists was Saburo Teshigawara, whose 1989 piece *Ishi-no-hana* (*Flower of Stone*), featured him dancing "on a mound of glass panes, stamping them into fragments, glass dust rising in alarming curls" (Meisner 2000). Another Japanese dancer that Laage sought out was Kumiko Kuniyoshi. Laage recalls being struck by her way of moving and staging, a very personal journey but closer to contemporary than butoh in its timing and sense of space.

Laage returned to Japan for her Ph.D. research in 1987 (Laage 1993). During this period, she interviewed dance critic Nario Goda and ingratiated herself to a number of Japanese butoh performers by hanging around after performances (Laage 1993, 34). She returned to Kazuo Ohno's studio and also watched Natsu Nakajima in rehearsal with Yukio Waguri. Laage saw an "invitation only" performance at Min Tanaka's farm (and witnessed Tanaka's group Maijuku's mid-night performance during the rain while Michael Blackwood shot his film *Body on the Edge of Crises*) as well as group performances by Hakutobo, Dairakudakan, Dance Love Machine, Harupin-Ha, Yuko Yuki, and Akira Kasai (Eurhythmy). She also saw solos by Masaki Iwana, Goi Teru, and Tomiko Takai, and later, Ko Murobushi, as he was beginning his series of dances with his body painted silver. Integrating herself into the community, Laage saw countless weekly performances in intimate theaters, "packing in up to one hundred and fifty people seated side by side on flat black cushions" (Laage 1993, 35). She also saw outdoor performances in Zushi Beach near Tokyo (Joan Laage, pers. comm., January 6, 2020).

Based on her experiences in Tokyo in the late 1980s and early 1990s, she concluded that "the underground spirit of the experimental 1960s is alive in Japan today" (Laage 1993, 35). She returned to the United States with these influences fresh in her own creative consciousness.

While living abroad in Japan, Laage had met her husband David Thornbrugh, a poet and editor. He eventually rejoined her in the United States, where she had been finishing her dissertation at Texas Women's University, while living with her father in El Paso, Texas. The couple eventually settled in Seattle. Laage says that she had always felt connected to the Pacific Rim and was drawn to the Pacific North West landscape. Says Laage, "there was no butoh scene here yet, but people knew about butoh here in Seattle because Sankai Juku had been here and many witnessed the fall to death of one of their company members" (Joan Laage, pers. comm., January 6, 2020). Kokoro dance may have been in Vancouver, B.C. around the same time, but she didn't become aware of them until later.

Laage is a pioneer of butoh in the Pacific Northwest, who established and helped build a community of dancers and audience members. Certainly, the community was bolstered by touring performances by Sankai Juku, who returned to Seattle every few years to perform, as well as the Ohnos and the duo Eiko and Koma. However, it was Laage who has given regular classes and maintained a consistent presence for butoh in Seattle since the summer of 1990.

Founding Dappin' Butoh Company in 1991, she remained Artistic Director for more than a decade. During her tenure, she produced the first Seattle International Butoh Festivals in 1998 and 2000. The first festival promoted the local community, as well as Vancouver-based Kokoro and introduced SU-EN to Seattle. The 2000 festival presented an impressive array of international artists, thanks to Kokoro's Vancouver International Dance Festival, in which Yukio Waguri/Kohzensha Butoh Company (Japan), GooSayTen (Japan), SU-EN Butoh Company (Sweden), Tangentz Performance Group (Hawaii), and Fujiwara Dance Inventions (Toronto) all performed. The festival also brought together artists from Seattle and San Francisco, with performances by Shinichi Koga/inkBoat's *Cockroach* and Degenerate Art Ensemble's *Rinko*.[9]

After 2002, Laage began to actively pursue solo work and research into her own ancestral roots. In 2003, she performed two seminal solo works at the New York Butoh Festival in 2003: *Black Widow* and *Infanticity or Every Baby is Jesus*, as well as a group work, *Imprints*. *Black Widow* is a dance that Laage has been working on in numerous iterations since 1995. She calls it a "slow burn" type of work, due to the fact that each time she performs it, her experience of the images becomes "more saturated." She works with a set structure, but the piece evolves through a series of images, and each journey is distinct. Then, Seattle-based noise artist Key Ransome/Small Cruel Party made the first music for this work, and later composer/photographer Steven Miller created the soundtrack with which she tours. She performed it in Tokyo and Kyoto, and the Red Cat Theater in LA, sharing the stage with Akaji Maro and Katsura Kan. It was an amazing experience for her, since Maro was her entrée into butoh. The ending section of the work features Laage eating and regurgitating red beets while embodying spider postures.

Infanticity or Every Baby is Jesus, first performed in Krakow, Poland in 1996, is based on the idea that "we are all born with innocence" (Joan Laage, pers. comm., January 6, 2020). The images were inspired by Laage's fascination with how and where people worship. She talks about how the buildings we build for worship radiate people's love and fear as they try to understand their place in the world. A particular church she visited in Bucharest was dark and smoky, with the Virgin and Baby Jesus icons decorated in pounded silver. She recreates this image on stage, with an iconic mother and child that she uncovers in the process of her dance, embodying Mary Magdalene and the Baby Jesus as she transforms through worship and iconography.

Another signature project of Laage's is *Earth Tomes*, which was born in 1993 in the middle of the night in an outhouse at a backcountry camp on snowy Mt. Rainier, Washington, while Joan sat listening to the sounds of nature and watching the shadows cast by her flashlight. She created the first solo for the Festival of One in Seattle and, also, performed it at the Seattle Fringe Theater Festival. In 2015, Laage created a new version as part of a symposium in Sweden organized by Susan Kozel, a Canadian/British dance artist. Performed in a greenhouse in Sweden's frigid winter, the audience sat on both sides, facing one another, in what she staged as an intentional yet subtle confrontation of one another. She describes the work as a birth, in which she enters as a tree and emerges as a body turned to earth. The piece for her is political, to remind us to remain connected to the earth.

Earth Tomes related back to Laage's roots in rural Wisconsin. She swam in the creeks in the summer, made igloos in the winter, traipsed through fields of cow patties, and tended a garden with her family. She says that when she began exploring butoh, it reconnected her with her upbringing:

> I felt like I was recovering my childhood, *that* body that was really *my* body . . . When I heard Goda Nario talk about Hijikata's one tatami mat dance and the children kept in a basket, whether or not it's true, it says something about the importance of one's childhood experience of space.
> (Joan Laage, pers. comm., January 6, 2020)

She likens her early experiences in life to her current gardening practice (and profession), and planting seeds that sprout later in life.

Initially a solo work, *Earth Tomes* became a project as Laage began inviting other dancers to join her. Since 2016, the project has been presented with local dancers in Seattle, Upstate New York, and several European cities. In many ways, it has become a community-based creative process that she can replicate wherever she travels.

Other projects have had a similar community-based improvisational feel, much like Hiroko ad Koichi Tamano's annual project in Berkeley, as well as other community-garden-based projects produced by other butoh artists (see

LEIMAY profile in Chapter 4). In 2010, Laage became a docent for the Seattle Japanese Garden, and annually presents a three-hour durational structured improvisational performance called *Wandering and Wondering* there and at Seattle's Kubota Garden.

Significant students who have worked with Laage include Helen Thorsen, who was a member of the original Dappin' Butoh from 1990 and continues to perform with her, and Douglas Ridings, who was a student and company member from 1993 to 1997 and went on to become a renowned yoga teacher and Odissi dancer with Urvasi Dance Ensemble. Another key Seattle figure who has collaborated with Laage on producing performances is Sheri Brown. Brown, previously a statue artist who encountered butoh when Laage's husband saw her on a bus and invited her to the 2000 butoh festival, has primarily trained with Diego Piñón and Katsura Kan. I mention Brown here because she is a primary organizer of butoh events in Seattle. There is a wonderful photo on Ridings' website of Laage, Brown, and Ridings in a 2009 improvisational performance; each has a different extreme expression that highlights their distinct aesthetics: Laage looks as if an invisible string has pulled from her lips through the top of her head and her eyes express a far-away look, Brown looks like a scary doll with her hand covering her open-mouthed cackle and her eyes are turned upward against a furrowed brow, and Ridings has a terrifying grimace on his face and is pulling red material from his mouth, á la classical Indian drama depiction of viscera. They look ephemeral, horrifying, and archetypal, respectively. Says Laage, something she finds really positive about the Seattle butoh community is that "people continue to work together, regardless of whether or not they share aesthetic similarities . . . participants see the value of working together to support a diverse community" (Joan Laage, pers. comm., January 6, 2020).

While living abroad in Krakow, Poland from 2004 to 2006, Laage took on the name *Kogut* [Rooster] to mark a moment of personal transformation in which she "claimed (her) artistic identity as an American of Danish/German heritage unfolding in a Japanese aesthetic" (Seattle Butoh Laage, n.d.). When asked if she calls her work butoh, Laage replies:

> I come from the butoh lineage. I consider myself a carrier [of this tradition]. My journey is to go deeper and deeper, and this is my path. The core is always butoh, the weight, the body, the space, etc. To say I'm influenced by butoh does not honor my history. I understand why others say that, and it's important for them to say that, but for me it's much deeper than that. Other things have influenced me along the way, but this is my lineage.
>
> (Joan Laage, pers. comm., January 6, 2020)

From Krakow, Laage and her husband moved to South Korea where appeared in several performance art festivals and absorbed new creative information from Korean dance and music traditions.

Resettling in Seattle, Laage joined Brown, Ridings, and several other dancers in founding DAIPANbutoh Collective in 2009, which became the producer of the Seattle International Butoh Festival. To date, the collective has produced 10 annual festivals, featuring numerous regional artists, including the Bay Area-based Tamanos, as well as Diego Piñón (2105), LimenButoh Theater (Warsaw, Poland, 2016), Natalia Cuéllar (Chile), and Ken Mai (Finland/Japan) in 2017, and Mushimaru Fujieda (Yakushima, Japan) in 2018.

Two dancers—Shoko Zama and Katrina Wolfe—sought out Laage in 2015 to study with her exclusively. Laage created pieces for Zama and Wolfe and a quartet with long-time student Consuelo Gonzales entitled *Stone Silence*, which premiered at the 2017 Seattle Butoh Festival and explored the condition of tinnitus. Zama and Wolfe continue to collaborate with Laage as well as creating their own work.

Laage continues to perform annually in DAIPAN's festivals, and directs and performs in annual Japanese garden performances, both of which have now been running for a decade. She has been a part of the European butoh community for many years (particularly in Italy, Poland, Germany, and Norway) and tours Europe annually (winter/spring) to perform and teach and create collaborations with local artists. Since 2015, Laage has returned to Italy to study with Atsushi Takenouchi in Pontedera, which is incidentally also home of the Jerzy Grotowski and Thomas Richards Workcenter in Tuscany, Italy.

Laage is an avid Tai Chi practitioner and gardener, which she has done professionally since settling in Seattle in 1990. She is deeply connected to the land and to weather, and feels that gardening has made her body into a barometer, with great sensitivity to changes in temperature, wind, moisture, etc. Much like her first teacher, Kazuo Ohno, there is no separation for her between art and daily life.

Diego Piñón (b. 1957, Tlalpujahua, Michoacán/Mexico, DF)

A profound connection to spirituality is the river that runs through Diego Piñón's (see Figure 3.3) life. Piñón was born in the colonial gold mining village of Tlalpujahua, home to several noted religious sanctuaries and convents, two-and-a-half hours north of Mexico City. He cites the religious fervor of his mother as his first memory that piqued his curiosity about the essence of being. He witnessed the way her body moved when she prayed or was in a devotional procession and it deeply moved him. He also remembers with crystal-clear clarity the religious ceremonial dance and song of his village in Michoacán, and the hundreds of people who would gather to celebrate the Virgen Mary of the village, Nuestra Señora del Carmen. The spirit he felt present during those moments animates his current search in dance: "for me, if there is no spirit present in performance, you might as well put a robot on stage" (Diego Piñón, pers. comm., May 14, 2018).

Figure 3.3 Paricutín (2004). Dancer: Diego Piñón.

Source: Photo by Isela Mora, reprinted with permission from Isela Mora

For Piñón, the force of religious practice and belief in Mexico is something that separates the practices of Mexican-based artists from those in the United States, especially artists of his generation. Even though his mother never forced him to engage in her rites, he learned to follow them and to probe the power inherent in this practice. His own search for a comparable experience brought him to art. For him, the quest had equal emotional intensity, in understanding humanity and our place in the universe.

And now, says Piñón, "the churches are closing, because their rituals are failing to convince anyone; we recognize that we need new rituals" (Diego Piñón, pers. comm., May 14, 2018). His dance proposes a contemporary ritual, drawing from indigenous roots, with the goal of personal and communal healing. Piñón went through a period of rejecting formal religion, as he realized that he felt something distinct in his own experience and body. Nonetheless, he says

> I think this is a major reason that butoh has had such an impact in Latin American countries, because we are still deeply religious in a pure sense of the word, we are looking for our connection to the sacred . . . not with a specific god or divinity per se, but still with the sacred.
>
> (Diego Piñón, pers. comm., May 14, 2018)

Added to the environment of religious ceremonies in his village, Piñón spent another significant part of his childhood growing up in a poor neighborhood in Mexico City, where popular dancers took to the street in social gatherings. There were some community centers, but most people could not afford to rent spaces so they danced outside. Piñón watched these dancers from his apartment window, fascinated. He asked his mother for permission to go down and join them, which she gave, and eventually people took him under their wing and taught him the dances. The music, particularly the percussive rhythm, brought him toward the spiritual sensation he was looking for, making him feel a vibration with all life forces. "Everyone feels this pulse" he says, "the priests, the old ladies, everyone . . . and this is dormant sensation underneath it all" (Diego Piñón, pers. comm., May 14, 2018). His father noted his passion and gifted him a transistor radio, through which Piñón's love of music grew: "I wasn't dancing to tropical rhythms," he says, "rather I connected to ballads, to melancholic and romantic music" (Diego Piñón, pers. comm., May 14, 2018). His father also bought the family a record player, and Piñón would play music and dance alone in his room. One of his favorite albums, which he still has in his possession, was of Italian accordion song that was the "soundtrack of my life for years and years . . . I danced to it, I cried to it, it was very emotional" (Diego Piñón, pers. comm., May 14, 2018). Through music he found a sense of catharsis.

He had intended to study music and to become a singer, but at the age of 16 was discouraged because his teachers said his voice would change and should not yet be forced. They wanted him to study many years of music theory and piano before pursuing voice, and the discipline of that training did not appeal. Moreover, his father wanted something else for him beyond music. Piñón chose Sociology instead as his academic career.

A life-changing encounter interceded between the ages of 17 and 20 years while he was studying Sociology. Piñón encountered Antonio Cué Ochoa, a Bioenergetic therapist who was experimenting with and teaching about corporeal energies. For Piñón, he was more a shaman than a therapist. Cué founded "the group SexPol (1974–78), which took its name from Wilhelm Reich's *Sexual Politics* reading that influenced the female, sexual, and homosexual liberation movements in Mexico" (Hernández 2019). Citing theories of Michel Foucault, Cué drew attention to religious and social oppression as enacted through our bodies. Says Piñón, Cué proposed a radical notion that the restriction on human expression can lead to sickness and death, and activists in leftist and homosexual movements cited his work in their own fight for human rights (Diego Piñón, pers. comm., May 26, 2020). For Piñón, Cué's work helped connect his individual search to the practice of collective group therapy. Cué introduced Piñón and other participants to the Meso-American, pre-Colombian cosmovision of the *Wixarica* (*Huichol*), centered in the North of San Luis Potosí.[10] They were one of the indigenous groups who had preserved their traditions and rituals, as well as sacred plants such as *hikuri* (*peyote*).

Through these deeply powerful encounters, Piñón notes that he was able to "open up and see beyond [his previous experiences of] social structures to things he could not explain but could definitely feel," and that it "revised [his] previous sense of the limits of everyday consciousness" (Diego Piñón, pers. comm., May 14, 2018). Piñón calls the process "a shamanic practice which opened a crucial understanding of the most universal principles of exchange," whereby the participant understands themselves as a vessel for said exchange (Piñón 2018, 4). When he later encountered butoh, the bridge was obvious.

Piñón was one of the few participants in Cué's exclusive groups[11] for more than seven years, invited to participate in private ceremonies with an indigenous guide. Huichol ritual involves immersive events, for example, a two-week walking meditation to San Luis Potosi, during which time the Huichol "hunt" the *hikuri* in the desert on their pilgrimage to Cerro Quemado [the Burning Mountain], a sacred Huichol site in the mythical land of *Wirikuta* (Carrasco 2014, 164; Diego Piñón, pers. comm., May 26, 2020). Other ceremonies take place in the *temazcal*, or the sweat lodge. Cué and his participants designed their own rituals—including meditation, pilgrimage walks, and fasting—with the help of the indigenous guide. The experiences marked Piñón significantly, as one can imagine, and pushed him to refine his pursuit of a vocation. Piñón knew that he was committed to fighting for human rights and combatting oppression, and he aimed to channel that impulse through a creative act. For Piñón, creativity is a holistic work of the body, mind, and spirit that produces something to be shared, a sentiment that resonated strongly with Kazuo Ohno's teachings when he would encounter them years later (Piñón 2018, 4).

During one of the ritual shamanic experiences with *hikuri*, Piñón had a vision. He heard a voice, which he interpreted as some form of a higher power. The voice said to him, "you don't belong in this space, you don't belong in this tradition, you have a work and a legacy there, in the space of your own society where you were born and grew up, your work is there." Not only did he find a clear directive to return to his community, but also it was absolutely clear to him that his work was through dance (Diego Piñón, pers. comm., May 14, 2018).

Upon graduating from university in 1979, Piñón taught Sociology in high school and college, but he was restless and sought to travel. After a period of years teaching and saving up resources, he went to Spain in 1980 where he was captivated by flamenco dance. Perhaps connected to the Spanish colonial culture in Mexico, he felt instinctively that "this [dance and music] runs through my blood" (Diego Piñón, pers. comm., May 14, 2018). The percussive rhythm, connection to the earth, and melancholic sentiment felt intensely familiar. While in Spain, he pursued all kinds of Spanish styles including flamenco through the community dance centers for several years. In that time, he encountered Pilar Urreta,[12] a Mexican dancer living in New York who had traveled to Spain to perform in a festival. Says Piñón, Urreta pioneered the fusion of Asian performance techniques within the Mexican contemporary dance scene. She encouraged him to pursue his passion for dance after watching him perform a masked dance as Lorca, in which he was a last-minute substitute covering for a sick dancer.

Urreta also introduced Piñón to Lorenzo Godoy, a Paris-trained Spanish dancer who had toured internationally and by 1978, was a significant figure in the development of contemporary dance (La Provincia 2014). Piñón went to study with Godoy in the Spanish Territorial Canary Island and again found resonance in this work with the dedication, discipline, and fervor with which Godoy approached his craft. He subsequently returned to Mexico City where he dedicated himself to the study of contemporary dance through a variety of studios and teachers. He encountered Bernardo Benítez, a Mexican dancer from his own village living in Mexico City, who had been invited to study with Lester Horton in New York and later went on to direct Ballet Danza Estudio in Mexico City. Piñón studied with Benítez and absorbed a great deal of technical information about dance and performance, during a wave of innovation in dance theater in the 1980s. Piñón then participated with two different dance theater companies, one of them Tropicanas Holiday (Graciela Henriquez, director), which created Vaudeville-esque spectacles, and the other was Andamio (Cristina Mendoza, director), a group of retired ballerinas (merely in their thirties) from the Mexican National Ballet, who were interested in theatrical experimentation.

The theatrical exploration within these projects drew his attention, and Piñón sought out further theater training. In 1985, he encountered Abraham Oceransky, the polemic experimental theater director who was the first Mexican director to present nude actors onstage, and also the first to introduce butoh to Mexico with Natsu Nakajima and later Ko Murobushi (see section on Oceransky in Chapter 2). The second director was Morris Sabariego, with whom Piñón studied from 1986 to 1988. Sabariego was a professor at Teatro de la Casa, an experimental theater school in Coyoacán. Sabariego's teaching was focused on the discipline of the actor and acting as a method of transmitting myth (Diego Piñón, pers. comm., May 26, 2020).

As in previous endeavors, Piñón continued to connect his performance research with his spiritual quest. In 1986, he encountered a theater group called La Rueca (The Spinning Wheel) (Susana Frank, director), who were the ones to introduce Eugenio Barba, as well as actors from the Roy Hart Theater, in workshops to Mexico. Piñón had read the books from these theater practitioners and asked to join the group as a performer. He was accepted and able to take the workshops and train with the company. For him, this was "one more petal of the flower" that confirmed his quest (Diego Piñón, pers. comm., May 14, 2018). At the center of the flower lay the essence of his work: "to open the most profound energies and memories of the human experience" (Diego Piñón, pers. comm., May 14, 2018). In a workshop with voice teacher Daniel Prieto, Piñón was struck by the direction to "open to the full range of your expressive possibility," which to him included the ability to unite the voices of his mother and father through his own vessel.

One of the acting teachers from Roy Hart Theater used an exercise in a workshop that Piñón found intriguing. When he asked the origin, he discovered that the company had adopted it from Japanese butoh practice. This was the third reference to butoh in his performance training, the first being through Oceransky, the second through Prieto, and now this one. Piñón recalls seeing images of Kazuo Ohno and Tatsumi Hijikata in 1985, in one of the first published butoh books. Subsequently, in 1986, he saw the photos of Sankai Juku in the Teotihuacán pyramids, which had been shot by famous Mexican photographer Paulina Lavista in 1981 when the company first toured to Mexico to perform at the Cervantino. Now encountering butoh through studio practice, Piñón's interest was piqued by this unfamiliar form.

His next encounter with butoh was in 1987 with Natsu Nakajima, a student of both of these founders, and her dancer Yuriko Maezawa in a performance of *Niwa*, in Mexico City. He describes the experience thus: "they danced a rite of access to a space of magic and mystery, outside the canons of conventional time" (Piñón 2018, 6). Her performance had a profound resonance, taking him "to an altered state of consciousness . . . [he] felt like he was witnessing his own essence" (Diego Piñón, pers. comm., May 26, 2020). As a spectator to Nakajima's performance, Piñón experienced something similar to what he had during the *Huichol* rites.

He continued working with the theater company La Rueca and was invited with them, along with numerous other companies working in a similar theatrical lineage related to Barba and Grotowski, to perform in an homage to Grotowski in Peru in 1988. While in Peru, he took workshops with Barba and continued studying with companies from this group that came through Mexico City, including an Italian street theater group called Teatro Tascabile di Bergamo. Piñón was struck by the social and political emphasis of the vast majority of the companies gathered in Peru. This festival was another significant moment for him, special in that he had firsthand access to so many theater artists working to develop and deepen a collective spirit, through a performance practice that felt like ritual (Diego Piñón, pers. comm., May 26, 2020).

Two years later in 1989, Piñón witnessed Kazuo and Yoshito Ohno live at the Cervantino in *Dead Sea* and *Waterlilies*. Witnessing that performance, Piñón says that he grasped a critical key in staging ritual practice for performance. He writes: "The power of his fragility on the stage, almost as if he were actually dying right there and then, transformed my understanding of what is possible in performance" (Piñón 2018, 6). He connected the liminal state he witnessed in the Ohnos to a state of rapture, or spiritual ecstasy that he had witnessed in his mother's devotional practice.

Piñón continued his research with the vibrant presence of Kazuo Ohno now a part of his consciousness. In 1992, he applied to the Japanese Embassy in Mexico for a scholarship to study with the Ohnos in Japan. Two catalytic interactions occurred in the interim while he awaited the results of his application: Mitsuyo Uesugi, assistant to Kazuo Ohno for 10 years, came to Mexico invited by the Japanese Embassy in 1992, and Byakko Sha invited Piñón to participate in a watershed performance they gave at the Anthropological Museum in Mexico City in 1993 (described in detail in Chapter 2). Watching performances by and studying with Uesugi, Piñón describes "how her soul expression emanated from a place of detachment from the [physical] body, from an intention to transmute and transform matter . . . surpassing the limits of civilized domestication" (Piñón 2018, 12). Piñón distinctly remembers her saying, "for me butoh is a sacred path, for me butoh is a way of reclaiming the sacred part of myself" (Diego Piñón, pers. comm., May 14, 2018). She had been the assistant of Kazuo Ohno for more than a decade, accompanying him on his tours, helping him paint his body and get dressed before performances. For Piñón, Uesugi drew parallels from the "mystical meaning" in Ohno's teaching with Piñón's own experience of Mexican folk ritual.

The Byakko Sha experience taught Piñón another layer of butoh methodology: "it required a level of concentration I had not yet experimented with. I was required to cultivate a state of stillness—feeling at my back the overwhelming force of the spectacle of Japanese butoh, [enhanced] by a dazzling scenic technology" (Piñón 2018, 14). Noted Mexican dance writer Emilio Rosales describes Piñón's role as a "gatekeeper" or sentinel (see description in Chapter 2); Piñón depicts it as "master of ceremonies" whose job, apart from remaining statuesquely still for prolonged periods, was to cut an infant's hair during the event (Piñón 2018, 14). He describes the preparations as "a very Japanese dynamic, as baffling as appealing for its uniqueness" (Piñón 2018, 14). He again experienced a strong bridge between these vestiges of ritual and folk practices from his childhood.

When the Japanese Embassy's invitation finally arrived, Piñón was surprised to find that it was not to study with the Ohnos, but rather to spend three months at Min Tanaka's farm, Body Weather Farm in Hakushu-sho. Nonetheless, he accepted, and along with Mexican theater artist Jaime Razzo whom he did not previously know, Piñón traveled to Japan in 1994 to embark on a journey that "push[ed] us to touch our absolute physical, mental, and emotional limits" (Piñón 2018, 14). He describes the training as "ego-crushing" and pushing his body to numbness, but by the third month of the intensive he found that the state of submission led him to find "compassion" in service of others through ritual. "I couldn't say that it was 'it,' however it was the way my being began to settle" (Piñón 2018, 16). The discipline and rigor of the training provided a distinct method to move beyond the daily ego–self.

When he arrived, Piñón joined a group of 20 new students, mostly European and North American, and one Brazilian. Many of them left by the end of the first or second week due to the difficult training regimen (Diego Piñón, pers. comm., May 14, 2018). Piñón, on the other hand, felt a responsibility to the granting agency to continue participating. He was also 34 years old, with a more mature perspective than some of his counterparts that were in their twenties that despite the challenges, it would be worthwhile to stay until the end.

While Piñón admits that he had many hard experiences during the training, he also had extraordinarily mystic experiences as well, similar to the shamanic journeys in Mexico. Tanaka invited Piñón to dance in the performance of *The Ancient Woman* with the company, which added to the intensity of the experience. Says Piñón, after a full day of farming, pulling potatoes from the ground and spreading animal excrement on crops to fertilize them, rehearsals would begin after dinner. Much like Hijikata's all-night rehearsals at Asbestos-kan, Piñón describes the preparation for the performance as three weeks of torment with very little time to rest. They rehearsed until 1:00 am and then began daily farming activities at 6:00 am. It pushed him beyond what he thought possible in daily life, confronting fears. Sometimes, he literally thought he would die; the risks seemed that extreme. In the performances, the men lit torches of dried cornstalks and attached them to themselves like a phallus. They were to walk across the space with the burning phallus as the flames got dangerously close to their bodies, dislodge the stalk, and then place it up on a pillar. At the end of the performance, the dancers destroyed a giant brick wall that they had constructed—they pushed from behind until it collapsed forward. Neither of these actions was rehearsed, which added to the element of extreme presence and also of danger, since no one knew if either action would be successful. Faced with one of the scariest moments in his life, Piñón says that he passed through fear and felt a freedom like "nirvana" (Diego Piñón, pers. comm., May 14, 2018). At the top of the show, Piñón had the sensation that he would certainly die, but once he began the performance, he "crossed the threshold, the rest was in ecstasy" (Diego Piñón, pers. comm., May 26, 2020).

The Ancient Woman was one of the most radical experiences of Piñón's life. Even beyond the performance, during the celebration following, he remembers vomiting because his body had been deprived of regular meals for the three weeks of preparation and simply could not handle the amount of food he had consumed after the show. Tanaka ordered the dancers to be served fish after fish, and, says Piñón, "you ate because he told you to . . . I threw up four times to make more room." But in the end, he felt content, and that the process had been worth the struggle.

As he prepared to leave, Piñón was called into the office where he met Horikawa. She asked him to join the company on tour in Europe, which to him felt like the fork in the road: After the experience with Tanaka from which he had just emerged, the decision felt quite charged. In a dramatic gesture, Horikawa placed a telephone on the desk in front of him, with the long cable stretched from another room, and said "if you need to arrange things, I'll leave you alone for a bit" (Diego Piñón, pers. comm., May 14, 2018). After consulting his friend and fellow dancer Louisa Racyk (Australian), he decided that he would look for a sign in his call home to Mexico. When his mother answered the phone, she was so happy to hear from him and told him "I hope that you complete all you have to do there" (Diego Piñón, pers. comm., May 14, 2018). That confirmation was enough to encourage him to stay. What he didn't know at the time was that he did feel the need to remain in Japan; his journey would take him away from Hakushu.

What followed was a brutal test, with the subsequent two weeks at double the intensity of the previous performance preparation. Moreover, he continued to be housed with the rest of the dancers who had not been chosen for the tour, and he felt such intense jealousy from his colleagues that it gave him nightmares. After two weeks of not sleeping, one early morning he went for a two-hour walk in the rain, and upon returning, he decided to respectfully tell Horikawa and Tanaka that this was not his path. From there, he went to study with Kazuo Ohno.

Following this portal through Tanaka's work, Piñón began to study with the Ohnos over a period of the next 20 years, in both the United States and Japan. Piñón was with the Ohnos about six or seven different times in Japan, and each time was like a chapter in his voyage that helped him resolve something in his own internal search (Diego Piñón, pers. comm., May 14, 2018). He characterizes his journey as "becoming, or unfolding, guided by a subtle and feminine path, much less rigid and crushing than Tanaka or Nakajima" (Piñón 2018, 19). The two extremes of his training allowed him to develop his own methods within performance training practice.

The Ohnos offered an entirely different view into butoh; they said to him, "since you are here, we are going to learn from you as well as you learning from us" (Diego Piñón, pers. comm., May 14, 2018). Says Piñón, "from this I learned something very important about teaching, that if you are to teach you must be open to the exchange . . . all of my teaching in the United States has taught me this as well" (Diego Piñón, pers. comm., May 14, 2018). Further, what he learned from Kazuo was not so much what Kazuo showed him how to do, rather he felt that Kazuo's grace and vulnerability exposed his being, his body, and his essence, and from that Piñón gleaned what lessons he learned.[13] Having witnessed firsthand the Ohnos' dance within their daily life, he understands the all-encompassing nature of the investigation; there is not an aesthetic or genre or brand with which he wishes to align his own work, rather it is a commitment to ongoing process and investigation.

In 1996, Piñón began teaching and performing under the guise of Butoh Ritual Mexicano (BRM), a name that solidified as he toured internationally. It was not his intention to create a particularly nationalistic rendition of butoh practice, rather the name was initially a connection between his childhood experiences with Mexican folk rituals and Japanese butoh practices. It was also a function of marketing by international presenters and likely helped build his cache.

Even as he was cultivating his practice in Mexico, Piñón increasingly built a following in the United States. He first performed in San Francisco in 1996, on a festival invitation from Brady Street Theater. Some of the Harupin-Ha dancers, including Terrence Graven, saw Piñón's performance and subsequently studied with him. The following year, Piñón taught a workshop at Prescott College in Arizona in 1997, which was the beginning of many lasting relationships in the United States. Among the Prescott College students were Mizu

Desierto, currently anchoring the butoh community in Portland Oregon, Nate Montgomery, currently based in Boulder, Colorado, and Christopher Mankowski, who continued to study with Piñón over the years and is currently his assistant. In 1998, Brechin Flournoy invited Piñón to participate in the San Francisco Butoh Festival, that year, themed "Global Butoh." He performed alongside Thailand-based Japanese dancer Katsura Kan, Argentine performer Gustavo Collini Sartor, Canadian company Kokoro, and several Japanese artists including the company Yan Shu and Abe "M"aria.

Piñón's participation in the 1998 San Francisco Butoh Festival gained him a review by respected American dance critic Rita Felciano. Following the festival, he was invited to teach workshops in numerous communities as well as through universities, including the University of California Los Angeles, UC Riverside, UC San Diego, Warren Wilson College, and Brooklyn College.

In 2000, he returned to the Ohnos' studio in Yokohama for an extended period of study, funded by a grant from Japan Foundation. Through their support, he was able to hire a translator, and glean even more information from the interaction, which has greatly influenced his teaching today. While there, he created and performed a new work, titled *Hñahñu*, doubly titled in the *Otomi* language, *Dumui (Broken Nostalgia)*. He returned to Mexico to perform the solo at Instituto Nacional de Bellas Artes (INBA), and also toured it to San Diego, San Francisco, and Vancouver.

Piñón opened his own center in Tlalpujahua, Michoacán, Mexico, in 2001, and since that time numerous students from around the world have studied there, seeking out his tutelage, which for many Mexican artists has become a rite of passage. Piñón is connected with the vast majority of the contemporary Mexican butoh generation, because they have passed through his doors at one time or another over the past 30 years.

Piñón has worked intensively with several small groups of dancers in workshops and research processes, and numerous of these investigations resulted in performances. In 2003, he created a group ritual project entitled *Espiritus en Transito (Spirits in Transit)*. Among the group of dancers were Espartaco Martínez, who danced with Dairakudakan for six years, and Tania Galindo (see profiles in Chapter 4).

Eugenia Vargas (see profile in Chapter 4) was in the audience for that piece. She had been a part of Piñón's workshops over a period of 10 years, together with a group of dancers with whom she worked closely. In 2006, Piñón formed another group and made a second synthesis of *Espiritus en Transito (Spirits in Transito)*, in which danced Vargas, Pepe Bravo, Cinthia Patiño, Constanza Herrera, Augustin Elizondo, and Laura Fernandez. The group performed in 2010 el Museo del Chopo, part of Universidad Nacional Autónoma de México, the organization that supported many butoh events in Mexico City over the years.

Tania Galindo, now director of Butoh Chilango (see profile in Chapter 4), had continued to study with Piñón and was also part of the research group in which Vargas participated. She did not appear in the 2010 performance but continued to work closely with Piñón as her mentor. Galindo produced the

Second Festival of Butoh in Latin America, in partnership with Susana Reyes, who had produced the first festival in Ecuador in 2013. Piñón suggested to her to make a bridge between Japanese butoh and Latin American performers following this link. Together they invited Masaru Susaki, director of the Japan Foundation, Mexico to present the historical aspect of Japanese butoh at a roundtable.

In the festival colloquium, Piñón pressed the question: "what is the integration or transformation of butoh that is occurring in Latin America?" Though it was controversial, he felt it was necessary to suggest that Latin American artists have the pride to express the force of their own culture, through this borrowed practice. The question for him is not what does Latin American butoh look like, but rather, where has 30 years of interaction with this dance in Latin America brought us? However, for Piñón, butoh is not a form that proposes a new movement vocabulary, nor an aesthetic. For him, it is "a proposal and a path for allowing an individual to cultivate silence and journey to their interior, toward the most profound liberation of the soul" (Diego Piñón, pers. comm., May 14, 2018). He adamantly encourages the current generation of dancers to pursue their own vision catalyzed by the inspiration of Japanese butoh.

Over many years of teaching in the United States, Piñón formed several significant relationships in addition to the ones noted earlier. In San Diego, Charlene Peener and Kata Pierce of Golden Corpse Ensemble were students and supporters of his work. Together with then–San Diego-based Shakina Nayfack, these artists shepherded Piñón's application for dual citizenship in the United States. In Chicago, Illinois, Piñón returned six consecutive years (2004–2010) to teach through Blushing Poppy in Chicago and performed a duet with protégé Nicole LeGette in 2009, who is considered "the mother of the Chicago butoh scene" (Out of Site Chicago 2014). He continues to teach in the Chicago community through Sarah Zalek.

Piñón began a collaboration in Portland in 2007 through Prescott College-alumni Mizu Desierto, choreographing another iteration of the *Espiritus en Transito* project. In 2013, Desierto organized a group under the name North American Body Ritual Movement Dance Ensemble through a residency at The Headwaters. The group has since performed the work in Portland and Eureka, California, and continues to invite Piñón to direct.

In New York, he initially taught through Ximena Garnica and Juan Merchan in the 1990s, then through Vangeline, and most recently Nick Fracaro and Gabby Schaeffer/Coney Island Butoh, with whom he directed the Coney Island Butoh Cabaret in 2017, 2018, and 2019. Other locations where Piñón has significant ties include Asheville, North Carolina (Julie Becton Gillum), Los Angeles, California (Willy Franco and Miki), Salt Lake City, Utah (Gerry Gardner, Associate Professor of Theatre, University of Utah), Miami, Florida (Helen Threvenot), and Seattle, Washington (Joan Laage, and Sheri Brown).

By 2015, after years of teaching abroad and fomenting an international community, Piñón determined that his work had truly transcended nationalistic determinations and renamed his work Body Ritual Movement, maintaining the BRM initials but now, curiously, titling his work in English.

For Piñón, there is not a butoh lineage per se to preserve. He feels quite strongly that although he studied with the Ohnos for quite some time, that he is not carrying on their legacy. His work is his own, as is every other artist's. Of his students in Mexico, he doesn't feel that they are in his lineage, only that he has planted some seeds in their path, as seeds have been planted in his. Similarly, he does not feel it is his place to judge that a performer is ready or not ready to perform butoh. He says:

> The practice I would like to support the sense to be present on stage and off stage in daily life in order to go beyond our ego-centric configuration, to offer the most pure energy that comes from our body's core. The goal is to expand our consciousness to develop a collective ritual process to restoring health.
>
> (Diego Piñón, pers. comm., May 26, 2020)

Now, the work that Piñón is doing at his center in Michoacán is focused on restoring health. For him, the most pressing problems of our time are due to our alienation from our bodies. He sees so much depression, so much violence, the dehumanizing effects of capitalism, and the attempt to solve our problems through a computer screen. He rejects this reality and proposes that the only way to heal is through the body. For this reason, his more recent workshops in Michoacán have specifically been promoted as "not for artists" but for anyone who wants to liberate their spirit.

Additional Anchor Artists

Other artists are integral to the development of butoh in the United States and Mexico during this time as well. It is beyond the scope of this text to cover all; however, it is important to note their names in hopes that other writers will pick up the torch and chronicle their contributions and body of work. At least in the case of Eiko and Koma, this has already been done by dance scholar Rosemary Candelario in her book *Flowers Cracking Concrete* (Candelario 2016). Other artists who warrant further research and archiving in the history of American butoh are Denise Fujiwara, a Japanese-Canadian dancer based in Toronto, and Kei Takei, who worked with both Hijikata and Ohno before arriving in New York in 1967 and forging her own path both there and in San Francisco. Descriptions of both artists' work are featured in Sondra Fraleigh's *Butoh: Metamorphic Dance and Global Alchemy* (Fraleigh 2010). Despite their stance outside of butoh, their influence on butoh is important as they have taught and performed throughout the Americas, sometimes in butoh festivals, and as such have impacted the aesthetics and methods of contemporary butoh practice as well as critical understanding of the art form.

Brechin Flournoy and the San Francisco Butoh Festival

Around the same time, these pioneering American artists were solidifying their craft, a savvy young artist/curator by the name of Brechin Flournoy was developing a distinct taste for the divergent. She describes her aesthetic at the time as "blood sport—performance art, all punk, lot of screaming on stage, Carol Lee Schneeman, that sort of thing" (Brechin Flournoy, pers. comm., December 11, 2017). Originally from Denver, Colorado, Flournoy encountered experimental dance and performance art through her interactions with professors at Antioch College, a globally minded liberal arts college outside of Cincinnati, Ohio. Her professor, Dimi Reber, guided her students to make socially conscious work, rooted in both the human and natural environments. Reber brought Maureen Fleming for a three-week residency, which Flournoy recalls with gusto: "Maureen had us be seaweed and I loved it because always wanted to be deeper and darker, I always wanted to be the black swan in ballet. . . . Being seaweed was the totality [of existence]." She had seen Sankai Juku's infamous hanging piece (*Jomon Sho*) in Cincinnati and was thoroughly intrigued.

Flournoy was introduced to arts administration through all of her externships, the first of which was at PS122 in NYC. She became enamored with the idea of curation, which at the time seemed like a viable career. Major companies had emerged and found stability through NEA funding in the 1960s and 1970s, and their prominence and success continued into the 1980s.

On Reber's recommendation, Flournoy spent a year abroad at the School for New Dance Development in Amsterdam, where she studied under Netherland Dance Theatre-founding member Jaap Flier, Deborah Hay, and Simone Forti. At SNDD, Flournoy met one of her formative collaborators, Anna Kristina Tischendorf, who had studied with Min Tanaka and Kazuo Ohno. With Kristina, Brechin recalls rehearsing outside in the rain, rolling on the ground in the mud. "I'm so uncomfortable!" she complained to her collaborator. "That's the point!" Kristina replied (Brechin Flournoy, pers. comm., December 11, 2017).

These "whispers," as Flournoy refers to them, eventually grew louder and she found herself wanting to know more. She contemplated studying in Japan, but then her mother took ill and she chose to stay Stateside. Her family was close, and, says Flournoy, they also had a significant influence on her desire to be an arts curator. Her mother had turned her on to the hippies; she herself had wanted to be a Beatnik and travel the country. Her parents met at Denver University. Her father was from Birmingham, Alabama, and had been on the front lines of the Civil Rights movements, including organizing housing for the Selma March. Her father, a preacher's son, was the one who had first discovered the bodies of the four young girls in the 16th Street Baptist Church bombing in 1963. Says Flournoy of her father, "As a black man who grew up in the South, he didn't share a lot of his stories because they were too painful" (Brechin Flournoy, pers. comm., December 11, 2017). His quiet presence impacted her nonetheless, particularly when it came to education. "In Black Southern families," she said, "education is a big thing, so there was no question that we were going to college" (Brechin Flournoy, pers. comm., December 11, 2017).

Flournoy's grandmother was a world traveler; she and her husband were the first American family to travel the length of the Panama Canal, where her grandfather was a foreman in charge of its construction. Her mother was three years old at the time. The Canal was completed in 1914, at the start of World War I. Following its completion, her grandparents became ministers and continued to travel throughout South America. When they returned home to Denver, they would present slide shows and artifacts from their trips at movie theaters. Flournoy credits some of her ideas of curation and presentation to her grandparents' productions.

When her mother passed, Flournoy focused again on her artmaking. She and her partner at the time moved to San Francisco to dive into the performance art scene. She had been to the city previously to visit a friend who had traveled out there with the Dead Kennedys as a band groupie, and who at the time was hanging with the Tragic Mulattos. Together they canvassed on Haight Street for Greenpeace. Flournoy had to go back to Ohio to finish school, but she had found her scene and knew she would one day return to the Bay Area.

The DIY culture of San Francisco in the 1980s and 1990s was the perfect petri dish for her risk-taking curatorial appetite. At the time, recalls Flournoy, artists were just having meetings to learn how to do things, and it was common for groups of people to just assemble and make a show, with little to no funding. Very early on in her time in San Francisco, Flournoy, and Japanese American dancer Takami Craddock recognized a mutual interest in creating some structure to the process, and together they formed the organization d-net (short for dance-network) in 1992.

The pair's ingenuity produced the first San Francisco Butoh Festival, fueled by Flournoy's interest in the avant-garde dance form and Craddock's ability to navigate Japanese culture. She and Craddock spent two years building contacts and developing support both through American funders and among the established Japanese butoh conduits for the butoh community, particularly Hijikata's widow Akiko Motofuji and Asbestos-kan, and Akira Kasai. Craddock served as the primary liaison with Japanese artists and trained Brechin in Japanese social etiquette. Flournoy, a highly detail-oriented person, remembers being surprised how important it was on which kind of paper she had printed an invitation letter and credits Takami for teaching her these critical details of Japanese culture.

Flournoy recalls the difficulty of gaining the trust of these very edgy artists, even the Tamanos, who had been living in the United States since the 1970s. She and Craddock worked diligently to present butoh "correctly," by researching the history, Hijikata and Ohno's work and writings, scholarly work, and critical reviews from abroad. Flournoy drafted richly detailed press packets, initiating the San Francisco Bay Area critics to this "new" art form.

Perhaps even more critical to the success of the Festival was building long-term relationships and a network to identify artists. Flournoy stresses that the

San Francisco Butoh Festival developed prior to the advent of ubiquitous internet access, and everyone she found, she found by following threads and obscure connections. "I didn't just open up some Rolodex," she quips, "these people were under rocks!" The organizers painstakingly researched and networked to locate and invite Japanese artists to the United States.

The dancer/administrator pair met and began planning for the festival in 1993. Over the course of the next two years, through carefully crafted letters and recommendations from contacts in the field, they slowly amassed the support and the network they needed to create a critically acclaimed international festival, the first of its kind in the United States. Their work ushered in a deeper understanding of butoh among American audiences.

By 1995, Brechin Flournoy and Takami Craddock shifted the San Francisco Bay Area butoh spotlight to the international stage with their introduction of the San Francisco Butoh Festival. Each year, the curators experimented with presenting a "different facet" of butoh, including "Women in Butoh," "German Expressionism and Butoh," "Global Butoh," and "American Butoh." Over the eight-year run, the San Francisco Butoh Festival presented 105 artists to thousands of audience members and hosted workshops for hundreds of students who came from as far away as Italy, the United Kingdom, and Brazil to come to this butoh mecca.

The first festival, titled "Butoh Prism" (Flournoy 2009), was produced in 1995 on a shoestring budget of $14,800 (SFBF 1995), with four soloists, three of whom were US-based: Tamano Koichi (Bay Area), Oguri (Los Angeles), and Maureen Fleming (New York). Flournoy and Craddock managed to secure funding to bring Kasai to the festival, thus introducing him to American audiences and beginning the most enduring relationship the festival had with any artist. The debut of the festival coincided with the 50th Anniversary of the Hiroshima/Nagasaki bombings, garnering extra attention for this Japanese art form that had grown out of the World War II aftermath. The Cowell Theater at Fort Mason was filled to capacity, with lines stretched out the door into the parking lot. Says Flournoy, "we did strike that gold vein in the mountain!" (Flournoy 2009).

When they finally launched the first festival after two years of preparation, the organizers had succeeded in securing some rather major players and brought together artists who had not seen each other in 20 years. Up until that point, these butoh dancers had diverged from the founding masters, and each company or artist was siloed in their corner of the world.

Flournoy recalls when Tamano and Kasai met backstage that they simply stared at each other for several minutes, and then moved on. It was a strange coming together, in Flournoy's words "almost as if wild and unruly forces had been harnessed and put in a bag together" (Brechin Flournoy, pers. comm., December 11, 2017). In one poignant memory, Flournoy sat crouched in her chair, gripping the chair legs with her hands, with eyes and mouth popping open. "That's not butoh!" heckled LA-based performer Oguri; Kasai retorted, "How dare you call this not butoh! I'm pouring my heart and soul into this moment!" (Brechin Flournoy, pers. comm., December 11, 2017). The heated banter validated for Flournoy that she and Craddock were delving into a juicy artistic conversation. The capacity houses and the crackling performance energy were the kind of liveness she was after.

In 1996, the second year of the festival, the curators chose to focus on notable women in butoh, drawing attention to a persistent underrepresentation of female artists in this form. The featured artists were Akiko Motofuji (Hijikata's widow), Setsuko Yamada, Saga Kobayashi, and Hiroko Tamano. They were marketed in alignment with historical traditions in butoh, beginning to define for American audiences the different aesthetics and adaptations butoh had taken since Hijikata's initial impulse. Press materials described Motofuji and Yamada as contemporary dance artists who were influenced by ballet, German *neue tanz* and American modern dance as much as they were by butoh. Conversely, the language used to describe Hiroko Tamano and Kobayashi emphasized connections to Hijikata's aesthetic. Incidentally, these two artists had danced together in Hijikata's *27 Seasons*. Hiroko left Asbestos-kan shortly thereafter to join Koichi in Harupin-ha, while Kobayashi remained at Asbestos-kan and danced in numerous subsequent productions under Hijikata's direction, including *Shizukana Ie* (Calm House), and helped establish Hakutobo with Yoko Ashikawa. These historical connections marked a pedigree system that is still referenced by many current generation American butoh artists, who define themselves by degrees of separation in the butoh family tree.

Motofuji, together with a team or organizers including Dairakudakan director Akaji Maro and photographer Eiko Hosoe, had assembled the Tatsumi Hijikata Memorial Archives at Asbestos-kan. Promotional materials for the archives included articles by Donald Richie and Mark Holborn, which Flournoy was able to source in her press releases as a way of educating American critics. Her press releases were extensive, and she cultivated relationships with reviewers and funders alike, introducing them to a more nuanced understanding of butoh than was previously known in the United States.

By 1996, they had raised $8,000 in grants and built enough of a following to make $18,000 in ticket sales. The following year, attention had ignited. San Francisco Arts Commission awarded the festival $30,000, and Grants for the Arts offered $6,000. Ticket sales dropped to $14,000 that year but workshop sales shot up to $17,000, proof that they had now built a following of students as well as audience members.

The third year of the festival (1997) drew attention to a critical sphere in the global butoh community: Germany. Not only did American audiences learn more details about the influence of German *neue tanz* on the butoh founders through press materials and program notes, but they also saw the continuing impact of German dance and healing arts, in the form of Rudolf Steiner's Eurythmy, through Akira Kasai's second appearance in the San Francisco Butoh Festival. After introducing Kasai to American audiences in the first festival and having had a second festival to start to define the contours of the butoh aesthetic, audiences were prepped to understand the nuances of Kasai's particular interpretation of Hijikata's inspirations.

1997 also marked an important year for the next generation of American butoh dancers: it was the year they met Germany-based Yumiko Yoshioka.[14] With a clearly traceable lineage[15] and a butoh farm of her own two hours north of Berlin, Yoshioka satisfied young artists' desire for connection to the past and also to the pulse of the future. Yoshioka was not only a solo artist as others presented in the festival had been but also had a company, Ten Pen Chii. She recruited Bay Area dancers and Tamano students Shinichi Koga and Alenka Mullin, then a husband and wife team who had also formed their own company, Uro Teatro Koku. In 1999, Yoshioka helped launch Koga as a choreographer, featuring him as one of eight artists in her annual eX . . . it! At Schloss Broellin. Yoshioka's festival and art colony became a butoh mecca for many Bay Area artists, including paige starling sorvillo, who later danced for Koga's inkBoat and collaborated with former Harupin-Ha dancer Kinji Hayashi before founding her own company, blindsight, and Megan Nicely, who joined Kasai's production of *Exusiai* in 1998 and his *Butoh America* in 2010 at Japan Society.

Yoshioka and her company also modeled the interdisciplinary collaborations that had been the hallmark of Hijikata's work and early Harupin-Ha collaborations. Ten Pen Chii was the brainchild of Yoshioka, German, large-scale sculptor Joachim Manger and American electronic noise musician Zam Johnson. Their work was impressive in scale and rigor, like Dairakudakan only more industrial, and fueled the visual aesthetics of several important emerging butoh choreographers, including Koga and Mullin, and Haruko Crow Nishimura, all of whom have staged their work in quite elaborate settings that often feel like industrial fairytales.

The events of the 1998 San Francisco Butoh Festival, marketed as "Global Butoh," were as far reaching in geographic representation as they were in Bay Area producing muscle. Artists from six different countries (Japan, Thailand, Mexico, Argentina, Canada, and the United States) performed at six different venues, including Cowell Theater, Asian Art Museum, and Yerba Buena Center for the Arts. The festival featured many outdoor events as well, including an indelible performance by Canadian Kokoro Dance at Ocean Beach. One review noted the beauty of "the image of the frozen, white painted bodies in glacially evolving movements against the gray sand and the turbulent ocean [that] carved itself into the soul" (Felciano 1998). The press release listed the Cowell Theater performance with artists from Thailand, Mexico, and Argentina as the "main event"; however, critical reviews claimed that space for Kasai's performance of *Exusiai*, which featured Takami, Flournoy, Megan Nicely, and Kristen Lemberg.

Exusiai opened with Kasai all in black against a black marley floor, taped in lanes with white tape in vertical lines moving downstage to upstage. The soundscore sounds like the electronic whine of an aircraft as it starts to taxi to its runway. Kasai's shiny black silk shirt and gold painted hair drew focus in the cavernous room. The women entered and exited as an ensemble, often crossing the stage laterally, in statuesque profile. At times, they lay prone on one side, propped on one elbow and gazing into the distance. They were dressed in silvery gray including body and hair paint, and they invoked a sense of cosmic creatures.

Dance critic Rita Felciano, who consistently reviewed the festivals as well as provided visibility and context for Bay Area butoh, praised Kasai's performance, calling him "an extraordinary performer able to command the various parts of his body with the skill of a conductor taking an orchestra from the softest whisper to a crashing tutti" (Felciano 1998). She also noted in her review certain stylistic trappings of the younger generation that she found distasteful. Felciano criticized Gustavo Collini Sartor for mugging and vamping around the stage, quoting from Ohno's *La Argentina* in both costume and posture but not, in her opinion, inner feeling. Her review commented that Collini's "theatricality . . . did not make up for an inexpressive body and lackadaisical execution" (Felciano 1998). Collini Sartor was an actor who had studied with Grotowski and also performed in Ellen Stewart's 1986 Italian production of *Oedipus* in Colonia. Felciano had praise for Mexican artist Diego Piñón, whom she had seen previously and not been as impressed; however, this time watching him dance the same piece, she commented that he was "focused, precise, and had impeccable timing" (Felciano 1998).

The 1999 Festival saw the return of two fusion butoh artists, Maureen Fleming and Setsuko Yamada, in a move that continued to align butoh with contemporary practice. This was important in the Bay Area because the Tamanos held the anchor with the Hijikata lineage, but their dancers (Koga being one of these next-generation Bay Area artists) were criticized for simply recreating the Tamanos' aesthetic shell without taking the ideas further.

Fleming and Yamada, both products of ballet and butoh,[16] brought a beauty to their work that gradually carved out a new aesthetic direction for younger dancers. These same younger generation artists that the festival sought to educate also gave a platform for their voices in the 1999 festival. There were several performances and films, under the title *Butoh Bash & Video Cafe*. Leigh Evans, former dancer with Harupin-Ha, struck out on her own. Joan Laage's Dappin' Butoh performed for the second time in the Bay Area after founding her own Seattle Butoh Festival the previous year. Anzu Furukawa performed *Crocodile Time*, and Koichi Tamano performed with his ever-evolving company of dancers, Harupin-Ha, which continued to build the Bay Area butoh community.

The next year, 2000, Flournoy emphasized group work and every piece was a large-scale ensemble. Furukawa returned with her German company in *VERWANDLUNGSAMT* (*Office of Metamorphoses*), featuring six dancers: Furukawa herself and the indomitable Yuko Kaseki, who would later become a member of Koga's inkBoat and important performer and teacher in the American circuit. The work they presented was *Goya—La Quinta del Sordo (House of the Deaf)*, with text by Franz Kafka and music by Steve Reich. The choice of music and text aligned Furukawa distinctly with pastiche dance theater.

Harupin-ha presented *Beauty of the Sky*, which featured Molly Barrons, who had become an assistant producer to Flournoy this same year, and Isaac Candelight, who later became Isaac Immanuel, and has since won several artist fellowships and prestigious apprenticeships.

In the 2000 festival, Flournoy also featured two emerging butoh choreographers, both of whom were former members of Harupin-Ha. First was Leigh Evans with *Red River Run Madly to the Sea*, addressing a persistent theme for Evans, that of plastics and post-consumer waste in general polluting our natural environment. Performers clambered in and out of metal shopping carts dragging rope fishnet capes laden with garbage. Evans had initially trained to be a dramaturg at the University of Michigan, had studied Brecht, Grotowski, and Suzuki, and was an avid yoga practitioner studying under Dharma Mitra in New York and Pattabi Jois in India. Her travels led her to discover Kathakali and Odissi dance in India, and Legong and masked performance in Bali. Butoh, through her work with the Tamanos and studies with artists such as Maureen Fleming, was another pathway of cultivating awareness and intensifying the "intersections of spirituality and performance" (Leigh Evans, pers. comm., December 2017). In recent years, Evans has focused that investigation almost exclusively through yoga, leading training sessions throughout the world in sacred sites and in nature.

Second of the Bay Area choreographers to have their own feature on the mainstage in 2000 was Shinichi Koga, presenting his first of three versions of *Cockroach*, featuring former Harupin-Ha and Pamela Z colleagues Evans and Kinji Hayashi, myself, Haruko Crow Nishimura and Joshua Kohl from Degenerate Art Ensemble in Seattle, physical theater performers Cassie Terman and Eugenio Brodbeck, and the performance rock band Sleepytime Gorilla Museum. It was a cacophonous array of "sonic butoh action theater," in which the musicians manned rolling tables with mic'd vegetables to amplify their chewing, as well as their rendition of Kurt Weill's "What Keeps Mankind Alive." Based loosely on Bruno Shultz's novel *Street of Crocodiles*, Koga wrote that *Cockroach* was "a testament to the unloved and marginalized" (SFBF 2000). The arch theatricality of Koga's work set him apart from his Bay Area counterparts, aligning more closely with developments with butoh in Europe, where he had increasingly begun to work and collaborate with other disciplines outside of dance.

Rounding out the program with her version of contemporary butoh fusion was Setsuko Yamada, who was by now a workshop favorite in the Bay Area. Yamada's style, influenced by her training with Kasai's Tenshi-Kan, emphasized fluid movement and attracted the attention of Bay Area dancers. The work, *Yumemiru Tochi* (*Land of Dreams*), premiered at the Theater Olympics in Japan and had its US premiere in Portland, Oregon, where Mizu Desierto had begun to develop a butoh community. Canada's Kokoro Dance also returned to the 2000 Festival with a free outdoor performance at the Yerba Buena Gardens, continuing their role of animating outdoor and natural environments for the Bay Area butoh community.

With the 2001 festival, Flournoy's next curatorial decision was an intervention for American audiences who were "still embracing traditional butoh and had a different interpretation of the term 'contemporary dance'" (Flournoy 2019, 321). To counter what many have dubbed the "classic butoh" aesthetic—ragged clothes, often kimonos in some stay of disarray, gnarled, floor-bound bodies, and dark expressions of humanity—Flournoy featured two uber-contemporary Japanese companies: Nibrol and Op-Eklekt, the latter of which one review called "one of the funniest duos on the globe" (SFBF 2001). Op-Eklekt's piece *Looking to the Far East* satirized traditional institutions through a farcical tea ceremony. Nibrol, which labels itself as contemporary dance, presented *No Parking*, shining a light on Tokyo as a "hectic, unfeeling, casually brutal place" (Hicks 2001). The group effortlessly blended video, absurdist dance to pop music (dancers in tight business suit skirts trying to take giant leaps, people knocking each other on the head and laying them flat), bouncy pop music, and irreverent animation (Ibid.). The San Francisco Arts Monthly notes that another artist on the bill, Yan Shu, "breaks ranks with the old style by incorporating humor and considers itself 'butoh pop'" (SF Arts Monthly 2001). Flournoy kept her finger on the pulse of new trends in Japanese contemporary performance and shared that with the increasingly savvy San Francisco Butoh Festival community. At the same time, she shared butoh's other directions in artists who had been influenced by the founders of the form and had chosen a different path. She included Kei Takei in that year's lineup, in her first performance in the Bay Area since a 17-year hiatus. Takei had worked with Hijikata and Ohno and rejected both to forge her own work in the United States, in the same way that Eiko and Koma had done. These perspectives were equally interesting to Flournoy as she felt her way through the forest of butoh.

With each festival, the language used to describe and introduce butoh became more sophisticated. The first festival in 1995 touted butoh as "one of the major developments in contemporary dance" (SFBF 1995). By the second festival, the organizers emphasized the interdisciplinary nature of the form, as this years' festival also featured an exhibition of the Hijikata Tatsumi Archive, which at that point was managed by Akiko Motofuji. "Butoh was not only a revolutionary dance but a magnetic sphere in which artists from various disciplines interacted" (SFBF 1996).

In a letter to dance critic Alan Ullrich, Flournoy made mention of 1998 being the 13th anniversary of Hijikata's death, citing this as an auspicious year in the Buddhist calendar. Since Hijikata was not Buddhist and this year could not have been significant to him, it rather signaled the continuing exotic status of butoh for American audiences, feeding into the fascination with Japanese culture since the 1960s. Flournoy craftily played with this appeal, while at the same time introducing new knowledge. Her focus remained on butoh as an art form, but a byproduct of her curatorial choices over time was a broader understanding of contemporary Japanese culture (and American consumption of it).

By mid-2001, Flournoy had decided to end the festival. Her curatorial interests lay in the cutting edge, but she had amassed an audience and student base that still clamored for "classic butoh," as she referred to it, that is, glacially paced, scantily clad bald dancers painted in white. Additionally, the student base began to shift, reaching a wider circle but also students with a more casual engagement in butoh.[17] At the suggestion of Kary Schulman, program officer at Grants for the Arts, Flournoy billed the 2002 festival as the "Grand Finale" and closed out the eight-year run.

The 2002 San Francisco Butoh Festival drew attention to not only the butoh diaspora, primarily that spread throughout the United States and into Latin Americas, but also SU-EN, who brought her "Nordic butoh" to the United States for the first time in 2002. As one can imagine with a Grand Finale that is intended to go out in a hail of fireworks, the performance offerings were extensive. Nearly 60 artists performed in three different venues, including Fort Mason Cowell Theater (mainstage and lobby installations), Yerba Buena Outdoor Gardens, and Flournoy's backyard garden. Highlights included *Women in Butoh*, featuring the "old guard" with Hiroko Tamano and also next-generation artists such as SU-EN and Kathy Rose, and "emerging artists" Megan Nicely and Molly Barrons. Additionally, Flournoy curated an evening entitled *New Visions* featuring Ledoh/Salt Farm, Michael Sakamoto, and Helen Thevenot. Among the numerous artists presented in Yerba Buena Gardens was Corinna Brown Hiller's New York-based Dean Street Foo, in which New York-based dancers Ximena Garnica and Christine Coleman performed.

In addition to presenting an aesthetic intervention with so many unusual and groundbreaking performances, the San Francisco Butoh Festival educated numerous American dancers who went on to make their own careers influenced by this work. Most of the workshops were organized through Dancers' Group, where Flournoy was Associate Director at the time, and ironically, I worked as an assistant, checking in many students for the festival before I even knew what butoh was. All of the names and dates in the following are drawn from class lists preserved in the San Francisco Butoh Festival Archives.

Students in the 1997 workshops comprised participants from far and wide. From Seattle came Joan Laage and D.K. Pan; Pan, initially a member of Dai'pan Collective, is a versatile artist/activist who participated in protests at the 2015 RNC with his group Infernal Noise Brigade and also directs Free Sheep Foundation to convert disused spaces into public art. From New York, came Jeff Janisheski, one of the co-founders of the New York Butoh Festival and currently the Chair of Theatre Arts and California State University in Long Beach, and Zack Fuller, a stalwart member of the New York butoh scene although he does not claim to be butoh since he is a student of Min Tanaka. Other New York-based dancers who participated include Irem Calikusu and Kristen Narcowich.

Many students were regulars throughout the festival years: Megan Nicely, who had danced in the Kasai's *Exusai* and later in his *Butoh America* and became a butoh scholar and professor at San Francisco State University, took numerous workshops. Vancouver-based Kokoro Dance co-director Jay Hirabashi frequently attended. Miami-based Helena Thevanot participated in numerous workshops over the years. An avid student of Diego Piñón, Thevanot was featured in the Grand Finale mainstage performances on the 2002 San Francisco Butoh Festival. Harupin-Ha dancers Molly Barrons, Martha Matsuda, Bob Web, and Christina Braun also frequented many of the workshops, and Barrons eventually became Flournoy's assistant director for the Festival. Jennifer Hicks often attended from Boston, where she would later found CHIMER-Alab Dance Theatre and also become a member of Katsura Kan's International Butoh Dance Company in 2001 (Dance-Tech, n.d.). Also from Boston was Alissa Cardone, who, along with Hicks, participated in a workshop with Akira Kasai in 2001 and later performed in his *Butoh America* piece at Japan Society in 2010. Seattle-based Haruko Nishimura attended Yumiko Yoshioka's workshop in 1999. Asheville, North Carolina-based butoh anchor Julie Becton Gillum attended workshops that same year with the Tamanos and Anzu Furukawa. In 2000, participants in Katsura Kan's workshop included Jennifer Hicks, New York-based Corinna Hiller (who later was invited to present her company Dean Street Foo in the Yerba Buena Gardens 2002 Festival), and Shinichi Koga. The 2002 workshop with SU-EN drew Denise Fujiwara, Sondra Fraleigh, Ximena Garnica, Kristen Narcowich, Corinna Hiller, and Christine Coleman. A second week-long workshop was added due to high demand, in which participated Helena Thevenot, Jennifer Hicks, Haruko Nishimura, Bob Webb, Martha Matsuda, Molly Barrons, paige starling sorvillo, and myself (both of whom were members of Koga's inkBoat at the time).

Notes Flournoy, "from 1995 to 2001, [The SFBF was] the only annual butoh festival of its kind in the United States and the sole American presenter that provided consistent training with master artists" (Flournoy 2019, 323). No less than 105 butoh artists from around the world graced the SFBF stages and ushered in a new generation of butoh artists. The festival became a beacon internationally as well, with 60 percent of students traveling from abroad to study each year, and many students were repeat attendees (Flournoy 2019, 323). Following the success of the San Francisco Butoh Festival, festivals emerged across the United States in Portland, Oregon, Seattle and Olympia, Washington, San Diego, Boston, New York, Chicago, Asheville, New Orleans, and many other places. Artists in Latin America produced the *Festival Internacional de Danza Butoh en America Latina* in Peru in 2012 and Mexico City in 2014. There are also festivals in Chile, Colombia, Costa Rica, Ecuador, and Peru, companies active in Argentina and Brazil, and a school based in the Lake Titicaca area of Bolivia.

Through her work on the SFBF, Flournoy feels proud that she and her collaborators "succeeded to bring butoh out of the shadows and connect[ed] the international community in an indelible way" (Flournoy 2019, 324). Her work was pivotal in educating audiences and critics, building an international community of students, securing funding, and linking a touring network for artists.

Notes

1 Fleming's father traced their ancestry back to discover that generations back in her paternal lineage, a Scots-Irish female slave owner's daughter had a child with one of the slaves, and their daughter was Fleming's great-great-great grandmother. This daughter's paternal grandmother was a slave. Fleming's video work *Black Madonna* created during Fleming's 2004 and 2016 artist residencies at Sacatar Foundation in Itaparica, Brazil honored Fleming's great-great-great-great-great grandmother (Maureen Fleming, pers. comm., August 14, 2020).

2 Deren and Erdman collaborated on a 1949 film titled *The Transformations of Medusa* but never completed the project. Erdman introduced Deren to her husband, Joseph Campbell, who subsequently published and wrote the foreword to Deren's second book, *Divine Horsemen: The Living Gods of Haiti* (1953). Deren was married to composer Teiji Ito, with whom Erdman collaborated (Keller 2015).

3 Fleming played Ismene and Hippodameia in the June 1985 production and would eventually perform as Antigon and Hippodameia alongside Korean actor Manhong Kang as Oedipus in a subsequent 1989 production of *Mythos Oedipus & Dionysus Filius Dei* in New York City (Press release, Feb 7, 1989, New York. Note: Fleming is listed as Maureen Williams, going by her mother's maiden name to distinguish her from another Maureen Fleming in the production).

4 Both Oguri and van der Ven currently teach Bodyweather, a training and technique developed by Min Tanaka at Hakushu, but no longer claimed by Tanaka as his technique (Fuller, Butoh Next Symposium, New York City, November 2019).

5 Orinska edited and published the interdisciplinary book BUTOH ("BUTŌ", 2015), in which the author wrote a short excerpt on butoh in New York and San Francisco, featuring a short profile of Fleming. As evidence of the interconnected and relatively small global butoh community, Joan Laage introduced Orinska and the author.

6 Kazuo Ohno (1977) in *Admiring La Argentina*, Photo by Naoya Ikegami.

7 https://enacademic.com/dic.nsf/enwiki/2626726, accessed Nov. 19, 2019.

8 Among Gnome's first dancers was SU-EN, who danced for Hakutobo under Tomoe Shizune's direction. She was with both companies from 1989 to 1994 and later went on to form her own school based in the Swedish countryside, carrying on Ashikawa's methodology layered with her own voice.

9 Koga and Nishimura performed in each other's works in the 2000 Seattle Butoh Festival, two of many collaborations between these two artists and companies. See Chapter 4 for profiles of both artists.

10 David Carrasco argues that Day of the Dead is one of the surviving rituals of pre-Colombian cosmology, merging indigenous beliefs and practices with those of the Catholic colonizers (Carrasco 2014, 169).

11 Cué conducted research with the Huichol for these 7 years, first inviting three men to participate with him in ritual practices. Later, three women joined the group.

12 Born in Mexico City, Pilar Urreta became a professional ballerina in 1969 with la Compañía de Ópera y Zarzuela de Salvador Quiroz. She was a scholarship student with Alwin Nikolais and Merce Cunningham, and was the first Mexican dancer to become a Certified Movement Analyst at the Laban/Bartenieff Institute in New York. While in New York, she also studied Tai Chi, Wu Shu, and Kung Fu (Pilar Urreta, n.d.).

13 Many students of Hijikata report a similar experience of learning more from simply watching the artist in daily life than they did from direct teachings. Interviews with numerous dancers, including Yukio Waguri, Hiroko Tamano, Saga Kobayashi, Ima Tenko, and Minako Seki, confirm this sentiment.

14 Yoshioka would first teach in Mexico in 2010 through Abraham Oceransky's Teatro T in Xalapa.

15 Yoshioka danced in Carlotta Ikeda and Ko Murobushi's company Ariadone, performing in the first butoh show outside of Japan in 1978, and then in 1988, she formed Berlin-based DanceLoveMachine with Minako Seki and Delta RA'I (Yumikoyoshioka, n.d.).

16 Fleming was a student of Kazuo Ohno and Cechetti master Margaret Craske (Maureen Fleming, n.d.), and Yamada studied ballet and also worked with Akira Kasai (Kasai 2013).

17 In a talkback after the 2001 SF Butoh Festival, SU-EN commented that there seems to be some shame, particularly when she teaches in America, about training the body to make it strong and compliant as a performance tool. For her, this is a natural part of the work. She talks about cleaning the floors in the studio, which she clarifies is more than cleaning the floors. It's taking care of the studio, dance, and ensemble. And this discipline she finds lacking in American dancers, or at least she did in 2001.

Works Cited

Anderson, Jack. "A Dancer Who Evokes The Sculptural and Spiritual." *New York Times.* Dec. 25, 1996.

Barclay, Michael. 2009. "Antony and the Johnsons," *Radio Free Canuckistan: Musical Musings from the Frozen North* (blog), January 27, 2009. http://radiofreecanuckistan.blogspot. com/2009/01/antony-and-johnsons.html. Accessed Nov. 27, 2019.

Barks, Coleman with John Moyne, A.J. Arberry, and Reynold Nicholson. 1995. "Shreds of Steam." In *The Essential Rumi*, 38. Edison: Castle Books.

Candelario, Rosemary. 2016. *Flowers Cracking Concrete: Eiko & Koma's Asian/American Choreographies.* Middletown: Wesleyan University Press.

Carrasco, David. 2014. *Religions of Mesoamerica*, Long Grove: Waveland Press.

Center for World Music. 2020. "Our History." https://centerforworldmusic.org/about-us/our-history/. Accessed Sept. 26, 2021.

Dance-Tech. n.d. "Jennifer Hicks's Page." www.dance-tech.net/profile/jenniferhicks. Accessed May 29, 2020.

Dappin' Butoh. Website. http://66.39.154.24/Dappin%20Archives.htm. Accessed September 28, 2021.

Deren, Maya. 1953. *Divine Horsemen: The Living Gods of Haiti.* London: McPherson & Company.

Felciano, Rita. 1998. "Butoh Bonanza: Festival Featured International Cast." *San Francisco Bay Guardian*, Sept. 2, 1998.

Finneran, Richard J., ed. 2002. "Mohini Chatterjea." In *The Yeats Reader*, 115–116. London: Palgrave McMillan.

Fleming, Maureen. 2013. "O Black Madonna.": Artist Statement, La MaMa's La Galleria, 2013, restaged at Riga Performance Art Festival, 2019.

Fleming, Maureen. 2018. "Wildflowers: A Feminine Genesis." Performance Program, La MaMa Experimental Theatre Club, Ellen Stewart Theatre, October 18–21, 2018.

Flournoy, Brechin. 2009. "Emergence of Butoh," Speech, San Francisco Library November 6, 2009.

Flournoy, Brechin. 2019. "Global Butoh as Experienced in San Francisco." In *The Routledge Companion to Butoh Performance*, edited by Bruce Baird and Rosemary Candelario, 313–324. New York: Routledge.

Fox, Margalit. 2020. "Jean Erdman, a Dancer Moved by Myth, is Dead at 104." *New York Times*, May 6, 2020.

Fraleigh, Sondra Horton. 2010. *Butoh: Metamorphic Dance and Global Alchemy*. Chicago: University of Illinois Press.

Gil, John. 2011. *Athens*. Oxford: Signal Books, unpaginated.

Gillespie, John. 2018. "Freeform Review of Maureen Fleming's Wildflowers, A Feminine Genesis." *Dance Enthusiast*, Oct. 18, 2018, www.dance-enthusiast.com/get-involved/reviews/why-audience-reviews/for-audiences/view/Review-of-Maureen-Flemings-WILDFLOWERS-A-FEMININE-GENESIS-October-18–2018. Accessed Jul. 5, 2019.

Hernández, Alonso. 2019. "Antonio Cué Ochoa 'El verdadero partero del Movimiento de Liberación Homosexual.'" *Ulisex MGZN*, Jan. 18, 2019.

Hicks, Bob. 2001. "New Wave of Energy Enriches PIPFest." *The Oregonian*, July 29, 2001.

Jowitt, Deborah. 1991. "Eros," *The Village Voice*, Jan. 22, 1991, unpaginated.

Kasai, Akira. 2013. "A Look into the Choreographic Art of Akira Kasai, Fifty Years after Entering the World of Butoh." Interview by Tatsuro Ishii. *Artist Interview*, The Japan Foundation Performing Arts Network, February 26, 2013. https://performingarts.jp/E/art_interview/1301/1.html. Accessed Sept. 27, 20188.

Keller, Sarah. 2015. *Maya Deren: Incomplete Control*. New York: Columbia University Press.

Klein, Susan Blakely. 1985. *Ankoku Buto: The Premodern and Postmodern Influences on the Dance of Utter Darkness*, Cornell East Asia Series. Ithaca: Cornell University.

La Provincia. 2014. "La capital dedica una plaza en Arenales al bailarín Lorenzo Godoy." *La Provincia*, Oct. 20, 2014. www.laprovincia.es/las-palmas/2014/10/21/capital-dedica-plaza-arenales-bailarin/640659.html. Accessed May 25, 2020.

Laage, Joan Elizabeth. 1993. "Embodying the Spirit: The Significance of the Body in the Contemporary Japanese Dance Movement of Butoh." PhD diss., Texas Woman's University. ProQuest, 9407788.

Le Figaro. 1996. "Eros" *Le* Figaro, Jan. 13, 1996.

Maureen Fleming. n.d. "Maureen Fleming Company: About the Artists." www.maureenfleming.com/pages/about.html. Accessed Sept. 27, 2018.

Meisner, Nadine. 2000. "At the Stillpoint of the Turning World." *The Independent*, May 12, 2000.

New Yorker. 2004. "Decay of the Angel." *New Yorker*, Apr. 12, 2004.

Orinska, Simona, ed. 2015. *BUTŌ*. Riga: Mansards.

Out of Site Chicago. 2014. "Blushing Poppy Productions." http://outofsitechicago.org/2014/06/blushing-poppy-productions/. Accessed Jun. 10, 2020.

Pilar Urreta. n.d. "Formación académica, dancística y de movimiento." https://pilarurreta.com/formacion/. Accessed Sept. 27, 2018.

Piñón, Diego. 2018. "Mi Paso Por Butoh" [My Passage through Butoh], Translated by Indira Percek, Edited by Christopher Mankowski. *INBA Danzaria Magazine* 54, Jul. 2018.

Seattle Butoh Laage. n.d. "Artist Statement." http://seattlebutoh-laage.com/about-the-artist/artist-statement/. Accessed Dec. 10, 2019.

Seibert, Brian. 2019. "Mortal Themes with a Light Touch." *New York Times*, Nov. 15, 2019.

Small, L.A. 1989. "Water on the Moon", *Village Voice* July 4, 1989.

SF Arts Monthly. 2001. "Three Festival Offerings." *SF Arts Monthly*, August 2001.

SFBF. 2001. Press Clipping. Source unknown, periodical name cut off. Accessed in SFBF Archives, December 11, 2017.

SFBF. 2000. Program. Accessed in SFBF Archives, December 11, 2017.

SFBF. 1996. Press Release. Accessed in SFBF Archives, December 11, 2017.

SFBF. 1995. Press Release. Accessed in SFBF Archives, December 11, 2017.

The Great Jones Repertory Company. 1988. "Mythos Oedipus: A Dance Opera." Performance Program, La MaMa Experimental Theatre Club. February 5–21, 1988. Accessed in La MaMa Archives.

Volli, Ugo. 1993. "Eros." *La Republica*, translated by Joel Brody, Jun. 2, 1993.

Yeats, William Butler. 2002. *The Yeats Reader: A Portable Compendium of Poetry, Drama, and Prose*, ed. Richard J. Finneran. London: Palgrave Macmillan.

Yumiko-yoshioka. n.d. "Yumiko Yoshioka is a Dancer, a Teacher and a Choreographer." www.yumiko-yoshioka.com/. Accessed Sept. 27, 2021.

4 Gen X Butoh

Introduction

The 1990s saw a new generation of American artists that had been influenced by butoh begin to form companies and collectives. There have been attempts to catalogue the plethora of American artists linked to butoh, including Tangentz Performance Group's Butoh Net website (last updated in 2009, included a list of 21 American artists and companies amid a list of 100 worldwide), CAVEArtspace's Butoh Nexus that launched in 2010 and featured an impressive user-driven database, and the Butoh Archive website that links artists in an intricate graphic map to their teachers and students (Butoh Archive, n.d.). There are so many more that it is quite difficult to count the number of artists who became invested in a butoh practice during this time.

The artists I have chosen to highlight in this chapter include two Mexican artists based in Mexico City, two Japanese American artists with strong roots on the West Coast of the United States, and a Colombian/Japanese duo who are living and working in New York. Each has had a significant impact on the formation of American butoh today, through some combination of their aesthetic interventions into butoh, or their teaching and producing and resultant impact on the wider butoh community.

These artists all share a cross-disciplinary approach to their work. In Mexico, Eugenia Vargas began in dance and then studied writing and cinema, before teaching movement to actors as the Director of the College of Movement in the Dramatic Arts Program at the Instituto de las de Artes de la Universidad Autónoma del Estado de Hidalgo. Espartaco Martínez began formal performance training in theater at Casa del Teatro but quickly connected his life-long interests in writing and painting to the imagistic aesthetic of physical theater and mime. Both artists foreground a spiritual aspect of their work, either through connection to indigenous knowledge or projects designed for community participation and healing. Shinichi Iova-Koga initially studied filmmaking before switching to theater and then eventually began performing in the Tamano's Harupin-Ha; he has also been heavily involved in the experimental music community in the San Francisco Bay Area and abroad, and the sonic aspect of his work is equally as important as the visual and the physical.

DOI: 10.4324/9780429028472-4

Crow and Joshua Kohl of Degenerate Art Ensemble began as musicians, traversing classical studies, punk, and performance art before beginning their stage productions. And Ximena Garnica was a child actress in Colombia before emigrating to New York to study theater, and Shige Moriya was initially a painter who began experimenting with video when he moved to New York. The pair are wildly experimental in terms of disciplinary boundaries, spanning light, sound, movement, character, physical objects, and performance environment.

Interestingly, the majority of these artists also do not label their work as butoh anymore. Perhaps due to their penchant for transgressing disciplinary boundaries, it is one lens through which their creative process has found focus. Many of them cite conversations with Japanese butoh artists encouraging them to "find their own butoh" as a key which spurred them to keep innovating.

At the same time, each acknowledges critical influence from key butoh artists: Martínez was a member of Dairakudakan for six years and continues to collaborate with many Japanese artists including Kumutaro; Vargas worked with Diego Piñón for more than 10 years as well as intensive tutelage under Natsu Nakajima and Tadashi Endo; Shinichi Iova-Koga worked most significantly with the Tamanos, Yumiko Yoshioka, and Ko Murobushi, and his wife and creative partner Dana Iova-Koga spent three years in Min Tanaka's company Tokason; Crow worked most significantly with Yoshioka and Mari Osani; Garnica spent a year in Japan studying with Akira Kasai, and among her other important teachers and collaborators are Murobushi and Osani.

While all of these artists have done some degree of presenting and hosting Japanese artists in their hometowns, Garnica and Vargas have produced large-scale festivals in New York and Mexico City, respectively. Their work has done much to build and educate audiences and artistic communities and continue the cross-pollination of creative ideas that informs butoh and performance in general in the Americas.

Most of these artists worked concurrently so it is difficult to order their profiles by hierarchy of age or experience. I have chosen to organize them geographically, beginning with Mexico and Martínez and Vargas and her festival Cuerpos en Revuelta, moving to the West Coast of the United States with Iova-Koga/inkBoat and Crow/Degenerate Art Ensemble, and ending in New York with Garnica and Moriya, the New York Butoh Festival, and their company LEIMAY. If we were to look at events chronologically, the New York Butoh Festival began and ended before Mexico's Cuerpos en Revuelta festival. However, all of these artists began working at roughly the same time and have crossed paths or tapped into similar sources along the way. Together they represent the new directions of what I am referring to as "Gen X Butoh" artists have developed this expression in the Americas.

Espartaco Martínez (b. 1972—Michoacán; Resides in Mexico City)

Espartaco Martínez is a performer forged in counterculture and protest. In his characteristic wry humor, he makes light of the fact that he was born in jail. His parents were political activists, and his mother was pregnant with him when she was incarcerated and beaten for being a part of the resistance in the 1970s. Martínez says he internalized the feeling of those blows while still in the womb. His father was one of *los desaparecidos*, a "disappeared" political prisoner.

In a dance film touching on his origin story entitled *Accion + Aislamiento: 15 ejercicios de liberación virtual—#12 (Action + Isolation: 15 exercises of virtual liberation)*, Martínez says that in La Fiesta Brava (Bull Fighting Festival), he identifies with the bull rather than the bullfighter, with being beaten, and perhaps with feeling a certain pride in withstanding pain (Teatrounam, 2020). He is not a stranger to violence and takes it up as a theme in his work, though in a Beckettian, Existential kind of way, coupled with circus music and occasional light movements that harken to mime. He springboards off his personal experience to challenge the viewer; looking straight at the camera, he asks: "when you are watching a violent video, who do you want to hit with your own hands?" (Teatrounam, 2020). There is no trace of anger or revenge in his face, rather a recognition of these edges of darkness that reside in us all.

In the short film, his narration of his life continues as he dances in a black and white striped one-piece shorts suit; he reveals that as a child in the *barrio* he learned how to hide until everything had closed and all was quiet. He comments that he feels safe when underwater, and the video closes with a striking image of his face as it submerges in water, air escaping from his mouth and nose.

Martínez's work has two strong roots within contemporary art in Mexico: both professional and popular performance. He is a distinguished butoh dancer, having created projects and collaborations with numerous notable butoh artists with which he toured to Germany, Switzerland, Korea, Japan, Colombia, the United States, Costa Rica, and Brazil. He has danced primarily with Dairakudakan, but also Russian-directed, Germany-based Derevo, and for theater director Romeo Castellucci. His own work has been produced at a high level in Mexico, including at the renowned Cervantino. At the same time, Martínez has a significant history in community theater, with countless multi-disciplinary works involving dance, literature, theater, and shamanistic ritual, geared toward social activism and personal transformation. He has also been a fixture of the Día de los Muertos (Day of the Dead) festivities in Pátzcuaro, famed center of these national celebrations, performing the role of the Angel of Death frequently. And finally, he has performed with the well-known Mexican hard rock band, La Castañeda (see Figure 4.1). He performed incredibly risky acts, like hanging from his ankles in the same way Sankai Juku did in *Jomon Sho*. Says Martínez, dancing with a band gave him an incredibly valuable experience of performing in an intense communal space, where the smallest gestures can carry archetypal significance to a crowd united by loud, throbbing rock music. He feels that it has been important for him to go outside of the typical avenues of presenting contemporary art, in order to have other visceral experiences of engaging with audiences of all kinds.

After Martínez's mother was released from prison, she went through a dramatic change, understandably so. She went to live in Berkeley, CA, to study

Figure 4.1 Angel de las Sombras, La Castañeda Concierto (2019). Photo of Espartaco Martínez.

Source: Photo by Silvestre Orzuna, reprinted with permission from Silvestre Orzuna

Anthropology. The children stayed in Mexico and lived with their maternal grandmother, who primarily raised them. His mother stayed in contact with her children but remarried an American and still lives in the United States. Martínez was able to visit her in the United States with her when he was 16. He lived with her for a time and also amid the hippy community of People's Park along Telegraph Avenue.

Martínez felt drawn to art from an early age and would write and paint frequently, searching for ways to express himself. His father was present in his life through the books he would send to his children while he himself was involved in underground political movements. Martínez read Antonin Artaud at a young age and also was drawn to a Mexican author, José Agustín, known as the "Jack Kerouac of Mexico." Also, among the writers he encountered in the library was Carlos Castañeda, which he says at first scared him because "it felt like witchcraft" (Espartaco Martínez, pers. comm., May 19, 2021). He eventually understood the significance for him that it was opening him to a different view of reality. Says Martínez, Agustín's writing connected to Castañeda in the sense that the Hippie Generation was in search of social transformations that were not just political but also spiritual.

One day while perusing *La Jornada*, he came across an advertisement for a literary workshop with Agustín who, it turns out, translated Castañeda into Spanish. The workshop was to be in Pátzcuaro, the town where Martínez would eventually land after returning from Japan in 2012. Strangely enough, Agustín was also detained in the same prison as his father, and Augustín had a son born the same day in the same year as Martínez. The two sons became best friends and continue in contact to this day. Agustín's son, Andrés Ramírez, is currently a Literary Director at Random House Mexico. The connections and crossovers in life stories were deep, and Augustín became a father figure for Martínez.

Martínez went to study there in Pátzcuaro in 1992, taking workshops in literature, rock and roll, and other avant-garde forms. The original name for Patzcuaro was Tzacapun-ansucutinpatzcauro, which translates to "door of heaven" or "place where the blackness turns to light" (Garcia-Gómez 2019). The city is the site of the most popular Day of the Dead ritual celebration in Mexico and has an incredible alternative arts scene, where many international artists have been in residence. The vibe, he says, was a mix of beat generation, indigenous tradition and pride, and worldly exchange through the many arts and cultural institutions in the city. Martínez attributes this to a community of bohemian "baby boomers" who have passed through, and attracted artists such as Andre Breton, Alejandro Jodorowsky, Ko Murobushi, Juliet Binoche, and many other elite artists (Espartaco Martínez, pers. comm., May 19, 2021).

In 1993, Martínez was present for the watershed moment for butoh in Mexico: Byakko Sha performing on the ruins in el Museo de Antropología. This event made a deep impression on Martínez. He thought they looked like ghosts of the Aztecs, martians, and some lost tribe that had just resurfaced in civilization, all in one breath. That sense of multiple meanings in one single piece is something he had sought through theater and dance training, but he never felt at home in either discipline. When he saw Byakko Sha, says Martínez, something shifted for him and for many performers in Mexico. "It left a massive impression of what was possible in dance," he said, "not only for dancers but also for theater artists who remember it as something magic" (Espartaco Martínez, pers. comm., September 19, 2019). Shortly thereafter in 1994, Japanese butoh dancers Yuri Nagaoka and Nike Minotau relocated to Mexico and began to present performances and teach. They introduced the Mexican dance community to Takuya Ishide, a direct student of Hijikata who later worked with Ximena Garnica (*Timeless Kaidan*) and Shinichi Koga (*c(H)ord*). The small ex-pat community of Japanese dancers began to grow in Mexico.

In 1996, Martínez went to a school for actors, Casa del Teatro, in Coyoacán, where he studied acting and physical theater. Martínez studied under and performed in the works of Rogelio Luévano (*Ulises en la Azotea*, 1996) and Héctor Mendoza (*Las Cosas Simples*, 1998), among others. While at Casa del Teatro, he studied with political theater group Bread and Puppet Theater, when founder Peter Schumann came as a guest artist. Martínez performed with the company in their Día de Muertos Performance at Teatro Callejero in Xico, Veracruz, in November 1996. He later worked with them in New York City in 1997, when the company invited him to join the off-Broadway production more. Casa del Teatro had received funding from the Rockefeller Foundation for the collaboration with Peter Shuman, which was Martínez's first contact with the funder. He would later receive several fellowships to conduct projects in the United States through the Rockefeller Foundation.

In his performance publication *Bitácora de Oriente*, Martínez notes that his own creative process was impacted by Bread and Puppet's approach: "We are not a school and we do not conduct classes, apprentices need to be self-motivated" (Martínez 2013, Intro). He has followed this trajectory rigorously in his own creative work.

Also, during his days at Casa del Teatro, Martínez encountered Swiss-born clown Daniele Finzi Pasca. The professors and students had gone to see a performance of Finzi's while he was in town, and then Finzi came to give a few workshops at the school. Martínez struck up a friendship with Finzi and was then invited to the house of Finzi's then-girlfriend, Mexican actress Dolores Heredia. On her coffee table, she had a copy of Mark Holburn's *Dance of the Dark Soul* (Holburn 1987), and it was here that Martínez first encountered images of Dairakudakan and many other butoh artists that he would later meet in Japan. While in Mexico, Finzi received an invitation to work in Canada, and then went on to create shows for Cirque Éloize, Cirque du Soleil, and Mariinsky Theater, among other illustrious credits. Finzi and Martínez remained in communication and reconnected in Tokyo when Martínez was in Dairakudakan and have maintained their friendship until this day. Martínez refers to him as a shaman who, throughout his own quest in theater, has always reminded Martínez to aim for the light, even when dancing between life and death.

At the same time, says Martínez, his experience at Casa del Teatro was fraught. Coming from a poor family, he felt a need to reject his background in favor of the Eurocentric cultural elite community at the school. While studying he made a performance for his father of which the school directors did not approve. Martínez had stayed in contact with his father's activist community, had met the Zapatistas, including Subcomandante Marcos, and been in contact with the indigenous community that they represented. Martínez invariably felt an allegiance with this community and the cause of indigenous rights. In the performance, he quoted the Red Hot Chili Peppers lead singer's appearance, naked with a sock over his genitals, with the addition of a Zapatista mask on his face. He spat gasoline and lit it on fire, which to him represented the revolutionary words of the indigenous peoples that are indeed like fire, in their anti-capitalist and anti-neoliberal globalization bent. The soundtrack featured a speech from Comandante Ramona, the main female indigenous leader of the group at the time. The performance certainly angered the school administration, and yet he was allowed to proceed (Espartaco Martínez, pers. comm., May 19, 2021).

In 2001, Martínez had occasion to travel to Washington, DC, in 2001, with a project that his mother conducted with the organization Mexican Solidarity and immigrants in the United States. The project spoke out against torture and the need for political asylum. During his performance, his mother actually broke out in hives, her own traumatic experiences triggered. She continued working with a church that was helping immigrants, which led her to conduct a project entitled *Visible Lines/Invisible People* at SUNY Brockport in Upstate New York. Martínez received a Rockefeller Foundation grant to work on the project and joined her at SUNY Brockport. They also worked with then Brockport professor Juanita Suarez, who introduced him to Sondra Fraleigh and also later came to Mexico City to work with Martínez. He spent time in New York City as well, adding to his experience of two richly experimental artistic communities in the United States. He characterizes the dichotomy of the two coast cities thus: San Francisco and Berkeley representing free love, good vibes, and hippies, and then New York as the dark underbelly, Velvet Underground. Both would influence his work over the years.

Martínez continued community work in Mexico. From 2001 to 2006, he had a job working for the Mexican Secretary of Education teaching theater classes in indigenous communities. He traveled throughout the country for six years in this capacity, and in the process, he learned a great deal about pedagogy that was different from his studies at Casa del Teatro, based in Jesuit, Eurocentric "elite" academic theater because in the pueblos terms like "nemesis" and "protagonist" were not legible. He learned how to adapt to local customs of carnival, calenda, fiesta, etc., in order to make the work relevant.

Through his connections in experimental theater, he became involved with the growing Japanese community in Mexico. By 2005, Martínez was helping to produce tours and workshops for Yuri Nagaoka, Takuya Ishide, also Taketeru Kudo, and Mushimaru Fujieda. He met his wife Sakiko Yokoo in Mexico through a Japanese friend, Nakano, who was a doctoral student in philosophy studying in Mexico. Nakano and Martínez met through a workshop with Diego Piñón. Martínez had invited Piñón to lead a workshop in one of his community projects, and another collaborator in the event was a Noise artist who invited Yokoo to join. She was in Mexico on a fellowship to study dance therapy and was working with students with Down Syndrome and Asbergers. The project was in Espacio Escultório de la Universidad de Mexico, a monument to pre-Hispanic cosmology located in the volcanic region. It is a round monument that resembles Stone Henge, if the monolithic rocks had been evenly spaced and dug into the earth, so they tipped outward a bit, like the petals of a sunflower.[1]

Yokoo was friends with Japanese butoh dancers, including the companies Dairakudakan and Sankai Juku, and it was through her connections and those of his friend Nakano that Martínez first studied with Sankai Juku in Toyama,

Japan on a short, 15-day trip. He also studied with Yuri Nagaoka and took classes with Yoshito in the Kamihoshikawa studio. When he returned, he applied to FONCA to study abroad in Japan, for which he needed a formalized school and plan for study. Though he laughed at the notion of study plan for butoh, being the avant-garde form that it is, Maro, director of Dairakudakan, agreed to write him a letter, and thus Martínez received the grant and embarked on his six-year journey to Japan. He notes that Maro and Dairakudakan insist on loyalty, such that when he did study with Yoshito or dance with Kudo, it had to be in secret. At one point, he traveled to South Korea and they explicitly told him that he would not say that he was their student until he had "calmed down."

Martínez danced with Dairakudakan for six years, from 2006 to 2012. He supported himself by teaching movement classes as an artist in residence at the School of Art and Design of Yoshibi University in Tokyo and working in a restaurant. His time with Dairakudakan was formative not only in terms of dance techniques but also in creative philosophy. Like many other butoh dancers have said of their experiences in companies, Martínez affirms the adage about learning more from his different teachers (Maro, Takuya Muramatsu, Daisuke Yoshimoto, Murobushi, Taketeru Kudo) when they were drunk and just rambling about dance and art and life. He also confirms the stories about the cruelty of training in the Company, during which dancers are routinely hit and aggressively verbally reprimanded for mistakes. It was a brutal experience, says Martínez, and at the same time it taught him. He was considered a student for the first three years of their work, and then in the fourth year he was asked to teach company workshops. During the whole time, he performed in several productions.

In addition to the rigorous training drastically changing his conception of performance, Martínez notes the challenge of living abroad in Japan for six years in a culture so distinct from his own. He felt the contrast of social codes, rules, and discipline culture present in Japan as opposed to the outward expression of joy in Mexican culture. At the same time, his experience in avant-garde performance in both countries was equally opposite, with what he experienced in Japan with Dairakudakan as beyond limits and constantly pushing boundaries, whereas he feels that much of the experimental theater in Mexico is pedantic and moralistic, and rather tame by comparison (Registro de Danza 2013).

During his time in Japan with Dairakudakan, Martínez also danced with other companies and choreographers, most notably Derevo in a piece called *Wheel of Power* (2007),[2] presented in a festival celebrating the 400th anniversary of the city of Mannheim, Germany. There were 30 dancers, artists, actors, and musicians from around the world, including St. Petersburg-based experimental theatrical "engineers" Akhe and Amsterdam-based multimedia industrial spectacle theater company Robodock. Martínez had met members of Derevo in a butoh marathon in 2006 in Yokohama, curated by Kae Ishimoto, in which Yoshito, Yan Shu, and many students of Kazuo Ohno also performed. Derevo founder Anton Adasinsky and lead artist Tanya Khabarova were students of Kazuo Ohno though from Martínez' account, it seems they have adopted the working methods of Hijikata more than Ohno: incredibly strict, everything is toward the staging of the piece with very little ensemble training practice per se, and no unnecessary talking or discussion either in or out of the rehearsal space. In this last aspect, however, Hijikata was known to host gatherings fueled by alcohol which lasted well into morning discussing art, politics, and life in general. Martínez also studied and danced with Daisuke Yoshimoto, who is another important thread in his butoh formation. Yoshimoto invited him to Korea, to the Demilitarized Zone between North and South Korea, which had quite an impact on Martínez. The two became friends and maintained connection even as Martínez was engaged with Dairakudakan.

He met up with Yokoo again a year and a half into his time with Dairakudakan. He was intrigued by her artistic practice. Though she was close with many butoh artists, she never considered her work butoh per se. Even when Martínez insisted that her work was akin, she countered that it did not have a name. She did community work with nonprofessional dancers and was mostly concerned with healing work. After seeing a work she did with Down Syndrome youth, he began to work with her in alternative youth communities in Tokyo in a similar fashion, with methods that were related to butoh but not exactly that.

In June 2011, he and Yokoo married in Japan. At their wedding, Yoshimoto offered them a dance as a gift. Other friends of them were planning performance offerings as well at the wedding, with Yoshimoto as the culminating event since he is such a revered teacher. Maro and his wife were of course also invited to the wedding, which did not seem like a problem to Martínez; however, when Yoshimoto found out that Maro was coming, he balked a bit. This shocked Martínez, because as he describes his elder, Yoshimoto is "brutal," which is Mexican slang for something like punk, unflinching, and extremely daring. But he also says that Yoshimoto is humble; he told Martínez that despite his accomplishments, the only thing he feels precious about is having been the stage manager for Hijikata and Ohno on *La Argentina*. Beyond that, he is quite fierce, says Martínez.

As Yoshimoto began to dance at the wedding, Maro joined him. From Martínez's account, they had a butoh dance battle. It was beautiful and felt like a space of respect for one another, says Martínez, but it was like a hip-hop cypher in that each dancer was showing their strength. They greeted one another, danced, said their goodbye, and then Maro exited. At the conclusion, Yoshimoto danced his way over to Saki and put his hands on her pregnant belly, sending his good wishes to their new family. The couple now has three children, two of which they had while in Japan.

When Martínez returned to Mexico, he contacted his professor from Casa del Teatro, Chamarco, who helped him get a position in community-based theater in Pátzcuaro which was ideal since both he and Saki shared this interest. Though he had previously worked in communities around Mexico, Martínez says that it was only after coming back from Japan and his time with

Dairakudakan that he felt able to truly reconnect to indigenous community and the power of pre-colonial Mexican cultural roots, through the work he did in Pátzcuaro. He and Yokoo worked in school, community centers, festivals throughout Michoacán, both teaching, performing, and presenting artists that came from Mexico City. They brought Kumotaro Mukai from Japan for a residency and also produced a collaborative project with Japanese yamabushis and Mexican shamans. Their children went to an alternative school, and their housing was within the cultural center. In many ways, it was an ideal life for the young family. However, the narcotraffic violence in the region was a constant stress. Moreover, the sociopolitical perspective of the center began to conflict with their own personal values. As it is a center founded by cultural elites, the overarching sentiment Martínez felt in giving community workshops was slightly patronizing, with the goal of exposing the uneducated masses to high culture. Martínez, coming from a strongly populist political background, chaffed at this notion. As the political leadership changed in 2018, this became an increasing source of friction.

At an opportune moment for them to make a change, in 2020, Yokoo was offered a position in a long-established Buddhist temple in Mexico City. They were able to move their whole family there, which is a welcome connection for the children to grow up surrounded equally by their Japanese and Mexican heritage, says Martínez. They continue their community and performance work through this practice. The temple had had previous artists in residence; Kota Yamazaki and Mina Nishimura were in residence at the temple for a full year in 2019.

In his home county of Mexico, Martínez strongly represents the Japanese root of butoh, having trained and performed so extensively there, both in companies and his own work. He was instrumental in organizing Dairakudakan's two tours to Mexico, the 2010 *Secretos de la Humanidad* (*Secrets of Humanity*) and October 2012 performance of *Haino Hito* (*Man of Ash*) there, and also danced with the company for the show. *Secretos* was the company's premiere in Mexico and a significant event, which further linked Martínez to his Japanese pedigree in the eyes of Mexican audiences. Each time, the massive group performed in Mexico City at Sala Miguel Covarrubias at al Universidad Nacional Autónoma de México (UNAM) and then at FIC. Their aesthetic was quite notable, distinct from earlier visiting solo artists and the relatively serene Sankai Juku, which had previously performed at FIC several times previously.

Martínez has also created and performed his own work extensively, including duets and group works in major festivals in Mexico, including the Cervantino in Guanajuato, and numerous butoh festivals in Mexico City. At FIC, Martínez has performed in La Plaza three separate years thus far, including a duet painted in all silver (2014), another duet entitled *La Bola De Carne* (*The Meatball*) (2017) that featured patchwork scaffolding and dancers clad in butcher's aprons. And in the 2018 Cervantino, Martínez created an ensemble piece entitled *Negro y Ninguno* (*black the color & no one the number*) featuring live singers and a cast of five physical theater performers.

Also in July 2018, he premiered *Temblor o La consagración de la nada* (*Trembling, or the Consecration of Nothing*) in nonconventional spaces in Bogota, Colombia, sponsored by the Iberescena Initiative. This was a multi-disciplinary effort featuring well-known Colombian theater and film actor Nicolás Cancino, musician and vocalist Juanita Delgado, Mexican dancer Malú Macareno, dramaturg Verónica Ochoa, Yokoo as co-choreographer, and actors Camilo Carvajal and Samuel Espinel. The piece was a heady mix of forms and aesthetics: social dances including the cumbia and champeta, primordial screams, traditional Caribbean music, physical theater, and butoh. Central to the work was the theme that Martínez had asked many times over in his life: "How do you face the earthquake and still come out dancing in the face of disaster" (*Nuevo Siglo* 2018).

Notable solo performances include *La Bestia* (2014), co-directed by Takuya Muramatsu of Dairakudakan, referring to the nickname Central American migrants have given to the dangerous train ride they take in hopes of making it across the Mexican/US border; *Inhumano* (July 2017), addressing the tipping point of violence in a country when it spirals out of control without limit or end in sight; and the short dance film by Manfred Lopez Grem "*Sclabo*," a play on words to indicate someone uneducated writing the word "*esclavo*," or slave. In the film, Martínez emerges from a wheelbarrow, where he is sleeping, cramped in a fetal pose. He is at once serious about his work and simple minded, moving among and on top of the bricks that are neatly spaced out on the dirt floor. At one point his own finger catches him like a fishhook and pulls him around the work site, and one can sense the overload in command. He becomes a stiff-legged and armed machine, rotating through his hip and shoulder joints mechanically to finish his job before he returns to his cramped sleeping quarters for the night.

Additional projects include collaborations with Japanese artists, such as Kumotaro Mukai *Hajimemashite* (*Nice to Meet You*) (see Figure 4.2) (May 2018) at Museo del Chopo, Mexico Butoh Fest. The premise of *Hajimemashite* is a shaman who invokes a spirit (presumably indigenous Mexican god) but got the incantation wrong and so a Japanese spirit appears. They played it as if there were meeting a martian, and "weren't sure if we should greet each other with the hand, head, rear end, or foot," says Martínez (pers. comm., May 19, 2021). The piece is quite theatrical, employing elements of clown and building on the convivial relationship that the two men already have.

Martínez also collaborated in *Dos Soles* (*Two Suns*) (November 2018) a group piece directed by Mukai, made as a reminder of the atomic bomb from which his own grandmother had perished. The project was funded by the Japan Foundation Mexico and featured Takao Kawagushi, Daiichiro Yuyama, Aime Irasema, Sheila Rojas, Martínez, and two of his children, Shizu Martínez Yokoo and Yiguen Martínez Yokoo.

In keeping with his perspective that theater is for everyone, not just the young and elite, Martínez has included his children in some of his productions. He invokes Bread and Puppet's notion of community theater as democracy and

Figure 4.2 Hajimemashite. Photo of Kumotaro Mukai and Espartaco Martínez, 2008.

Source: Photo by Cesar Alberto Guzman, photo courtesy Cesar Alberto Guzman

thinks it is good for both audiences to see children in plays and his children to participate in theater. The first piece his oldest daughter was in was Romeo Castellucci's Tokyo performance of *Inferno* in 2009 when she was just over a year old. There is a room full of children in a clear, plexiglass room onstage in one scene. In another, their parents play with them, but the lighting and music choices are meant to invoke something more ominous, like little demons attacking the adults.

In *Dos Soles*, his eldest daughter Shizu appeared in a flashback scene of a child sitting and reading a didactic book explaining the bombing to children. The scene begins as an ordinary day with a child in school and then suddenly the scene goes black, signifying the absolute upending of reality. In another scene, the dancers represent the impact of the atomic bomb on human flesh, rotating violently around one another until they disintegrate into "one giant ball of meat" (Espartaco Martínez, pers. comm., May 19, 2021). Says Martínez, something he appreciates about Dairakudakan is the ability to be precise and clear in theatrical content, particularly in social or political critique that is funny and at the same time leaves one feeling like they've been hit in the stomach.

Martínez sees butoh in Mexico as creating an opening for performers to create their own techniques and express their own voices. He says that due to the history of colonialism in Mexico, Europe is the standard against which Mexicans measure themselves. Where he sees this manifesting in theater training is most professional schools are somewhere connected to European traditions, particularly Grotowski. While he agrees that this physical theater training opens a space for something like butoh to take root, it is still tied to European intellectualism and tradition. "This is the dilemma of modernity" says Martínez. "Butoh," he continues, "gives the space in which we can say no." The Japanese who came to Mexico are not at all interested in colonial Mexican culture, rather they are solely interested in the indigenous. There has been so much mixing that it's not really possible to know what tribe one comes from. But at the very least, says Martínez, butoh allows him to explore these connections in an embodied way.

Martínez cites the methods and philosophies of numerous artists in his own approach to dance, among them Kazuo Ohno: "what technique can I teach? Life is the training" (Martínez 2013, unpaginated). He eschews definitions of butoh and studies of lineage, quoting his director, Maro: "Those who are concerned with butoh destroy butoh, because there's no butoh in butoh, there's no dance in the dance, no science in the science, no nature in the nature. Nothing" (Martínez 2013 unpaginated). Instead, Martínez says of his own approach, "I have accepted that one has to, among other things, forget mental strategies in order to open to your own doorways" (Martínez 2013 unpaginated).

He feels that the point of Noguchi Taiso is to listen to the body and to live well, to sustain oneself through old age and promote a healthy and pain-free life. It's a funny sort of math in Noguchi gymnastics, however. It's not that one moves slowly and with care in order to prevent injury and promote functional alignment. It's rather that one taps into a life force that is beyond what one thinks is possible, and that life force sustains through seemingly impossible tasks. For example, Martínez describes training for a performance with Dairakudakan, and when he completed the series and was standing in a puddle of his own sweat with what he felt like was nothing left to give, Muramatsu directed him, "again." He of course obliged, because the implication was that if one wanted to be a part of the company, that was the culture. When he finally went to sleep that night, completely drained and broken, he recalls thinking, "ok, I'll quit tomorrow," and yet somehow in the night his body had returned to its ready state, eager to return to training. Time and again he had this experience, such that he realized there is a different edge or limit which he is capable of reaching by tapping into *ki* energy, the sense of the body as a resilient water bag, and other images as impetus for his dance (Espartaco Martínez, pers. comm., May 19, 2021).

> I realized that the body has no limits . . . all is possible . . . of course we are not superhuman and we need to choose the things in which we invest carefully but we are capable of so much.
>
> (Espartaco Martínez, pers. comm., May 19, 2021)

It's not without its risks, he says, and although when he was younger, he perhaps took foolish risks, and now he feels like he does so with "respect for life and death" and in many ways, an understanding that "life is pain" (Espartaco Martínez, pers. comm., May 19, 2021). He attributes his perspective to his birth, and being present for his own mother's torture, both in and outside of her womb. He did in fact seek out extreme experiences in his youth, inspired by poets such as Rimbaud; he says, "I sought fire, and sometimes it burned me." But through his work in communities with indigenous ideologies, and training with artists such as Daniele Finzi, he has found a tenderness with which he approaches that edge.

Eugenia Vargas (b. 1967, Mexico City)

Eugenia Vargas is a product of both urban, cosmopolitan and rural, indigenous Mexico. Born and raised in Mexico City, Vargas' father was an agricultural engineer, and her mother was a lawyer. Thanks to her father's profession, she spent a significant period of her childhood visiting the countryside a few hours outside of Mexico City, in Hidalgo, where she would later teach. She always felt a deep connection to and respect for the land, as later became important in her artistic work. From a young age, she learned how to care for plants from seedling through harvest by tending the garden at her house in Mexico City.

Vargas had determined that she wanted to be a dancer even when she was a little girl. She was also deeply intrigued by indigenous culture and the connection of humans to nature. Her course of study combined these interests and lead to her current investigations in butoh.

Vargas first began studying Jazz dance intensively when she was about 15 years old, and from there she discovered contemporary dance. In the 1980s, she studied at several of the most important dance schools in Mexico City, including Ballet Nacional de México (directed by Guillermina Bravo). At 18 years old, Vargas completed a three-year program at Grupos Especiales para la Enseñanza de la Danza Contemporánea, which was a part of Bellas Artes and would later form into the renowned Escuela Nacional de Danza Clásica y Contemporánea. The majority of her training at these schools was in Graham technique or ballet. She also took Graham-based classes at the Ballet Nacional de México. Following that, she attended Ballet Teatro del Espacio (directed by Michel Descombey), where she continued to study Graham and ballet. In the late 1990s, she would add study in Horton, Cunningham, and Limon techniques to her lexicon.

At the time, Bachelor's degrees only existed for choreographers but not for dancers in Mexico. Instead, dancers would undergo rigorous training for five years, and then afterward they would audition to dance in companies.[3] Vargas danced for a few companies in Mexico City but ultimately felt disillusioned with her role. As a dancer, she felt that her job was to simply learn a sequence of steps and then execute them. To her disappointment, dancers were not involved in the creation process.

Realizing that she was more interested in choreographing and creating new work, she supplemented her dance studies with education in creative writing and cinema. From 1990 to 1992, she completed a diploma program at Escuela de Escritores (SOGEM), a prestigious school for theatrical, creative, and technical writers, receiving a degree in Creative Literature. Following that, she enrolled in the Cinemania diploma program for "Cine, Arte y Comunicación" from 1998 to 1999, receiving a degree in Cinema, Arts, and Communication. The cinema studies in particular allowed her to explore the relationship of images and movement more fully.

Vargas recalls two different encounters with butoh in 1993. The first was seeing Byakko Sha in their fabled presentation at the Museo Nacional de Antropología, which included Diego Piñón. The second was a workshop with New York-based Shigeko Suga, who was touring Mexico with an adaptation of Yukio Mishima's novel *Sotoba Komachi* as a performance entitled *Sotoba Komachi, Teatro Flamenco y Butoh.*[4] Suga, who has made an artistic career out of the blending of butoh with flamenco, is a resident artist at La MaMa. The workshop featured her blend of these techniques.

Vargas remembers being intrigued by both artists, however, was still quite focused on contemporary dance. She was accepted into the Bachelor's program for Choreography at the Escuela Nacional de Danza Clásica y Contemporánea, which she attended from 1998 to 2002. During the final year of her studies, theater director Abraham Oceransky was a guest artist at the school. His workshop emphasized the use of imagery in performance, and Vargas noted its significance in her future endeavors. Oceransky had organized Natsu Nakajima's first workshop in Mexico, the impact of which was quite significant on his subsequent work and he invited her to return numerous times after that first encounter. Additionally, Oceransky brought Ko Murobushi to Mexico for one of their many collaborations, during which time Murobushi gave a 10-day workshop at Bellas Artes. This was Vargas' first real exposure to butoh training. After four years of intensive study in classical and contemporary dance composition, this new, experimental work began to draw her attention.

Upon graduating, Vargas says that she "felt like an orphan without the structure of school" (Eugenia Vargas, pers. comm., August 11, 2020), and she was searching for a new configuration for her studies. While walking in the Bohemian Mexico City neighborhood of Coyoacán, she encountered a flier advertising one of Diego Piñón's workshops and decided to attend. She remembers being impressed with his training, which she says, "helped her deepen her own artistic voice" (Eugenia Vargas, pers. comm., August 11, 2020).

Vargas found a strong connection in Piñón's work with ritual and land. She studied with him for a decade (from 2002 to 2011), as part of the second official group or "la Célula" (the Cell) of Butoh Ritual Mexicano. This process culminated in Piñón production of *Espíritus en Tránsito* (*Spirits in Transit*), in 2010 el Museo Universitario del Chopo, in Foro del Dinosaurio, in a butoh series produced by Director Jose Luís Paredes Pacheco. In the same series,

Vargas presented a solo she had choreographed for Carlos Cruz, entitled *Haiku: Cuerpo Poético* (*Haiku: Poetic Body*).

Vargas's contact with Piñón connected her to a new community of artists, among them, Nora Manek. Manek was concurrently teaching dance and movement studies at Casa del Teatro in Coyoacán, Mexico City, and at the Instituto de las Artes de la Universidad Autónoma del Estado de Hidalgo in Real del Monte, three hours northeast of the capital. Invited by Manek to take her place in Real del Monte, Vargas became the Director of the College of Movement in the Dramatic Arts Program at the Instituto de las Artes de la Universidad Autónoma del Estado de Hidalgo from 2004 to 2007. The director of the Department of Dramatic Arts was Indira Pensado also worked with Piñón for many years as part of the first group of Butoh Ritual Mexicano. Pensado had previously worked with Roy Hart Theater and was also a voice teacher at the school. Vargas and Pensado met while studying with Piñón. This community of artists involved in similar research began to weave closer together.

Says Vargas, working at Instituto de las Artes was an exciting time of experimentation in her creative development, in which she collaborated with artists from multiple disciplines. All of the students were acting students and were quite open to the work that Vargas brought them in movement. As this was her first time working with actors, she was very interested in their approach to the body and was curious about how their expressive possibilities were unique from her experience with dancers. Says Vargas, there were many interesting artists that converged there and built the degree program from the ground up during Vargas' tenure. As it was a new program, all of the faculty and students were open to all kinds of investigation and made adventurous cross-disciplinary work.

Her time at the university also brought her back to her childhood roots in the countryside. The town of Real del Monte is situated on the edge of the mountains and forests. Being so close to nature, she was able to pursue her two interests in dance and the land. She worked intensively with a group of students from the school, often out in nature. They trained together and were invested in a similar search for openness and authenticity in the body. Says Vargas, "If it was butoh or not butoh, I don't know, but we were involved in this search . . . and we always had the idea that it was a laboratory" (Eugenia Vargas, pers. comm., March 13, 2018). Performance work in the studio was informed by explorations outdoors, including *velaciones* (fire rituals), *temazcales* (sweat lodges), and *aguas termales* (thermal baths in hot springs). She recalls spending the whole evening tending a fire and watching the night sky change. Vargas describes her immersive research as a revelation of the sacred even in the smallest of things. A particularly apt example of this for her was the seeding of corn through the process of planting, tending, and harvest. As the national crop, corn has indigenous heritage and significance in Mexico. Her process connected to deep roots of Mexican culture.

During 2004 in her first year at the university, Vargas formed a group of theater students that she continued to work with over the course of her time there. Each year, this group presented a culminating project of their work, titled *El Polvo del Camino: Lo Sagrado Habita en lo más Pequeño* (*The Dust of the Journey: The Sacred Exists in the Smallest of Things*), referencing the farming process and the sacred indigenous practices involving cornmeal (Eugenia Vargas, pers. comm., March 13, 2018). There was an outdoor version presented in Hidalgo, and later she and her students presented another version in the theater at Foro "Los Talleres" in Coyoacán, in Mexico City. Vargas continued her trend of intertwining country and city, and the slowness of tending plants with the bustle of the international metropolis.

This intensive performance study group would become the foundation of Vargas' company, and as such she dates the official founding of the company as 2004, when she began to direct her own intensive research. In recognition of the collaboration among actors and dancers, in particular, she named the group Laboratorio Escénico Danza Teatro Ritual (LEDTR) (Ritual Dance Theater Scenic Laboratory). Founded with seven students, three students remained with Vargas after her four-year tenure at the school, when she began to work in Mexico City again.

Among the dedicated group of students who Vargas trained, Carlos Cruz was perhaps the most active of those who continued to work with her after graduating. Cruz had come in as an acting student, as the others had, and worked with physical theater methods of Roy Hart Theater and Eugenio Barba, through his teachers Indira Pensado and Rogelio Luévano.

Together with Cruz, Vargas traveled in 2007 to eXit! at Schloss Broellin, Germany, the butoh mecca produced by Yumiko Yoshioka and Delta Rai. Here, they met Tadashi Endo and Yuko Kaseki, who Vargas would later host in residency in Mexico. During the intensive three-week festival, Vargas choreographed and performed a dance with Cruz entitled *Celebration*, a duet on the theme of earth and corn.

By 2008, Vargas' company had secured support from the prestigious FONCA, for the project entitled *El sueño de la muerte o el lugar de los cuerpos poéticos* (*The dream of death or the place of poetic bodies*), which was inspired by the writing of Argentinian poet Alejandra Pizarnik. The piece was a series of vignettes with movement and voice, abstracted from Pizarnik's poetry. The performers included actress Sandra Celedón (graduate of Casa del Teatro), Gisela Cortés (one of the three original dancers in LEDTR, and a graduate of Instituto de Artes de Real del Monte), and Feldenkrais teacher Laura Zermeño. Piñón and Indira Pensado assisted as outside eyes, offering guidance on the performance and voice work, respectively.

At the outset of the project, Vargas embarked on a year-long investigation in which she and her performers boldly plunged into a year of research. Together they participated in indigenous ceremonies related to the *Camino Rojo* (Red Path), which refers to indigenous ritual practices among communities stretching from Patagonia to Alaska. Vargas and her group of women participated in indigenous rites such as a shaman-directed vision quest, which involved four days of fasting solo meditation in the wilderness and began and ended with sweat lodges (*temazcales*). Says Vargas, her focus for the year was to intertwine art, spirituality, and life in the creation process, such that making a dance was "more like a life journey, in which the dances were informed by this consciousness of life and death. You dance through it. It's a form of prayer, an appreciation of the mystery of life" (Eugenia Vargas, pers. comm., August 11, 2020). At the end of the year, the group presented *El Sueño de la Muerte, or the place of poetic bodies* at Foro Los Talleres, the theater founded by Isabel Beteta. For Vargas, the ceremonial practices "opened a spiritual dimension and sense of existence in which death is essential to an understanding of life" (Eugenia Vargas, pers. comm., January 7, 2021).

Though the group participated as part of the dramaturgical research for a performance, Vargas continued to participate in vision quests and other rituals over a period of four years. Other such rituals include the Dance of the Sun and Dance of the Moon (La Danza del Sol and La Danza de la Luna), which entail dancing all day or night for four days, respectively, and sleeping when the sun or moon has set. These rituals are also punctuated by sweat lodges and participants fast for the duration. Says Vargas, they really had no previous experience with these practices, and committed to the adventure nonetheless. Of the original group in *El Sueño de la Muerte*, Zermeño continues to perform the Dance of the Moon rite, which has become an important practice among Latin American women seeking to connect to the power of feminine energies.

Vargas' creative research led her to take a workshop with Natsu Nakajima in Guanajuato, organized by dancer Lola Lince in 2007. Lince, a former ballet dancer and successful experimental choreographer, had developed an international presence with her vivid, image-based performance. Lince had begun collaborating with Nakajima in 2004 and had fostered an active community of butoh and experimental dance artists in Guanajuato by the time Vargas encountered Nakajima's work. Vargas felt she had found an important teacher for her and continued to seek out her training.

Vargas continued teaching in academic settings, including los Talleres Libres (Open Workshops) de la UNAM and at la Unidad de Vinculación Artística de la UNAM, an interdisciplinary school dedicated to the study of art, history, and resistance.[5] Though her work spanned many practices, she gradually began to just go by the name of butoh. Says Vargas, "It seems that people always need labels, and wanted a name for what I was teaching, and so I started calling my classes butoh" (Eugenia Vargas, pers. comm., March 13, 2018).

In 2009, Vargas and her company designed a series of workshops for the performance community that addressed many of the investigations she had pursued over the years, including but not only limited to butoh. These included butoh with Diego Piñón, Gabrielle Roth's movement meditation of 5Rhythms with renowned actor Gerardo Trejoluna, Roy Hart voice work with Indira Pensado, as well as Feldenkrais. Vargas also taught a workshop entitled "Presence, Impulse, and Energy." All of the trainings were linked by their interest in expressive possibility. Together with her collective of dancers and growing student community, she continued investigating modes of performance that touched on ritual and a deep authentic experience.

Vargas joined another workshop with Nakajima in 2009 at Ballet Teatro del Espacio in Mexico City, organized by Jessica Sandoval, the creative and life partner of Vargas' fellow Hidalgo professor, Gerardo Trejoluna. Following the workshop, Vargas was then asked to be a stand-in for an actress who could not attend all of the rehearsals in a project organized by Trejoluna and San-doval in which Nakajima was the choreographer: *The Tempest*, presented at El Galeón Theater in 2009. The project attracted esteemed Mexican theater director Rubén Ortiz, who had directed Trejoluna in previous projects and had made a name for himself in post-dramatic theater. Chicago-based butoh artist and student of Piñón, Nicole LeGette had come to Mexico for the workshop and remained for part of *The Tempest* rehearsals, in which she served as an assistant. Vargas spent time with LeGette both in and out of the studio, sharing meals and outings outside of the city including to Tepoz-tlán, the reputed birthplace of Quetzalcóatl. Says Vargas, LeGette helped her immensely in understanding Japanese butoh culture in general and in understanding Nakajima in particular. The project was well received and also launched Vargas into a pivotal relationship with Nakajima, as her assistant and producer in Mexico.

By 2010, Vargas had begun to present Nakajima's workshops in Mexico City and throughout the country and continued presenting her until 2013. During this time, Vargas produced nearly 20 events for the Japanese dancer. Highlights include conferences in collaboration with UNAM, a residency with Isabel Beteta at Los Talleres that culminated in the piece *Chasing the Shadows of Birds* for Beteta's company (2011), an homage to Nakajima at Diego Piñón's center in Tlalpujuhua (2011), and a commission for Nakajima's choreography *The News* on LEDTR (2012). *The News* was supported by CaSa, the Oax-aca State Government, Japan Foundation Mexico, and the theater company la Compañía TeatroSinParedes. Nakajima had made a name for herself in Mexico through her collaborations with theater director Abraham Oceransky, Lola Lince, and as she branched into the dance community, she attracted institu-tional support.

The News was a cross-cultural investigation; it was a collaboration between Nakajima and Vargas, and included dancers Eugenia Vargas, Ireli Vázquez, Alam Sarmiento, Carlos Cruz, Priscella Uvalle, Malú Macareno, and Aura Arreola (a long-time member of LEDTR who would become co-producer of the Cuerpos en Revuelta Festival). The performance offered a critical view of modernity through the lens of current events, with dancers draped in newspa-pers among other references to contemporary life. It was originally staged by Nakajima and Yukio Waguri and remounted on the group of Mexican dancers referencing relevant local culture. The work drew from numerous influences, including images of visual artist Shinzaburo Takeda, a Japanese artist who emigrated to Mexico in 1963 and has become an important artist and educator in Oaxaca, Mexico, training generations of young visual artists through his faculty position at Universidad Autónoma Benito Juárez de Oaxaca.[6] The piece also employed text from prominent Mexican peace activist Javier Sicilia, who at the time was leading a highly publicized peace movement that marched to Mexico City to call for an end to drug cartel violence (Brito 2011).

The process was a charged one for all of those involved, due to the political climate and personal life situations. Vargas describes the rehearsal process as one in which the performers "permanently broke their ego." It resulted in a strong performance piece, one that left them all changed. Additionally, for Vargas, who was assistant director, performer, and producing partner, this was the most ambitious project she had taken on to date, with multiple institutional partners and performances in two cities.

Following the performance, Nakajima and Vargas went their separate ways. Nonetheless, she was one of Vargas' most formative teachers. She credits Nakajima with imparting strong technique into her previous investigations with butoh:

> With Natsu, I also learned many concepts, many sensibilities, in particular in *The News* after spending many weeks with her assistant, Akiko, learning all the details down to how I move my little finger. I thought I had it perfectly but when Natsu arrived after several weeks, she thought we were horrible and had no idea what we were doing. It was a very interesting process of how to forget the score . . . she would say things like "I don't want to see Eugenia perform this, you need to be more of a thing, more material."
>
> (Eugenia Vargas, pers. comm., March 13, 2018)

Vargas had first experienced Nakajima's process during rehearsals for *The Tempest*. One of the dancers in the piece was a virtuosic contemporary dancer. They were learning a walking choreography in which the image was an old woman wearing black, who is barely visible in the darkness, walking alone in the night. This dancer got frustrated with Nakajima for continuously correcting her. She asked to be taught the steps, to which Nakajima responded that she couldn't do that. Says Vargas, "how can you teach anyone to feel, especially to feel such a mysterious image?" (Eugenia Vargas, pers. comm., March 13, 2018). The training she received from Nakajima, she says, was precisely how to express the essence of the material she wished to portray, without adding anything superficial to the embodiment.

Through both experiences, Vargas gleaned concrete working methods—a "strange and enigmatic technique that called me strongly"—that she carried forward into her own choreography. Says Vargas:

> These are the first things you learn about butoh, no? To be smoke, to be the wind. But [with Nakajima] this was another process, super mysterious,

thrilling, sometimes paralyzing, but without a doubt, the richest process I've lived in my life. Her method is relentless, without compromise.

(Eugenia Vargas, pers. comm., March 13, 2018)

Following this experience, Vargas invited Tadashi Endo to work with LEDTR. Working with Endo brought out a different spirit entirely, says Vargas, one that was much lighter. Endo also worked with improvisation as a methodology and performance technique, which was a new experience for her. She continued to invite other artists to Mexico and also took workshops with traveling butoh artists, including Murobushi, who continued to be a regular presence in Mexico. Teachers that LEDTR produced included Hiroko and Koichi Tamano, SU-EN, Sherwood Chen, Makiko Tominaga, Kae Ishimoto, Yukio Waguri, Yuko Kaseki, Minako Seki, Taketeru Kudo, Atsushi Takenouchi, Yuri Nagaoka, and Seisaku, among others.

Vargas began to notice that though each teacher had their own method, all seemed to be aiming for a notion of the "empty body." Says Vargas, "the principle or the essence [among teachers] is the same. It was always a question of transformation. With Diego is was similar, the empty body, and how to arrive at that empty body that was not just an intellectual question" (Eugenia Vargas, pers. comm., March 13, 2018).

A pivotal piece in this period was *Espejo Negro* (*Black Mirror*) (see Figure 4.3) created in 2014 through an artistic residency commission with Tadashi Endo,

Figure 4.3 Laboratorio Escenica Danza Teatro in *Espejo Negro*. Dancers left to right: Aura Arreola, Malú Macareno, Eugenia Vargas, Ireli Vázquez.

Source: Photo by César Alberto Guzmán, photo courtesy César Alberto Guzmán

supported by FONCA and presented in the Foro del Dinosaurio at Museo Universitario del Chopo. The piece featured dancers Malú Macareno, Aura Arreola, Ireli Vázquez, and Eugenia Vargas (all of whom danced in *The News*), with assistant direction by Teresa Carlos, Vargas' long-time collaborator. Experimental composer Eduardo González created the music.

The promotional materials for the work reveal the dramaturgical inspiration as the legend of Aztec deity Quetzalcóatl in his "mythical journey to Mictlán to meet the smoking mirror, the obsidian mirror" (Museo Universitario del Chopo, n.d.), a metaphor for his own awakening just before death.

LEDTR had become one of the foremost names in butoh in Mexico. The company has been involved in almost every major butoh festival that was produced in Mexico prior to 2016 including el Primer Festival de Danza Butoh de la Ciudad de México, organized by el Museo Universitario del Chopo (2010); el Festival de Danza Butoh, organized by el Centro Cultural Los Talleres (2012); el Festival Internacional de Danza Butoh en el Museo Ex—Teresa Arte Actual, organized by Coordinación Nacional de Danza (in 2013); Segundo Encuentro de Butoh Latinoamericano (in August 2014), organized by Tania Galindo; and Muestra Internacional de Butoh y Expresiones Contemporáneas, organized by Anzar Danza (in 2014).

In 2015, Vargas received funding that allowed her and two company members—Aura Arreola and Teresa Carlos—the momentous experience of traveling to Japan. The trio participated in the Performance Studies International conference, held that year in Aomori, the birthplace of Hijikata Tatsumi. Vargas recounts the impact of the trip as a clarifying experience, one that allowed her to "smell the fragrance of what I had been hearing about for so long . . . it was something mysterious and profound but also had a strange familiarity" with the vision quest work she had previously undertaken in the Mexican countryside. She felt a kinship with Japanese culture; though it was so distinct in social practices, she found many points of similarity, "the people are so generous," she says. It left Vargas with the desire to investigate further, to meet more teachers, to understand the lineage, the terminology, and more of the intellectual dimensions of Hijikata's provocation. The Keio University Hijikata Archive was one of the main organizers of the events and had presented an exhibition in the museum. Vargas met head archivist Takeshi Morishita and invited him to come to Mexico the following year.

In 2016, LEDTR's producing of workshops and performances by foreign guest artists coalesced into its own large-scale festival, Cuerpos en Revuelta: Festival Internacional de Danza Butoh, presented in March and April 2016. For Vargas, the idea of the festival was to "give students a training and a framework so that butoh was not just therapy" (Eugenia Vargas, pers. comm., March 18, 2018). With the support of Museo Universitario del Chopo, LEDTR organized an impressive month-long series, featuring invited Japanese guests Hiroko and Koichi Tamano, Yukio Suzuki, and Kumotaro Mukai, which, the organizers noted in press materials, represented three distinct generations of butoh in the lineage of Hijikata. Also drawing performers from the new generation of dancers in Mexico, the festival featured Espartaco Martínez, and Vargas and her company LEDTR. And building the dialogue across Latin America, the festival invited Chilean performer Natalia Cuéllar, director of Compañía Ruta de la Memoria, and organizer of the Chilean Butoh Festival FiButoh.

My descriptions and analysis of the festivals are informed by reviewing extensive archival footage of the proceedings for the 2016 and 2017 festivals, and my own participation in 2019.

The first iteration of Cuerpos en Revuelta in 2016 coincided with the 30-year anniversary of Hijikata's death in 1986, which the presenters took as an opportunity to create an homage to his life and work. Supported in part by the Japan Foundation Mexico, they were able to secure the participation of Morishita, director of the Hijikata Tatsumi Memorial Archive at Keio University. He brought with him several seminal pieces from the archive, including Hijikata's red dress from *Nikutai no hanran* (*Revolt of the Flesh*), the cast mold of Hijikata's foot, the acupuncture wall tapestry from *Bairu no iru* (*Rose Colored Dance*), along with numerous photographs and videos to share with Mexican audiences. Just as the San Francisco Butoh Festival had done in 1996, Cuerpos en Revuelta hosted the Hijikata Archive to introduce audiences to contextual and historical materials including costumes, photographs, performance programs, and other artifacts. Morishita gave a keynote speech and an extended panel talk as a detailed introduction to the collection, both of which had attendance at capacity. Morishita had begun work on cataloguing the butoh-fu at that point and introduced the library of movements to Mexican audiences. Simultaneously, he introduced Yukio Waguri as a living archive of the choreographies. LEDTR subsequently presented a special conference in between festivals focused entirely on Waguri; he taught, gave lectures, and set a solo piece on Vargas.

Vargas and her producing team foregrounded cross-cultural collaboration, through dual-led choreographic workshops, and also with the performance collaboration between Mukai and Martínez, who had previously danced together in Dairakudakan. Their piece *Hajimemashite* (*Nice to Meet You*) used humor and archetypal trappings of their two cultures to highlight the dual responses of fear and admiration of the Other. Martínez wore a leather thong covering adorned with feathers, and only his hands and forearms were painted white. Mukai was in full white body paint, wrapped in a loose brocade fabric, perched atop *geta* sandals, and carried a paper lantern. The pair carried on in several antics of misrecognition to Chaplin-esque ragtime music; at one point Martínez, his own face obscured in a serape blanket, balancing a pillow and a skull on top of his head, offered his hand coquettishly to Kumotaro, who took it and began to lead him in a dance.

Also, in the 2016 inaugural festival, Vargas and LEDTR presented *Voraz* (*Voracious*), a treatise on violence, particularly against women, in Mexico. The all-female cast directed by Vargas included Carlos, Arreola, Raquel Salgado, Marcela Vásquez, Liliana Segovia, and Fernanda Palacios. The dancers crawl out from a black fabric that covers the entire stage; one woman emerges barely from the waist up, through a hole that leaves the rest of the fabric around her waist like a skirt. They share their place in the shadows, their subjugated existence. In one scene, a woman is sprawled on the ground with her clothes pulled down around her ankles. Another woman crouches over her, as if trying to identify the body. These are horrifying images of the plight of women in Mexico, which have become all too commonplace. A central image in the work was a mandrake, a medicinal plant used in ritual practice that causes hallucinations. Vargas related the theme of femicides to this surreal experience because, she says, "our land is sown with dead bodies, fertilized by all of these disappeared bodies," a horrifying presence which she feels under the surface of daily life. LEDTR had begun work on *Voraz* in 2014 when they presented a version at the Segundo Encuentro de Butoh Latinoamericano.

Also, as a part of the 2016 Cuerpos en Revuelta festival, the producers created and screened a short documentary that was a moving tribute to the life and work of Ko Murobushi. Murobushi had sadly passed away of a heart attack at the airport in Mexico City the previous year. The series of slides from his archives are underscored by an indigenous funeral dirge, "Música para los muertos" (Music for the dead), giving him a proper Mexican send-off to the beyond. Audiences were treated to a visual history lesson in the process: the first group images in the film show him in 1972 with the founding members of Dairakudakan, all shirtless and glowering at the camera, and a 1974 sultry shot of founding female dancers of Ariadone, his collaboration with Carlotta Ikeda, lounging among costumes with an equally hardened stare. There are also numerous quotes from Murobushi peppered throughout the four-and-a-half-minute video. Mexican scholar/artist Jonathan Caudillo had published a book that elaborated on references to Nietzsche, Foucault, Deleuze, and Artaud in Murobushi's writing and dancing: *Cuerpo, crueldad y diferencia en la danza butoh: una Mirada filosófica*, in 2105. Not only was Murobushi a beloved dancer in Mexico, but there was also a Spanish-language text about his work that helped make him even more legible to these audiences. Theater director Oceransky also produced numerous symposia with Murobushi over the years. In many ways, the tribute to Murobushi was a primer for understanding the materials brought by the Hijikata Archive, made more familiar by the deep local connection to this artist.

The first festival was a resounding success, with sold-out houses and workshops at capacity. Co-organizer Teresa Carlos notes that the performances attracted curious people off the street, moving butoh well beyond the typical avant-garde dance audience. With this success, LEDTR was able to secure renewed support from Museo el Chopo, as well as critical funding from FONCA.

The Second Festival of Cuerpos en Revuelta was again organized with the collaboration of el Museo del Chopo and featured Japanese dancers Makiko Tominaga (former Dairakudakan dancer based in Berlin, and the first butoh teacher in Chile), Atsushi Takenouchi, Takao Kawaguchi, and Taketeru Kudo.

Kawaguchi performed his *About Kazuo Ohno* homage, in which he replicated movements of the muse from videos of his work, giving a new generation of dancers the chance to experience the pieces in some fashion (Ohno had performed at the Cervantino in 1989).

Natalia Cuéllar (Chile) returned for a second year in a row, strengthening the connection between the Chilean and Mexican butoh communities. Noted Mexican contemporary dancer Lola Lince performed *The Human Animal*, influenced by her work with Natsu Nakajima since 2007. The press release described it as Kafka-esque. Lince, in all black clothing with bright red lipstick, danced, spoke, and buried herself in furniture. And El Laboratorio Escénico Danza Teatro Ritual performed a site-specific installation work entitled *La Noche del Mundo IV* (*Night of the Earth IV*). The piece was set in a museum and featured the large black cloth that had been used in *Voraz*, with a dancer placed high on a pedestal.

Within the 2017 Festival, the organizers chose to call attention to those artists who have been influenced by butoh profoundly, though they may not consider themselves to be butoh dancers as such. This program, entitled "Variaciones Butoh," featured all Mexican artists in a showcase-style performance of short pieces. Choreographers presenting included José Bravo, Marta Arellano, and Carlos Cruz. One dancer was painted head to toe in shiny, black, tar-like paint with a jaguar mask. Others had masks and clothing that drew connections with Mexican indigenous cultures. One trio of female dancers in red dresses, directed by Bravo, danced in a more contemporary dance style, mixed with cat-like gestures.

The academic symposium featured two luminaries, Mexican dance writer Emilio Gustavo Rosales and American butoh scholar Bruce Baird, discussing the globalization of butoh and also the specific permutations in Mexico. Rosales grounded their joint conversation by discussing the antecedents of physical theater in Mexico, through Jerzy Grotowski and Eugenio Barba, as well as the influence of surrealist filmmaker Alejandro Jodorowsky.

Shortly following on from the May 2017 festival was a residency with Yukio Waguri in August of the same year. Waguri gave workshops and presented a conference on Hijikata's butoh-fu, which he had begun to re-create for a photo and video library at Keio University, along with dancer Moe Yamamoto, under the direction of Morishita.

Waguri also directed Vargas in a solo which would premiere at Los Talleres in August 2017 and then was presented again in the third Cuerpos en Revuelta Festival. Waguri's choreography departed from Shakespeare's Ophelia, "a woman threatened by shadows of loneliness, melancholy, and insanity" (LEDTR 2019). Vargas worked with Hijikata's butoh-fu (interpreted through Waguri), drawing from visual images from Francis Bacon, Paul Delvaux, and Hans Bellmer. The dance was entirely choreographed and featured several elaborate costumes. Recognizable Hijikata cum Waguri butoh-fu appeared in the dance, including the stamping bull and hands as lotus blossom. Rendered on Vargas' body with her long flowing black hair, expressive face, and black and white Spanish-style dress, the choreography took on a distinct quality of theatrical tragedy.

The next major project for Vargas was a residency with Tadashi Endo, during which he choreographed the second piece for *Umbría* [loosely translated as *Shadows*] (which would become the first section of the trilogy when performed) (see Figure 4.4). She worked with Endo intensively for a period of several weeks. The final piece was largely improvisational in nature, using the working methods of Kazuo Ohno. Vargas appears in a voluminous black dress with irregularly placed bright red accents. Her movement resembles an insect, segmented, moving one isolated "feeler" at a time. Her face reads less of the open-mouth pathos than the section with Waguri, and her eyes lead the facial dance in this section. A black fishing net serves as the main prop. It is wrapped in a ball at the top of the piece, and she pulls it apart as if alternately looking for insects and weaving it anew. In the end, it becomes the dancer's cocoon or tomb, as it envelopes her body.

Following these two residencies, Vargas choreographed her own response to the work, using as inspiration the instance of so-called veiled births, when a baby is born in a closed amniotic sac and must emerge a second time into the world. Wearing a pure white dress and covered in a clear plastic tarp, the dancer was pelted with red liquid that dripped from above. She fought against the coverings and writhed in the muck, which to her symbolized red earth

Figure 4.4 Umbría. Photo of Eugenia Vargas, 2019.

Source: Photo by César Alberto Guzmán

and a connection to the land. In a reference to the violence of birth, she notes, "life is raw, cruel, but also marvelous" (Eugenia Vargas, pers. comm., July 22, 2021). Unwittingly for me as a viewer, it also called forth images of violence in contemporary Mexican life and connected to earlier themes in her company piece, *Voraz*. Vargas presented the *Umbría Trilogy* during the Third Cuerpos en Revuelta festival, this time organized in collaboration not with El Chopo but rather the Coordinación Nacional de Danza at Centro Cultural del Bosque, a part of the Instituto Nacional de Bellas Artes.

Featured guests in the Third Cuerpos en Revuelta included experimental Japanese choreographer Kakuya Ohashi, whose works express an uber-contemporary take on Hijikata's choreographic prompts, butoh luminary Saga Kobayashi, one of the most important female dancers in Hijikata's Tohoku Kabuki period alongside Yoko Ashikawa, and Berlin-based Minako Seki, original member of DanceLoveMachine and founder of Tatoeba with Yumiko Yoshioka and Delta Rai. This wide-ranging program gave Mexican audiences yet further iterations of butoh inspiration as applied to Ohashi's contemporary dance, Seki's physical theater, and Kobayashi's presenting of the absurd in a Becket-esque cabaret style. The academic portion of the conference featured talks by philosopher/theater director Jonathan Caudillo speaking about Murobushi and Butoh in Mexico, myself speaking about butoh in the United States, and Doctor Francisco Gómez Mont, director del Centro de Investigación en Neurohumanidades, speaking about neuroimagery and the arts.

The advent of COVID-19 pushed 2020 events online; however, Vargas and her team embraced the challenge and produced a number of virtual dance performances and workshops. As they have reflected over their past festivals, Vargas says that the producing team is interested in presenting artists for a longer period of time, to foster deeper collaborations and experiences for the growing Mexican butoh community. One special project that Vargas is cultivating is a collaboration across three generations of female butoh artists: Makiko Tominaga, Rhea Volij, and Natalia Cuéllar. For future research, Vargas is interested in Hijikata's butoh-fu that is currently being catalogued at the Keio University Archive. Vargas is also interested in branching out to related techniques, such as the methods of Japanese theater director Tadashi Suzuki. The appetite for butoh and similar styles and techniques remains strong in Mexico.

Shinichi Iova-Koga/inkBoat (b. 1968 Santa Clara, California, Current Residence: Lucerne, Switzerland)

Shinichi Iova-Koga's inkBoat[7] is arguably the most prominent performance company to have grown out of the San Francisco Bay Area butoh scene launched by the Tamanos. Iova-Koga has cultivated a presence throughout the United States and abroad, mostly in Western Europe but also in Japan. His company has been awarded numerous prestigious awards and grants including several National Endowment for the Arts, Mellon Foundation, and Rockefeller MAP grants. And he has successfully garnered support in the "mainstream"

American dance world when he made it onto the coveted Dance Magazine "25 to Watch" list in 2007, the first American butoh dancer to ever receive coverage in the magazine (Felciano 2007).

Having collaborated with and been influenced by artists as diverse as Ralph Lemon,[8] Anna Halprin, and Ruth Zaporah, Iova-Koga waivers on his identification with butoh. "Certainly it's an important piece of me," he says, "but it's not the complete picture." He is often marketed as a butoh dancer, but he uses the term less and less frequently in his own publicity materials. Iova-Koga's work is cohesive, poetic, and highly crafted. It has also had many chapters in the course of his career, with the promise of new chapters yet to come.

Iova-Koga found his way to butoh through a performance by former Hoppo-Butoh-ha dancer Yuko Yuki's company Suzuran-toh at NOHspace in San Francisco in 1991. The piece was *Ezo-men*, choreographed by Bishop Yamada, leader of Hoppo-Butoh-ha. Iova-Koga recalls, "My attention remained riveted to the smallest motion. Energy and gesture were brutally economized" (Iova-Koga 2019, 533). At the time he was pursuing his BA in film production at San Francisco State, where he also took numerous theater courses. The butoh performance spoke to his developing "dark, shadowing aesthetic . . . in my photography of dead, decayed, rotting rats; my films of lonely people gathered in dank cellars, cutting onions and crying" (Iova-Koga 2019, 534). Koga had previously studied photography at Cal Poly San Luis Obispo from 1986 to 1990. Just three months shy of graduating from the photography program, he transferred to the Film program at SF State. He was also very active in theater during his time at Cal Poly, where he had founded Vox Theater which included inkBoat set designer Frank Lee and the current Chair of the inkBoat board, May Yong.

The physical rigor of butoh appealed to Iova-Koga, as he had grown up practicing judo with his father, Yuzo Koga. His father had emigrated to the United States in 1963 to compete in the US Judo Nationals, which he won in his weight group from 1964 to 1968.[9] Says Iova-Koga, "I was in the dojo as a baby. Judo was all around me. Japanese martial arts were just a part of my growing up" (Shinichi Iova-Koga, pers. comm., May 11, 2021). He studied with his father and other members at the judo club from eight years old until he was 17. Throughout the course of his career, he would explore numerous traditional Japanese arts, including *shakuhachi* (with Masayuki Koga, no relation), Aikido (black belt, teachers include Jan Nevelius, Jorma Lily, and Cornelius Jaeger-Herzog), Kagura (Shinto ritual ceremonial dance), Nihon Buyo (classical dance that forms part of Kabuki), and most significantly Noh theater, which he continues to study and practice.

Exposure to butoh and Suzuki Method of Actor Training marked the beginning of Iova-Koga's conscious pursuit of Japanese performing arts. At San Francisco State University (SFSU) in the early 1990s, he was primarily taking theater classes with Professor Yukihiro Goto, who introduced him to Tadashi Suzuki's training methods and also brought in guest butoh teachers. Goto organized a workshop for Yuko Yuki when she came through San Francisco on tour, and also brought the locally based Tamanos in for a masterclass. Goto invited Haku-tobo dancer Akeno Ashikawa to teach and perform at the university over the course of a week, and at that point Iova-Koga began to take much more notice of his alignment with butoh methods and aesthetics. His interest piqued, Iova-Koga sought out the Tamanos classes and began to train with Hiroko in 1991.

After graduating from SFSU in 1992, Iova-Koga began to study more intensively with Hiroko. His induction into Harupin-Ha is indicative of the organic way in which that company grew and established community: Iova-Koga describes standing side by side with Hiroko preparing *onigiri* for a *taiko* festival. In the middle of their rhythmic meal production, Hiroko paused momentarily and asked: "Hey, do you want to dance with us?" to which he replied "sure" to which she replied "good" and then they went back to scooping and pressing the *onigiri*, with the matter settled (Shinichi Iova-Koga, pers. comm., May 11, 2021). For the next few years, he too would be pressed and molded, like the *onigiri*, into the lineage of Hijikata's butoh.

It is worth noting that he was not exclusively practicing butoh or even Japanese styles, perhaps indicative of his continued fusion of forms. From 1993 to 1997, he also performed in Larry Reed's Shadowlight Theater in San Francisco. Through dedicated practice Reed had become recognized as a Shadow Master in Balinese shadow puppetry. Reed then began to adapt the intimate traditional work, projecting onto giant video screens at Fort Mason's Cowell Theater. For Iova-Koga, it transformed the result into a different art form, heavily influenced by the original yet something wholly unique. I find this significant in Iova-Koga's own trajectory as an artist, in that he himself has digested myriad forms and re-imagined them through his own lens. In fact, the article he wrote for the *Routledge Butoh Companion* was titled "Burn butoh, start again" which to me sums up his improvisational path through his career. It's not to say that Iova-Koga is at all casual about the forms he studies; in fact he is quite the opposite, diving deeply into intensive study for periods of time. But with a true improviser's practice, he draws on the skills he has studied and puts them into motion in the moment.

Iova-Koga officially joined the Harupin-Ha's production of *Goblins* in 1993,[10] which performed in Nevada City, La Criee National Theater of Marseille, and San Francisco at Theater Artaud. Iova-Koga recalls being impressed with the placement of butoh in large mainstream theaters in France; they performed in a venue where Merce Cunningham was the next engagement. In each location, *Goblins* employed additional chorus dancers. In contrast, butoh in the United States was then and remains largely in "experimental" theaters. When *Goblins* returned to San Francisco's Theater Artaud, Molly Barrons[11] joined the production and became one of the longest standing company members to work with the Tamanos. Through the production, Iova-Koga met his first wife, Alenka Mullin, who was one of the primary dancers in the Harupin-Ha and toured along with Iova-Koga and the Tamanos to Marseille.

Iova-Koga and Mullin began collaborations in life and art, and by 1994 they had formed their own company, Uro Teatr Koku. Their first works included a solo *Silent Mind* for Shinichi, and the ensemble piece *Desert Body*. One version of that piece was presented for the Street Theater Festival and included musicians Dan Rathbun, Nils Frykdahl, Eugene Gen (all of the band Idiot Flesh), and Carla Kihlstedt. A second version was their Uro Teatr Koku collaboration with Kihlstedt, Rathbun, and Frykdahl, which also featured performer Erica Blue (soloist). They performed at 964 Natoma Gallery which was a rather unusual space; there was a second floor above and a dropped floor below where Rathbun was flaring up an arc welder, setting off sparks and making a deafening industrial sound score. Iova-Koga notes "It was the kind of stuff that would be totally illegal in any normal theatrical context" (Shinichi Iova-Koga, pers. comm., May 25, 2018). In this and other production elements, Iova-Koga and these musicians tested the limits of performance in their early work.

The collaboration with Idiot Flesh was noteworthy for numerous reasons, not least of which is the fact that Iova-Koga repeated the Tamano's late 1970s/early 1980s practice of incorporating avant-garde musicians as physical theater performers in his work. Idiot Flesh was a giant of the avant-garde scene in the 1990s, and Iova-Koga performed with them in loud, unruly rock clubs, affording him a similar kind of experience as early butoh practitioners had in cabarets. People were drunk, talked over your act, and occasionally spilled things on you. The stakes were high and one learned quickly how to hold an audience's attention.

Iova-Koga became involved with Idiot Flesh because of a chance encounter with guitarist Gene Jun, who worked in a record store where he had gone looking for a copy of Belgian composer Nicholas Len's *Flamma Flamma*, or *Fire Requiem*, a contemporary operatic tour de force originally produced in 1993. The two struck up a conversation, and Shinichi revealed that he was a butoh dancer, which elicited an invitation back to their live/work studio The Nursery, where lead vocalist/guitarist Nils Frykdahl had photocopies out of *Butoh: Shades of Darkness*,[12] plastered all over his wall. The connection was instant. The first performance of Iova-Koga and then-wife Alenka Mullin did with Idiot Flesh was at the Stork Club in Oakland, dancing on a pool table during the musical set.

Idiot Flesh was an exemplary performance/prog rock music group that was highly experimental in their shows, often beginning with the band members and other performers processing through the audience. There were puppeteers, acrobatic fire bearers, and characters of all sorts in this motley parade. Iova-Koga performed in numerous shows and recalls walking around with a torch in his mouth from time to time. The revelers would enter the venue from the street and surround the audience before performing their opening number, *Dead Like Us*. One Bay Area musician and future inkBoat lighting designer who was present for numerous Idiot Flesh shows described it as "Burning Man before there was Burning Man" (Allen Willner, pers. comm., May 1, 2021). The musicians wore fantastical costumes and Goth makeup, and put on an epic show.

Iova-Koga performed with Idiot Flesh and their subsequent band, Sleepy-time Gorilla Museum, in the Bay Area and on tour. Their extreme, driving rhythms were matched by his daring physicality. In one act they created to the song *Sleep Is Wrong*, the band is asleep at the mic and mumbling incoherently, while Iova-Koga tosses and turns in a full-sized bed on the stage. As the song picks up speed, Iova-Koga is slowly dragged out of bed upside down, where he dangles by his ankles, thrashing for the majority of the seven-minute song.

Iova-Koga/Mullin's company Uro Teatr Koku was essentially their duets performing with members of Idiot Flesh (see Figure 4.5). Also involved was the exceptional violinist/vocalist Carla Kihlstedt, who was the partner of Idiot Flesh drummer Wes Anderson and also a member of the Bay Area band Charming Hostess, with Nina Rolle and Jewlia Eisenberg.

Both Mullin and Iova-Koga joined Yumiko Yoshioka's workshop in SF in 1996. Yoshioka then invited them both to join a project she was doing in a stone quarry in Graz, Austria. When Yoshioka saw their work, she commented that Iova-Koga looked like "a little Tamano" (Iova-Koga 2020, 536). Rita Felciano reviewed Uro Teatro Koku's *Desert Body* negatively for this very reason which was challenging but nonetheless he felt that she was "spot on." As his work progressed, Felciano became one of his biggest supporters. Though Iova-Koga

Figure 4.5 inkBoat in *Falling Dust* at Orph Theater, Berlin (1999). Performers left to right: Carla Kihlstedt, Andrea Splisgar, Crow Nishimura, Shinichi Iova-Koga, Dan Rathbun, Nils Frykdahl.

Source: Photo by Marcus Lieberenz, reprinted with permission from Shinichi Iova-Koga/inkBoat

and Mullin had many ideas about making new work for Uro, reflecting back on it, Iova-Koga feels like the movement style was "copying as a way to learn, as a process of finding who I am in dance" (Shinichi Iova-Koga, pers. comm., May 25, 2018).

What took his dance in a new direction was interaction with Germany-based Yumiko Yoshioka. Iova-Koga and Mullin were also members of Yoshioka's company, TEN PEN CHii, based at their center Schloss Broellin two hours north of Berlin in Germany. They lived in Germany, performing, training, and developing the networks that would help give inkBoat its international presence. In 1997, Iova-Koga and Mullin performed in Yoshioka's site-specific piece in a quarry, *Der Letze Klang der Erde* [*The Last Sound of the Earth*], in which also participated the Russian butoh company Do Theatre. During this performance, they met Ksenia Vidyaykina, a member of Do Theatre who later collaborated with Iova-Koga on *We Ain't Got No Home in this World Anymore*.

The Iova-Koga/Mullin duo performed in TEN PEN CHii in numerous subsequent performances, including *DA-PPi*[13] (Graz, Austria, 1998), *Jikken No. 11* (Germany, 1998), and *Test Labor*[14] (Germany and Stettin, Poland, 1998). Yoshioka's partner Joachim Manger created industrial sets for the company, such as giant water tanks in which the dancers submerged, swam through, and climbed out of, wet bodies clinging to harsh metal frames. The sets were punishing, and Iova-Koga remembers being bruised throughout the creative process. The visuals were quite stunning and combined the frailty of human bodies, strong as they may be, with the gigantic, unforgiving steel structures. They performed in several important experimental theaters, including Orpheum Theatre in Graz, Tacheles in Berlin, and Theatre am Halleshes Ufer in Berlin, famous for well-funded experimental arts productions.

By 1998, Iova-Koga and Mullin's marriage had unraveled, and they dissolved their company. Yoshioka had invited them to teach and perform in the butoh festival she produced at Schloss Broellin, eX . . . it! at the end of 1999, but only Iova-Koga went. Among the other choreographers at the 1999 eXit! were Imre Thormann, Sabine Seume, and Kokoro Dance (Vancouver). At that festival, Crow was a student in Koga's workshop and performed in the first work-in-progress showing of *Cockroach*. Crow then performed in multiple versions of *Cockroach* in San Francisco, Seattle, and toured with inkBoat to Germany. Iova-Koga was impressed with her, saying that though she was still young in her butoh training, she had amazing instincts and was "tapped into something" (Shinichi Iova-Koga, pers. comm., May 25, 2018). I joined the company at this time as well, having met Iova-Koga in a three-month Ruth Zaporah training beginning in January 2000.[15]

After the dissolution of Uro Teatr Koku, Mullin worked in Germany for a period, designing costumes for Yoshioka and also Minako Seki. It was in this capacity that she became a collaborator in Iova-Koga's new company, inkBoat. Mullin co-designed costumes for *Cockroach* and *Onion*. She also hosted the company in residence near Mendocino, California, where she was living in an arts collective.

Cockroach was a large-scale performance, with a cast of 15 including Sleepy-time Gorilla Museum playing live as characters in the piece. The first version, presented in the San Francisco Butoh Festival in 2000, featured the band members in rolling tables with mic'd food that they ate in time with the Kurt Weill song *What Keeps Mankind Alive*. Wearing protruding bellies made of tire innertubes, the roaches (Kinji Hayashi, Leigh Evans, Iova-Koga, and myself) emerged out of a slit in a giant lace dress that was hanging from a 15-foot ladder, while its wearer (Cassie Tunick in San Francisco and German tour, Eugenio Brodbeck in Seattle, bedecked in pearls and sporting a beehive hairdo) gasped and feigned horror. Degenerate Art Ensemble's Crow emerged from a decrepit playpen and discovered some cake which she gleefully ate. DAE's Joshua Kohl entered as an exterminator complete with an old-fashioned canister and gassed the roaches. Nils Frykdahl, in characteristically tongue-in-cheek bravado, sang "Cockroach, your problems are not mine/I love life but with you I draw the line/not to flaunt my superior design/but next to you I'm practically divine." The piece ended with the roaches coughing up the poison and clamoring through the audience, in search of more food.

The work toured to the Seattle Butoh Festival and then on to Germany, where the company was in residence at Schloss Broellin and Fabrik Potsdam, and also shot a film in Sanssouci in Potsdam directed by Eric Koziol[16] (HGun, Stanford). Following the creative process of *Cockroach* from beginning to end, Koziol crafted another work entitled *The Duchess*, using the characters and actions from *Cockroach*. Some original cast members could not join the tour: Hayashi had visa restrictions, and Sleepytime Gorilla Museum had a conflicting touring schedule as a band.

inkBoat was in Berlin on 9/11. We were scheduled to perform on September 13 and instead were attending peace rallies at Brandenburger Tor. The flood of support from Germans for Americans was impressive during this scary time, especially for those of us who were abroad and could not get home because all flights to the United States were grounded. Four members still performed an improvisational piece, and the rest were too shell-shocked to be on stage. Years later when I studied the origins of butoh as a protest movement against American Occupation and rapid capitalistic spread, I would find it ironic that this was only a fraction of the experience in post–World War II Japan, when nearly 300,000 lives were lost in a matter of hours and the nature of a culture changed radically within a decade. Life seemed so vulnerable and precarious. A punk-inspired reaction like butoh seemed apt.

Following the tour, the cast shifted, and Iova-Koga recruited Kaseki to perform the role of the Duchess in *Cockroach* in the final version of the piece at Theater Artaud. Kaseki and Iova-Koga began collaborating on several new pieces, including the ensemble piece *Onion* (with Crow and Sten Rudstrøm) and their duet *Ame to Ame* (with director and lighting designer Marc Ates). Iova-Koga and Kaseki had met during the 2000 San Francisco Butoh Festival when she was a dancer in Anzu Furukawa's company. She was based in Berlin, and the two had reconnected when inkBoat was on tour in 2001.

Iova-Koga pursued a number of different collaborations in the next few years, including one with Takuya Ishide and Yuri Nagaoka in Tokyo, and with Kaseki, Minako Seki, Sten Rudstrøm, Yael Karavan, Tadashi Endo, and Nils Willers in Berlin: a site-specific group called adapt. One of their breathtaking stagings included *Glass Anatomies (2002)*, a re-make of material from *Cockroach* performed above a glass-domed ceiling with the audience watching from below. Iova-Koga also joined Germany-based Russian physical theater troupe Do Theatre as a dancer for numerous productions of *Bird's Eye View* and *Nonsense* in 2004 and 2005, touring in France, Germany, Italy, Monaco, and the United States.

Iova-Koga met his wife Dana while teaching an outdoor workshop in the mountains of Montana. Dana had danced ballet from the ages of 4 until 11 in Asheville, NC. Her parents encouraged her creativity. She studied theater, dance, visual arts, creative writing, and finally narrowed down her preference to theater. She attended North Carolina School of the Arts in high school for Theater, and then went to New York University from 1994 to 1997 and studied in the Experimental Theater Wing, where she discovered her affinity for physical theater. She studied butoh with Maureen Fleming (her first butoh teacher), Viewpoints with Mary Overlie, Grotowski Plastiques with Steven Wangh,[17] voice with Jonathan Hart (Roy Hart's son), Feldenkrais, Contact Improv, and many other forms. Her teacher and mentor Tamar Rogoff told her about an audition with Min Tanaka for the *Poe Project* inspired by the work of Edgar Allen Poe. Iova-Koga was cast, as was New York-based artist Zachary Fuller, and she traveled to Japan for a three-month workshop with Tanaka's company. Dana fell in love with the process of farming as training, and the slow cultivation of patience and attention. Tanaka asked her back into a second project inspired by Antonin Artaud and the conquest of Mexico, entitled *La Conquista*. She was working for an import/export company in India at the time (through another contact of Rogoff's) and traveled back and forth to Japan for the next few years when Tanaka invited her into various projects. In 2000, he founded a second company, Tokason, and invited Dana to join.

During her time with Tanaka, Dana experienced farming as training, some MB (mind–body/muscle–bone) work, and then a great deal of autonomy to create her own movement sequences. Tanaka would give them a title/theme and a time limit, and the dancers would go up to a small studio up the mountain and create something independently for Tanaka to then shape. The shared community brought an added intensity to the research. Though Dana did not have previous farming experience, she grew up gardening with her parents, and her grandfather was a farmer, so the work was not foreign to her. The dancers in the company at that time were Dana, Fuller, Milvia Martínez, Macarena Ortuzar, a Brazilian dancer by the name of Jorge, two young Japanese dancers/farmers named Kiku and Yuji, Tanaka's Partner Rin, and the four main dancers of Hakushu: Maureen Phelan, Yasunari Tamai, Kazu, and Keshi Suzuki who helped found the new dance company and tea farm an hour away. Dana and the other dancers from Tokason helped with the rice harvest and miso production at Hakushu, and the dancers there came to help with the tea, so there was definite cross-over between the communities. At the same time, the new company was part of Tanaka's separation from Body Weather and exploration in new directions. The work Dana was involved in was much more subtle than Piñón's descriptions of running into brick walls and lighting corn husk phalluses on fire; in one piece, she describes being covered with delicate shards of bamboo charcoal, and their task was to dance without breaking a single piece. In another piece, they had to smile the entire time for over an hour. The challenges were subtle yet sustained. Though less brutal than Tanaka's early work, there was still an element of disquietude in the space throughout the creative process. Dana identifies the experience of being comfortable with discomfort as fundamental to Tanaka's process, as well as an ability to be alone. These were radical lessons for her as a young performer, who had been accustomed to being in community and needing validation from others; "it was good for me" she emphasizes (Dana Iova-Koga, pers. comm., June 7, 2021).

Following her time in Japan, she moved to Maui at the end of 2002 to help care for a family friend's land. It was the total opposite experience, one of balance and harmony, and she simply cared for the land and did not feel compelled to make much art other than landscaping.

In 2005, she felt ready to dance more seriously again and found a workshop that Shinichi was giving at CounterPulse in San Francisco. She was eager to study again but what really caught her eye about the announcement was a picture of Shinichi as a child wearing a yukata; "I fell in love with little tiny Shin" she says (Dana Iova-Koga, pers. comm., June 7, 2021). At the conclusion of the two-day workshop, he announced an upcoming longer workshop in Montana. Though she already had plans, she canceled them and attended. At the conclusion of the Montana workshop, he proposed.

One of the Iova-Koga's shared dreams was to have a studio out in nature, on some land where they could grow food and be inspired by their surroundings. It so happened that Sleepytime Gorilla Museum's bassist Dan Rathbun's parents had such a place in the Lost Coast region of Northern California, and so Shinichi and Dana went to live there with their young daughter Zoë and serve as caretakers to Rathbun's aging parents. While there they planted a sizeable garden, planted many fruit trees, and refinished a raw barn structure to serve as a dance studio. For many years, they held annual Dance on Land workshops where participants camped on what they had dubbed inkGround and spent a few weeks dancing in nature.

Says Dana, "learning to wait and to watch and to observe are some of the greatest gifts I got from Tanaka." Though Tanaka and most Japanese butoh artists eschew any connections to Buddhist practice, Dana sensed a connection in methodology:

> Being on the farm is very much what I imagine being in a monastery is like, except that we weren't being trained to sit and observe our thoughts but rather to dance. So *how* we washed the dishes, *how* we cooked the rice,

how we weeded, *how* we dug the potatoes . . . all of that was *it*; it wasn't like it was supplemental, that *was* the training.

(Dana Iova-Koga, pers. comm., June 7, 2021)

Dana adapted these lessons into her own practice, which interestingly had been informed by the Buddhist inflection of Experimental Theater Wing (ETW) director Wendell Beavers, who later went on to direct the Performance Program at the Tibetan Buddhist Naropa Institute in Boulder, Colorado. Says Dana,

It's about patience, presence, paying attention, understanding what your body is doing, understanding all the forces around . . . if you're living your life as if everything is informing you, or everything is training, I think that makes you present in a certain way . . . I got the feeling that for him, everything was important, and with that kind of being, there's a there-ness.

(Dana Iova-Koga, pers. comm., June 7, 2021)

The ways in which they have shifted since coming together are marked. When I was with the company in 2000, the aesthetic was more along the lines of highly stylized radical performance art. The turn Shinichi has since taken is along a beautiful, subtle, delicate path. I initially thought this was Dana's influence until I talked with them individually again and realized that they met at a time when they were both ready for a shift in their own practices. And both artists have expressed their growing interest in the healing arts as a means of discovering subtlety and practices that will sustain them in the long term.

Dana met the legendary dance artist Anna Halprin through Tanaka when Tokason went on tour and in the California leg of their journey they danced on her deck at her Mountain Home Studio. Looking back, Dana finds it so strange that the two artists were friends, because they were vastly different. Both worked in nature but from such different approaches. Later, when Dana worked with Halprin with inkBoat, she felt like her studies with Tanaka became integrated with her previous practices. Studying with Halprin, a pioneering female artist whose influence flowed through a generation of teachers that Dana had studied with but had not been aware of the roots at the time, felt like going to the source of sources for Dana. She noted that as Halprin was of her own American culture, the lessons from Tanaka from dancing in nature came home to her in a different way in her study with Halprin.

Shinichi made *Milk Traces* in 2007, inspired by the birth of his daughter Zoë. Based on a positive review in the SF Chronicle, Anna Halprin decided she wanted to meet him. She contacted Sherwood Chen, a butoh dancer who had worked with Halprin years before, and asked him to arrange a lunch meeting. They hit it off, and Halprin invited the company to rehearse *c(H)ord* at her studio and get feedback from her in the creation process.

It was in *c(H)ord* (performed at Yerba Buena Theater in San Francisco) that Iova-Koga really began to integrate vocal work from his training in Action

Theater, and also singing/screaming/toning by Dohee Lee. This was also the first company piece that Dana Iova-Koga performed in. Another Min Tanaka student, Sherwood Chen who was in Maijuku, also began collaborating with the company.

In addition to the innovation of voice work, Iova-Koga welcomed the influence of Anna Halprin on his work. In addition to having her guidance on his own creative process, he became involved in hers. For Halprin, Iova-Koga served as the Associate Director on *Spirit of Place* and *Parades and Changes*. Subsequently, she made a duet for Shinichi and Dana entitled *Song of Songs* or *In the Fever of Love*, based on erotic drawings that her husband Lawrence sent to her during wartime. The story of these drawings is fantastic and romantic. According to the story, Lawrence was headed into battle and made her a series of drawings, not knowing if he would return. He tossed them to a passing ship for delivery to Anna. The drawings were dutifully sent to her in New York, but she had already left to come to San Francisco. Both Lawrence and the drawings made it back to her eventually. After he died, Halprin wanted to make an homage to their relationship, and this was the work she choreographed on Shinichi and Dana.

From Halprin, Iova-Koga feels like he got a new point of view, specifically the process of framing a work with the Resource, Score, Valuation, Performance (RSVP) Cycles scoring process, developed by her husband Lawrence for landscape architecture, dance, or any creative endeavor, whereby all of the different players involved in the process understood the intentions and resources necessary for realizing the project. The RSVP Cycles shifted the director's role from one of simply giving orders to one of revealing the entire process with the collaborative team. Iova-Koga then used that same process in his making of *95 Rituals*, his homage to Anna Halprin. This shared ownership of the creative process was one that Iova-Koga had long been interested in and attempted to instill, but frequently in the larger ensemble pieces the cast members would want him to "just direct." In the making of *95 Rituals*, with a cast of 12 people, many of whom were directors of their own work with strong opinions, the RSVP Cycles served to develop the language and method for these creative voices to share points of view and an aesthetic diversity in the creation of a single event.

Following the time with Halprin, Iova-Koga experimented with levels of control as a director, determining various levels of autonomy for the performers, particularly with his students at Mills College in Oakland, California, where he was full-time faculty from 2009 to 2017. He taught butoh, composition, and Japanese avant-garde performing art perspectives. He would direct works with students by either setting each movement precisely or providing improvisational scores for dancers to inhabit. He describes each as equally satisfying, which is an interestingly fluid process to see within one artist.

Iova-Koga sought out other great artists as mentors/collaborators, including Ruth Zaporah, Ralph Lemon, and Ko Murobushi. With Zaporah, he had begun the Action Theater training in 2000 when I first met him. He continued collaborations with master Action Theater teachers Sten Rudstrøm and Cassie Tunick, including *Onion, Our Breath is as Thin as a Hummingbird's Spine*, *95 Rituals*, and an ongoing (22 years at the time of writing) improvisation series with Tunick entitled *The Smallest Country*. Certified Action Theater teachers train with Zaporah every May for an intensive period, and Iova-Koga began joining this group in 2014. He received certification to teach Action Theater in 2016.

Iova-Koga began a four-year collaboration with Ko Murobushi in 2008 that would culminate in *Crazy Cloud* (see Figure 4.6), premiering at Theater Artaud in San Francisco, and playing subsequently at The Bride in Philadelphia and CAVE in New York. Their work began at inkGround in the Northern California Lost Coast. In 2010, they were in residence at the Maggie Allesee National Center for Choreography at Florida State University, an epicenter of contemporary dance creation. Again, Iova-Koga was the first butoh dancer to cross into the mainstream contemporary dance scene, with Kota Yamazaki following in 2017. The performers in *Crazy Cloud* included Murobushi, Dana, Shinichi, Sherwood Chen, and Peiling Kao, a student of Iova-Koga when he was on faculty at Mills College. I observed their creative process in May 2010 at Florida State University, as they worked on the new piece inspired by the irreverent and controversial Zen monk Ikkyu Sojun.

Even as an enlightened and practicing Zen master, Ikkyu was known to frequent brothels and bars, and was an outspoken critic of what he called "false

Figure 4.6 inkBoat rehearsing *Crazy Cloud* (2012). Pictured left to right: Shinichi Iova-Koga, Peiling Kao, Ko Murobushi, Sherwood Chen.

Source: Photo by Pak Han, reprinted with permission from Shinichi Iova-Koga/inkBoat

piety" within the Zen establishment (Sanford 1980, 276–7; Keene 1966/67, 61–2). Ikkyu scholar Sanford suggests that his unorthodox behavior was his method of modeling a true "unity of opposites" and living the non-duality which Zen espoused, revealing the "artifaces and distortions" of his colleagues who also visited brothels but preached celibacy (Sanford 1980, 277).

Says Iova-Koga, the influence of Ikkyu was an evolving force in their work. Ikkyu was known to parade around skeletons, to remind us that we all die. In the first version of *Crazy Cloud*, the dancers held skulls in their hands in one scene, orbiting them around their bodies as if smudging their bodies with the awareness of their mortality. "Death and dying were constantly on our minds in the making of the piece," says Iova-Koga (Shinichi Iova-Koga, pers. comm., May 11, 2021). When they began working on it, Kazuo Ohno was still alive, though on his death bed. In one scene, they called to him in whispered hush, invoking his name and the liminal space he inhabited at that point in his life. In another scene, Tom Jones crooned "What's New Pussycat?" while the ensemble lay on their side, quivering and trembling for the entirety of the song. The juxtaposition of campy, flirty vocals and tortured bodies and blank stares underscored the absurdity of human passions.

Of Murobushi's influence, Iova-Koga says: "Murobushi helped me strip away the tendency to add more and more. He knew how to cultivate a simple moment" (Iova-Koga 2018, 536).

In a final scene, Sherwood Chen walked upstage slowly, facing away from the audience while Shinichi faced the audience, struggling to control the muscles of his face. A torrent of sand fell on Shinichi's head and knocked him to the ground as Chen silently soldiered on. Murobushi entered with a cardboard box and asked wryly, "tough day? I've been there." Murobushi proceeded to pull human skulls from the box and set them down in a line, reciting their names: "my father, my teacher, etc." The scene evoked the sands of time as we are called one by one to leave this earth.

After revisiting his dialogue with butoh through the interaction with Murobushi, Iova-Koga felt called to study traditional Japanese arts in order to "get into the sources of my sources . . . I wanted to get into Noh [in particular] because it was a foundation for the Suzuki training" that he had studied in college with Goto. He notes that both butoh and Suzuki's method are avant-garde forms, and as such do not have such a long history compared to something like Noh which originated in the 1400s. That history resonates with his Japanese heritage.

In Summer 2012, the Iova-Kogas traveled to Kyoto on a US-Japan Friendship Commission grant with their children in tow, where Shinichi studied Noh, Kagura, Shakuhachi, Aikido, and Nihon Buyo. He became especially interested in Noh vocal techniques. In Spring 2013, Jubilith Moore was offering a three-month Noh intensive training at NOHspace in San Francisco. Iova-Koga attended and this started him on a path to a focused training in Noh Theater with one of the five renowned Japanese training schools, Kita School. He subsequently studied with Kita school master teachers Akira Matsui, Kinue

Oshima, and Rick Emmert at the Noh Project Summer Intensive in Blooms-burg, Pennsylvania. (Incidentally, this renowned program was the same one that Jeff Janisheski, one of the producers of the New York Butoh Festival, had completed previously.)

In 2011, Iova-Koga collaborated with Korean experimental vocalist Dohee Lee, a traditionally trained Korean singer who had begun playing with sha-manic vocal practices, to create *Line Between*, presented at ODC Theater in San Francisco and Vancouver International Festival (2012). The work is an explora-tion of the liminal state between sleeping and waking, and vocal work bridges the places of meaning and abstraction. Dana directed and Peling Kao came in as an additional performer, creating silent tableaus to their chaotic scenes. The second iteration of the work was presented at Seoul International Dance Festival at Sejong University and featured Jubilith Moore, who brought a new edge to the vocalization with her expertise in Noh singing. The movement style seems to draw from Iova-Koga's Action Theater training, in which his body becomes the kinetic expression for the yips, shouts, and intonations of the different vocalists. The sonic range is impressive, arrhythmic, and multi-tonal. In places, Iova-Koga's dancing is not unlike his performances with Sleepytime Gorilla Museum, in which his body is shoved around by constantly changing rhythms and chords.

Following *Line Between*, Iova-Koga performed in two Noh recitals, one with Hosho school director Fuji Masayuki at San Francisco's Marines Memorial Theater in 2016, and another with Moore and Lluis Valls (a Catalonian artist who he first met when they were students together at SFSU, who had been study-ing Noh since that time) at the Haiku Festival in Ukiah, California, in 2017.

Moving deeper into traditional forms, he began to study Qigong in 2014 with Damo Mitchell of Lotus Nei Gong and David Wei of Wudang West, investigating the development of the physical, energetic, and mental aspects of human life through the lens of Daoist Internal Arts.

In 2016, he began practicing Dao Yin, Nei Gong, and Qigong more inten-sively with Mitchell, initially for the health benefits, but he quickly recog-nized the benefits of this pathway toward greater internal awareness. Some of the exercises felt familiar or parallel to work he had done with the Tama-nos, though framed differently. Gradually, his engagement with the spiritual aspect of the Daoist Arts grew, which, according to Iova-Koga, works with the physical and energetic processes of the body as the foundation to cultivat-ing a more refined consciousness. He contrasts it with Buddhist practice that starts directly with consciousness (i.e., through meditation). There are multiple metaphorical prompts in Daoist arts like "dragon playing with pearl" ("dragon" refers to spine, "pearl" refers to lower dan tian), which Iova-Koga finds simi-lar to *butoh-fu* in their dual layers of physicality and metaphor. He notes that he finds greater physical power in release rather than the bound, contractive tension that he utilized in judo. He now feels that he is currently focused on power within softness, expansive (vs. contractive) tension, coiling, and releasing within structure.

When asked: *What are you interested in doing with butoh as you take it forward?* he says:

> It's hard to say about butoh as a whole. I break things down to primary components, to foundations. Noguchi Taiso is quite interesting and useful in this regard because it looks at fundamental movement using the image of a water body. to encourage a state of being. This is in contrast to [my work in] Qigong and Action Theater, which are both more concerned with *things as they are* than things as I imagine them to be. However, using imagery allows you to be non-mechanistic, outside of linear logic. I'm deconstructing that. My interests are in the area of the "what is." Butoh was about erasing and disappearing [myself]. At a certain point I thought "well where does it go from there?"
>
> (Shinichi Iova-Koga, pers. comm., May 25, 2018)

It is going many places indeed. The Iova-Kogas began collaborating with performance artist Ann Carlson. She wrote and directed a short piece for them which brings together their explorations with text, narrative, and physical theater, called *These are the Ones We Fell Among*. They showed excerpts of this and another new work at Klein Theater in Luzern, Switzerland, in May 2021. Both pieces indicate that there is much experimentation afoot, and while clearly inflected with the depth of butoh imagery work, there is a distinct effort to create narrative, however, absurd and surreal.

These Are the Ones We Fell Among

These Are the Ones We Fell Among[18] opens with Shinichi and Dana rushing in as if late for rehearsal, blathering excuses in English and German and hurriedly changing into their outfits, which consist of gray hooded sweatshirts turned upside down. They step into the sleeves with their legs and secure the wide bottom around their chest with elastic suspender straps, leaving the hood dangling between their legs, a phallic appendage. There is mention of baby elephants; their costumes evoke something of this as well. They settle into a seated position, facing away from the audience, with Shinichi's arm resting on large purple gymnastics ball. A playful melody rings out, and the pair fall over, asleep. Shinichi pops up and proceeds to roll the ball around the stage like a baby elephant, fingers curled in so that his hands look like feet. At one point, he balances all four limbs on the ball, and the baby circus elephant comes to life in stunning clarity. Old-fashioned circus music replaces the sweetness and the two dancers lumber around the stage, the one holding the other's "tail." The sound of thunder interrupts their rhythm, and they are pulled from the dreamscape back to the flustered explanation. They forgot their socks, the year is just off in general, the equinox happened early, etc. They talk over each other, a little out of sync but repeating the same words until Dana turns to Shinichi and asks "are you *copying* me?" to which he replies "are you copying *me*?" They fall into a rhythm of "when . . . where" repeated cyclically, punctuated by "when will it get better?" juxtaposed with "where is my pencil?" A particularly lovely labyrinthine word passage turns the phrase "get ready" inside out, playing with "when will we be ready," "we're never really ready," and "get ready to get ready," coupled with physical actions like covering the face and peeking out the hands like shutters, and throwing a baseball repeatedly while spinning in a circle. Their banter continues, talking over and under each other, questioning each other, cajoling each other, and agreeing with each other.

Their final passage involves an attempt at a romantic interlude, which they wave off saying in English and German they won't be good at it, that they asked some French friends, a joke aimed at their intercultural existence and audience at the same time. It is a neatly wrapped up piece, and rightly described in the program notes as "inhabiting a world reminiscent of Samuel Beckett and Dr. Seuss" (Luzerntheater).

A second piece on the same bill demonstrates the seams of their experimentation. Shinichi skillfully performs Noh theater text, song, and dances. Dana explores her larger store of resources in theater such as character and voice work, and is interested in ways to allow energy to travel through rather than remain in bound flow. The juxtaposition of the two is at turns comic, beautiful, and poignant.

We Meet Again

In the piece *We Meet Again* (2021), Dana is on a bench in oversized sweats, legs spread wide, hood flopped down. Head bopping to sound on headphones. Shin floats in full Noh regalia and settles. Begins to sing. Dana busts out a surprisingly skilled popping and locking solo to the tune only she can hear, and then dances off. Shin finishes and leaves, and Dana returns with a briefcase and oversized overcoat performing a clown routine. Shin walks through in Japanese undergarments eating a banana. Shin returns in an oversized vest; both dancers are wearing top hats and proceed to greet one another in a playful lifting the hat up and down, pretending to sit, walking in a circle funny courtship. Dana leaves, and Shin spreads out on the bench. He falls off of it and rolls to the spot where he had been singing before, and starts his Noh song again, rolling back and forth to the bench and each time he hits the downstage left spot it's like his antennae pick up a former radio station and he chants again. Eventually, he crawls off the stage with a whimper of his song, crossfaded with Dana returning, tiredly singing an echo of his song. She is dressed in a black mesh top, ruffled sleeves, black petticoat, yellow boxing gloves, and a black motorcycle helmet that fogs up a little as she sings. He enters, and she stumbles past, issues a "hey, c'mon" gesturing him to a fight with her boxing gloves, and then throws a punch that leads her off stage. He watches her go, perplexed, and then recites his Noh lines sounding like a samurai and sitting there in black pants, white shirt, and bare feet. Dana walks through on demi point in a red dress, clicking her tongue like the sound of high heels and Shin loses his place. He is interrupted by a Sleepytime Gorilla Museum song—*1997*. "Mother fucker you're going down tonight . . . tonight we're gonna party like it's 1997" Shin re-enters in his red suit, shaking and strutting to the music. Dana reaches into her leopard print purse and grabs a stick, tosses it into the pile, and Shin runs out on all fours and retrieves it like a dog, complete with panting. She exits, and he continues panting. Dana interrupts, back in her suit which she soon strips down to an old timey striped swimsuit, and Shinichi soon returns in one as well. They make a play of getting ready to dive in and then running off to get one more thing that will make them ready: boot, top hat, handbag, facemask, etc., but eventually give up and never swim. The final section is more meditative. Dana balances the curly twigs into a delicate sculpture and Shinichi dresses into formal wear and does a fan dance. There is a beautiful quiet connection between the two, as they rotate their objects in space.

Degenerate Art Ensemble/Haruko Nishimura a.k.a. Crow (b. 1970, Kashiwa City, Japan) and Joshua Kohl (b. 1970, Berkeley, CA)

One of the most successful experimental touring companies to come out of Seattle in the early 2000s is Degenerate Art Ensemble. They are an eclectic group whose movement vocabulary and training are butoh, but they were musicians first. Haruko Nishimura (hereinafter referred to as Crow) and Joshua Kohl met at the New England Conservatory of Music, where she studied classical piano and he studied classical guitar.

The daughter of a Japanese diplomat, Crow had lived in Australia and Syria, and spent her teenage years with an American host family in Seattle while her father served in a post in the 1980s in Lebanon during the Civil War. When she and Kohl announced their decision to marry, her father excommunicated her. "Heartbroken and lost" according to her own account (Crow, pers. comm., January 29, 2020), she decided to return to Seattle area to a familiar and formative community. Struggling with what she describes as "depression and identity crisis," art became her world. As a coping mechanism, she threw herself into creative practice and became engaged in the experimental scene with students from Cornish College, where she took classes part time and Kohl enrolled full time at Cornish College to study composition in 1993.

Cornish professors Jarrad Powell (Director, Gamelan Pacifica) and Pat Graney (Choreographer, Pat Graney Company) brought together composers and choreographers in an intensive seminar, where they had to make a new piece each week, through a collaborative composition class with musicians and dancers. Influenced by this collaborative creative process, a group of performers continued to work together after graduation in 1996. Among them was Crow and Kohl's first company, The Young Composers Collective (TYCC), with Joshua Kohl conducting. It was a highly experimental group encompassing music and avant-garde performance. Members included classmates at Cornish, notably Reggie Watts (comedian/musician and bandleader for James Corden's *Late Late*

Show), guitarist Tim Young (member of the *Late Late Show* band), violinist Eyvind Kang (Co-Director, Musical Arts/Experimental Pop Specialization in the CalArts School of Music), cellist/composer Brent Arnold, and dancer/ performance artist Saiko Kobayashi, who studied at the Cornish College. As a group, they did a silent film score for Fritz Lang's cult favorite, *Metropolis*, with their 17-person collective. Originally, they were playing in rock clubs like the OK Hotel, the infamous venue where all the Grunge bands played. Kohl describes TYCC's unique style as "Big Band Garage Orchestra" with performance art, which they continued throughout the 1990s. Their members were a rich mix of classical, jazz, world music musicians and improvisers, modern dancers, and visual artists. They were all quite open to ideas and experimented freely across disciplines and genres.

In addition to the musicians, there were visual artists who contributed to the work. Among them were painter/photographer Junko Yamamoto, set designer Akiko Sato, sculptor Niklaus Weisend, sculptor/graphic artist Thomas Rude, and costume designer Kikuko Dewa. Crow's current imaginative aesthetic and love of highly inventive fashion is influenced by her collaborations with Dewa. Dewa was originally from Kyoto and had a large collection of valuable vintage kimono that she would reconstruct into hyper-modern clothes. She had clothes in boutiques but came to the TYCC to experiment further with even bolder designs. Crow spent hours and hours in her studio assisting her in designing the costumes, and describes Dewa as an aunt-figure who took her under her wing.

When the group first began, Crow was the piano player. She quickly realized she wanted to engage in the performance art aspect of the company's work instead and threw herself wholeheartedly into that end of the creations. Performing in rock clubs like OK Hotel made the stakes even higher, says Crow, as she immediately felt the audience's response as to what worked and what didn't in her presentation of characters.

As TYCC, they had a period of obsessively reading Ikkyu, an irreverent Japanese monk and poet who staged parades of skeletons to remind people that they were going to die. The group painted themselves white and staged three-hour-long processions through the streets, during which time they described intense audience reactions including people throwing stones at them, drunk college kids from the bars they passed pouring drinks on them, and the like. Crow describes the events as "terrifying and fun at the same time" (Crow, pers. comm., January 29, 2020), and driving them to their edge, which she, like many butoh performers, identified with successful performance.

Prior to this group, Crow had been studying Japanese traditional folk dance and when she met Kobayashi, the two found a common interest in the tragically haunted characters in Japanese ghost stories. When Crow and Kohl were 18, they had gone together to an exhibit in the British Museum of work by Kawanabe Kyosai, a painter and satirist who is largely credited with inventing manga in 1874 with his irreverent demon images lampooning Imperial Japan's engagement with the West and subsequent rapid modernization. One such image, *He-gassen* (*Fart Competition*), was completed the same year as the

Meiji Restoration and pokes fun at Japanese people "straining to become Westerners," stuffed in Western-style clothes and affecting a "dignified, pseudo-Victorian demeanor" (Arn 2018).

Crow and Kohl were smitten with the work. They recall walking into a gallery and seeing an entire theater curtain (56 feet wide by 13 feet tall) with a painting of a demon with a long neck stretching oddly out of its kimono, and an equally long tongue stretching out of its mouth. They began researching the artist's life and work, and discovered that in addition to his fantastical imagery, which Crow called "punk," he also hosted painting parties in which he would invite audience to watch him and a group of artists paint. For them, this was an early version of avant-garde art. Crow wove Kawanabe's images together with her interest in ghost stories, supernatural, and Traditional Japanese folk dance, and together these threads were the fabric of her early performance art.

TYCC's Kobayashi, herself trained in modern dance, was the one who introduced Crow to Jean Viala and Nourit Massine's photobook *Shades of Darkness*, and it spoke to Crow's self-proclaimed quest for "spine-chilling beauty." Her interest peaked, Crow then saw a performance by Butoh-sha Tenkei at On The Boards (OTB). Then she started going to the San Francisco Butoh Festival and taking Yan Shu's workshops, led by Kinya Zuru. Says Crow, she was fascinated because they were young Japanese who were "punk, just did whatever they wanted, [their] attitude was so refreshing" especially in comparison with her own upbringing (Crow, pers. comm., January 29, 2020). She also saw Kazuo Ohno perform *Water Lilies* at the Moore Theater in Seattle in 1993.

TYCC was strongly invested in Asian American culture, particularly the avant-garde edges of the arts. At the same time, traditional arts had an important role in their experimentation. Taiko drummers also worked with TYCC at its inception. Kobayashi was instrumental in the founding of the Asian American Arts Alliance in Seattle, an organization that produced events in the Seattle area for many years in the 1980s and 1990s.

While with TYCC, Crow began vocal experimentations purely based on music she had heard and liked, such as "Noise Rock" band Melt-Banana, fronted by a female singer. She also listened to Japanese punk band Boredoms, fronted by screaming vocalist Yamantaka Eye. The loud, nonsensical vocals felt right for her young adult angst, excommunicated from her family and confused about her identity.

Kohl and Crow realized by the late 1990s that they had a shared vision for theatrical productions and they gradually began learning the technical aspects of stage performance. They began creating narrative theatrical shows with TYCC such as *Hell's Cauldron* in which a nerd boy hatched from a pod, traveled the underworld in the lair of a Hell's Princess, and was seduced by her male courtesans. TYCC's big band played the role of an army of Nerd Boys that performed a score that included biting and spitting apples to the beat as part of the torture of the Princess' Hell's attendants. This work and *Rinko*, about a girl living in an apocalyptic future with a mutant, were small-scale shows but were the first to be presented on theatrical stages with full lighting. Many of the musicians in the group had other gigs, and the demands of technical rehearsals and theatrical shows were difficult with that schedule.

Eventually, in 1999, Crow and Kohl formed a new group, Degenerate Art Ensemble, with the express purpose of pursuing theatrical stage shows. The group took its name from the 1937 modern art exhibition entitled "Entartete Kunst" ("Degenerate Art") held by the Nazis to justify their persecution of the most radical modern artists of their time.

Scream!LionDogs was the first new work by the company, presented at On The Boards in early 1999. They still toured as a "punk big band" as well, with Crow on vocals, which have been described as a cross between Bjork and Yoko Ohno (Upchurch 2009). The designation of "punk" comes up repeatedly in Crow and Kohl's description of their own work and that of those who inspire them. Says DAE of this first work:

> The creation of *Scream!LionDogs* was motivated by the brutal murder of an Asian American teenager by neo-nazi skinheads, which struck close to home, as the killer was married to the sister of our close friend. In responding to the murder we created *Scream!LionDogs*, a performance work that dove into the psychology of hate, which began our journey of investigating broader aspects of human nature through art, using archetypal symbols from dreams and fairy tales while also drawing inspiration from our obsession with cinema, comics, punk, protest, and the supernatural.
> (Crow and Kohl pers. comm., January 29, 2020)

During the 1999 World Trade Organization (WTO) protests in Seattle, Washington, Kohl joined a protest marching band called the Infernal Noise Brigade. This group formed from another activist collective, eco-punk group ¡Tchkung!, composed of musicians from Oklahoma who had moved to the Olympia/Tacoma region, combined with Seattle-based musicians. D.K. Pan, dancer and director of the butoh company P.A.N., brought the artists together at a nightclub above a Vietnamese restaurant, and all of them hit it off. The INB went on to travel internationally and was an active force in the global protest scene, while Kohl and Crow continued to hone their performance craft through more art house theater events.

The duo's sonic and visual aesthetic carried over to Degenerate Art Ensemble, with all pieces including live music, vocals, dance, and performance art. In *Sonic Tales*, Crow wears a weeble wobble dress with a curved, round bottom that she has to spin to maneuver around the stage (see Figure 4.7). The dress, created by sculptor Colin Ernst, is outfitted with numerous hollow metal tubes that both she and the two other performers strike rhythmically, producing the soundscore that accompanies the piece. The pipes are differently pitched, making the song melodic as well as percussive. And the characters are clearly in battle, turning their music playing into a stylized dance.

Crow threw herself into butoh training, particularly following Yumiko Yoshioka as a teacher. She also took many isolated workshops, among them,

Figure 4.7 Degenerate Art Ensemble in *Sonic Tales* (2009). Performers left to right: Crow, Joshua Kohl, Jeff Houston.

Source: Photo by Bruce Tom, reprinted with permission from Degenerate Art Ensemble

with Mexican artist Diego Piñón. Of Piñón, Crow felt inspired by the raw expression she was able to find through his practice. And with Yoshioka, she was drawn to her theatrical constructions. Crow studied with her in Seattle and then followed her to Vancouver for an intensive training. Following that, Yoshioka invited her to participate in eXit! in Broellin in 1999, at which Crow met Shinichi Iova-Koga.

Following that meeting, Crow began collaborating with Iova-Koga's company, inkBoat, first in *Cockroach* at Theatre Artaud in 2000. It was during this performance process that Crow started training with Yuko Kaseki in between rehearsals, and then began to study with her and Minako Seki in Berlin, Germany. Crow felt at home in the dance-theater aesthetic of these artists and was inspired with the ways in which they were classically trained by Japanese butoh "masters" yet had all made their own way with a variety of performance styles. When asked if she identifies her own work as butoh, Crow says "I just went where people wanted me, and for many butoh festivals I feel I am not butoh enough. I certainly cite my teachers as Japanese butoh dancers, because that is indeed where they come from." This worked for Crow especially because she was almost entirely self-taught in terms of performance work outside of classical piano.

Throughout their formation as a group in the 1990s, they worked closely with OTB curator Mark Murphy and lighting designer Chris Fleming, who helped them transition from performing in rock clubs with little beyond a soundcheck to performing in theaters with a methodical technical rehearsal. They also learned quite a bit from their collaborations with Koga, as they were involved with productions he did throughout the country and in Europe, including *Onion*, *c(H)ord*, and *95 Rituals*. Robin Held, the curator for the Frye Art Museum, was also instrumental in DAE's development, supporting their efforts to produce the sprawling parade performances they wanted to create in and around the museum exhibition of their work in 2011. The couple credits this opportunity in their growth as artists because it necessitated their own writing about their work, and also leadership experience in directing a team of production and marketing staff to realize their vision.

More recently, Crow has been studying Qigong, Taiji, Noguchi Taiso, and Bagua, all forms of martial arts or gymnastics. She had studied Noguchi with Yoshioka and Kaseki while in Berlin, and then made a connection with Mari Osani, with whom she studied in various workshops in Portland and Seattle, and then spent a month training with her in Aomori, Japan in 2014.

As a company, they are able to support themselves through a variety of activities, primarily touring and grants but also some teaching, such as a collaboration Crow began with Colorado-based visual artist Senga Nengudi. Nengudi cast Crow in an installation of her work in Seattle and then invited Crow back to Colorado Springs to teach and continue working together on a multidisciplinary project called *Boy mother/faceless bloom*. They are collaborating with the Department of Innovation at Colorado College, where they will also teach while in residence.

The cumulative effect of the duo's efforts has been great. In 2012, Crow was awarded a Guggenheim Fellowship, and DAE was commissioned by Robert Wilson to create an interpretation of *Einstein on the Beach* at Baryshnikov Arts Center in New York. And on a personal level, Crow feels she has truly reclaimed her sense of self through the generative process of making art. In 2017, she renamed herself Crow in the process of making her latest work about violence, familial trauma, and the silencing she fought hard to overcome. The following section describes this haunting and poignant work.

Skeleton Flower

The opening image is Crow walking as if on the moon down a soft hallway of light. A voiceover tells a story of a waking dream of her mother as a moth, fluttering her wings at Crow, scattering dust that chokes the young girl "muting my will to speak." The hallway is emblematic of all of the generations that brought her here. Harsh front light makes a shadow of the dancer on the wall, and she ripples and flutters her arms in a gossamer costume that gives the impression of wings on the upstage wall. Not just a fragile insect, she stomps once loudly, to announce her presence. To the sounds of her own haunting, breathy vocals, Crow settles onto her side and writhes her arms and legs like that of an injured insect, incessantly. At moments, she echoes Anna Pavlova's dying swan with one leg folded and the other outstretched, arms spiraling, and then in the next contorts her body into an unstable balance, twisted upside down.

A book falls from the sky, and she begins to read with childlike wonder and laughter. A mic in the book picks up her gurgling noises with perfect clarity. It is clear that the sonic environment is as important as the visual for these artists. We learn from the voiceover that the book is a gift from her mother who, despite their toxic relationship, imparted her love of fairytales on the young girl. We continue watching and listening to the girl's laughter and gasps amid increasingly rapid speech in Japanese, until the book sticks to her face. She dances thus, eventually freeing one body part only to have another stuck or trapped by the pages. What makes this section so compelling is in part her precise physical theater but also the fact that the musicians play live and are incredibly sensitive to her shifts and dramatic moments. It cannot be overstated the impact of live music that molds to the dancer. It is like hearing the inner monologue of the performer as it unfolds in real time.

The next section featured Crow dodging behind panels of projected build-ings that grow ever skyward, as the voiceover tells of physical abuse at the hands of her family and from school kids in each new foreign city that the family temporarily calls home.

Red shoes fall from the sky. They too are mic'ed. A possession dance ensues. As she struggles to remove the red shoes, a video screen drops down, covering the action. On it is projected an imaginary Japanese TV program, with a fam-ily of Godzilla creatures around a dinner table. The scene is at first humorous but quickly turns violent, complete with Godzilla drinking a Sapporo beer and throwing plates at Mother Moth (whose costume includes multiple patterns of gingham, wings, and what looks like red strainers molded into eye cover-ings). It is intended to be fantastical and dark at the same time, removing the trauma from a personal story to one that resonates for others. With cartoonish characters, the piece is able to portray the scenario but not re-traumatize the performers or audience through this alienation effect (a la Brecht).

Crow returns to the stage clad in a white costume that looks like a paper cutout, with moth-like tendrils, cone-shaped head, and screen-box skirt, on which is projected light, moving water, dim shadows. Her text in the voiceo-ver traces stories of generational trauma that she questions over and over again, "why is it so hard to break free?" She talks of learned behavior, passed down through generations of women, walking the same steps as their mothers before them.

Crow returns again in her gossamer gingham outfit, this time with a mir-rored swan that she partners with expert puppetry skills. A beautiful narrative of love, play, loss, grief, and solace unfolds before our eyes. I am reminded of so many other birds that have appeared in butoh pieces, as objects to be sacrificed. This one is a friend and is revered. Even the white peacock in Sankai Juku's

Kinkan Shonen is an object to behold but not an actual collaborator in the piece that creates empathy in the way that Crow masterfully does with this mirrored wooden swan.

In a third and final fairytale, we enter a psychedelically checkered castle—is it Bluebeard's? The woman finds herself in "the forbidden room" with a curious stench, where body parts are displayed along with the instruments used to remove them. She recognizes and then refuses this fate. The voiceover monologue rings out an anthem about taking back power, saved from too much sentimentality by a stirring rock ballad, with Kohl on electric guitar and Crow belting out a song about head, bodies, arms, and legs. What seems like a pile of store mannequins comes to life, reassembles, stands, and dances. They are human women, dancers, dressed in white, performing a martial art *kata*. The voiceover recounts going to a police station, identifying a man, Crow appears in the backdrop video holding a Molotov cocktail, hurls it, and the entire three screens explode in flames. The crescendo smolders, and Crow reappears onstage, dressed head to toe in flowers, draped over the same pointed hat and box skirt of her earlier white moth costume, walking down that same corridor of light, having bloomed, and now claiming the control over her own path. She is singing what sounds like a bird whistle with water in it, chortling really, beautifully, and harmonically. Her voice is as much a wonder as her dance, with the ability to swing from screaming, barking jenglish punk that sounds like she herself is a hurdy gurdy machine, to this gorgeous melodic lullaby that closes the piece.

DAE has become a versatile performance group that spans traditional theaters, public spaces, museum installations, and music venues/recordings with grace. Their strategy to engender this success has been to remain flexible to the given venue and create multiple iterations of a piece that can be presented in different spaces with distinct audience experiences. *Red Shoes*, for example, was a street performance and also a stage show, and additionally was part of a museum exhibition of the costumes at the Frye. *Skeleton Flower* has a stage performance, a band that performs some of the music in the piece as well as other compositions, and a museum installation with costumes and sound.

Kohl talks about being in Kazuo Ohno's studio in early 2000 and as a musician he thought he would just observe class. But as he sat down, Ohno ushered him onto the dance floor, saying "you could be dead soon, come dance!" (Joshua Kohl, pers. comm., January 29, 2020). These two artists have done just that, never missing a chance to explore, experiment, and challenge their ever-expanding edge.

LEIMAY Ensemble: Shige Moriya (Osaka, Japan) and Ximena Garnica (Bogota, Colombia,) (b. "When Do You Want Us Born?" Based in New York City)

The work of this artistic duo[19] has been vital to the contemporary development of butoh in New York. Their story is a labyrinthine tale. Both came from abroad in search of artistic experimentation and found butoh through happenstance. They have played a pivotal role as curators and community builders, and now as artists who are forging their own path, inspired by those they have encountered along the way.

Shige Moriya

Shige Moriya emigrated to New York from Osaka, Japan, in 1993. Moriya's father, a respected visual artist himself, helped land Moriya a position in a SoHo gallery where he had connections. Moriya began to build a network of likeminded artists who wanted to experiment with cross-disciplinary work in ways that the downtown gallery scene did not yet support. Together with action painter Naoki Iwakawa (see Figure 4.8) and painter Satoshi Imagawa a.k.a. Grande, Moriya converted a 3,000-square-foot former auto body shop at 58 Grand Street in Williamsburg, Brooklyn, into a live-work studio with two gallery spaces. Says Moriya, "We called it CAVE because it was freezing cold and we had to make open fires to keep warm indoors" (Garnica et. al. 2016, 8–9). In the early years, the space hosted weekly salons as well as monthly gallery

Figure 4.8 CAVE Gallery showing Naoki Iwakawa Action Painting, CAVE circa 1980. Pictured left to right: Ximena Garnica, Naoki Iwakawa.

Source: Photo reprinted with permission of CAVE/LEIMAY

exhibitions that were open to the public. The majority of the artists came from the visual arts and music, and they were experimenting with different media including paint, fabrics, projection, and a wide variety of instrumentation.

The space attracted and fostered further experimentation in artistic genre. Among the artists involved in these early years of CAVE was Ben Armstrong of Laddio Bolocko, a group of experimental rock musicians. Armstrong collaborated in numerous exhibitions of Naoki Iwakawa's action paintings. Additionally, Tim Wright of the American band DNA, a part of the no-wave experimental music scene, frequently performed at CAVE events. Wright worked with Brian Eno and David Byrne, and he was fascinated with mummies and Mexico, two themes that Wright would find in common with Ko Murobushi when they later met. Also Jack Wright, a free jazz saxophonist who frequented CAVE events, performed there with Azumaru of the Japanese butoh company Dairakurakan.

CAVE proved to be the laboratory that Moriya was seeking. Through his adventurous curation and collaborations, Moriya's own creative work expanded from visual art to installation art. As he became more interested in durational experiences and live spaces, it was a logical next step to begin working with dancers. Moriya attended a butoh workshop in Upstate New York with Atsushi Takenouchi in 2001, where he met Ximena Garnica, Juan Merchan, and Zachary Model, the latter of whom had been studying with Diego Piñón in the United States and Mexico. Moriya was working on an installation called "The Things We Step On" when they met, and he asked Garnica to organize a performance intervention in the midst of his structure, and thus they embarked on their first collaboration (Shige Moriya, pers. comm., November 8, 2018).

Ximena Garnica

Ximena Garnica was involved in theater at an early age in her home country of Colombia. She was a child television and stage actor, and had also been exposed to the distinct Latin American physical theater tradition that was based on Eugenio Barba's work. Garnica says that this was her inroad to contemporary performance as well. She was reading Barba's book, *Theater Anthropology*, in which he describes Japanese *buyo*, and this led to a fortuitous mistake later in New York. From Colombia, she went to Denmark to research at Odin Teatre, to continue investigating physical theater (Ximena Garnica, pers. comm., November 8, 2018).

In 1998, Garnica moved to New York to study English and later on to pursue theater studies. She attended the Lee Strasberg Theatre & Film Institute and completed her BA in Theater at City College of New York but was left wanting a different approach to performance. "I was studying Uta Hagen but I don't fit with the Latina roles" (Ximena Garnica, pers. comm., November 8, 2018). Specifically, the most common roles for Latina women were frequently hyper-sexualized, playing opposite a macho Latino man.[20] Says Garnica, "To be able to be in the theater, my body would have to be reduced to its identity, and that was the problem I had and what [later] attracted me to butoh." Though she feels she gained important skills at City College, she continued to search for other training and performance styles.

Garnica went to a butoh workshop by mistake, thinking it was the *buyo* that she encountered in Barba's book.[21] That workshop was led by Mexican dancer Diego Piñón. Because Garnica and Juan Merchan, whom she met at the workshop, spoke Spanish, they began to organize workshops for Piñón in New York. Garnica and Merchan became creative partners and brought other artists to New York as well. Says Garnica, their producing was a matter of necessity because at the time both she and Merchan were undocumented at the time. If they left to go study with a teacher outside the country, they would not be allowed to return. Instead, they began bringing teachers to New York so that they themselves could train.

After meeting Moriya and collaborating on *The Things We Step On*, Garnica and Moriya embarked on a new chapter in their creative work as they became increasingly interested in exploring the intersections of their different disciplines. Garnica and Moriya also became life partners, and she became a resident at CAVE.

Garnica notes that when she first came to CAVE, she and Moriya were already exploring art that was made live in front of an audience: action paintings, action installations, and action interventions. It wasn't butoh, per se, it was performance that explored liveness and chance. They even wrote bios for the studio cats Franny and Zooey in the programs, as the "action lickers" who would regularly walk through and become part of the art-in-progress (Ximena Garnica, pers. comm., November 8, 2018).

The following sections chronicle how Garnica and Moriya built a festival to investigate their creative interests in butoh, and then how their research developed into a unique performance ensemble, LEIMAY.

New York Butoh Festival

In 2003, the butoh workshops that Garnica and Merchan had been producing at CAVE flourished into a bonafide festival, with the team of Garnica, Merchan, Moriya, Zachary Model, and Jeff Janisheski at the helm. Garnica recalls the meeting in which the organizers decided to produce the festival in a theater; they were not sure they could actually pull it off. Says Garnica, "it wasn't a romantic idea of making a festival, it was just out of need that if we wanted to study, we had to bring teachers to us" (Ximena Garnica, pers. comm., November 8, 2018). Luckily, the group of friends and collaborators had many contacts, including Janisheski who had studied with the Ohnos for a number of years in Japan and also knew Yukio Waguri. The first festival featured headline performances and workshops with Waguri, SU-EN, and Joan Laage, all at Theatre for the New City on the Lower East Side, as well as New York-based artists performing at CAVE Gallery. SU-EN secured sponsorship for her own travel. Through family connections, Model was able to offer a $20,000 loan, and thankfully the festival earned $20,400 (Garnica et. al. 2016, 10).

The program promised that "The New York Butoh Festival will serve as an East Coast hub for growing regional and international network of butoh performers and audiences" (NYBF 2003), and indeed the festival accomplished that and more. With this initial offering, the producers merged generations, East and West Coast communities from the United States, and foregrounded collaborations with musicians and visual artists. Waguri brought his protégé company, Shinonome, and also performed a duet with Garnica. SU-EN, Laage, and Dawn Saito represented a second generation of established butoh dancers. San Francisco-based Shinichi Koga performed a solo and also an improvisational piece with the author and another Bay area dancer, paige starling sorvillo. Theater for the New City, an iconic East Village theater founded in the 1970s and known for fostering experimental artists, was a perfect setting for this fledgling festival. The opening events at CAVE Gallery featured local artists, including CAVEnsemble's *In Illo Tempore*, a durational piece in which dancers hung on a wall in CAVE Gallery in the center of canvases painted by Iwakawa.[22]

The New York Butoh Festival galvanized a new hub for butoh in the United States. Since Kazuo Ohno's first New York performance in 1981, the touring networks had disseminated butoh through numerous US cities, and it had flourished in San Francisco. With the 2003 New York Butoh Festival, New York was once again established as a beacon for butoh. As the San Francisco Butoh Festival had just presented its final season in 2002, it felt as if the center of gravity within the American student community shifted and would now begin to flock to the East Coast for training and performances. As one of many artists that moved from San Francisco to New York in the early 2000s, I saw many of the same students in New York who had previously participated in the San Francisco and Seattle Butoh Festivals.

Though the stress of producing a festival every year was more than this small nonprofit wanted to undertake, they smartly continued to build audience through workshop offerings and intimate performances. In Spring 2004, they offered a cluster of workshops with Akira Kasai, Yuko Kaseki, and Atsushi Takenouchi. There were also studio shows at CAVE by Kaseki, Takenouchi, Zendora Dance Company (of which Merchan was a member), dancer/drummer duo Claire Barratt and Tatsuya Nakatani, and Boston-based Jennifer Hicks (a member of Katsura Kan's company), and Seattle-based Degenerate Art Ensemble. The studio shows at CAVE in particular engendered a feeling of Hijikata's Asbestos-kan, the tiny Tokyo stage that was the crucible of butoh. Only 50 audience members could fit into the tiny space, which meant that most shows were quickly sold out and demand grew.

This new generation of students was also hungry for more information about butoh and was eager to attend film screenings, academic symposia, and artist interviews. CAVE put significant producing muscle behind these endeavors and partnered with other New York presenters to expand the scope of what the festival could offer.

Buoyed by the success of the first festival and the growing student community surrounding CAVE, the producers created the 2005 festival as a multi-week, multi-venue endeavor, featuring key Japanese artists including Akira Kasai, Yumiko Yoshioka, Masaki Iwana, Katsura Kan, Daisuke Yoshimoto, Azumaru (Dairakudakan), and Yuko Kaseki. The festival co-director's program note commented "because we are currently the only festival in the United States presenting butoh's international spectrum, this is a rare chance to see a number of these legendary dancers perform, some for the first time in New York" (NYBF 2005). Theater for the New City was again the host of the mainstage festival events.

The performances made a lasting impression with critics and audiences alike. Dance critic Claudia La Rocco commented on the wildly different collection of individuals who presented solos: "Moods shifted from silly to sinister to sublime and back again in cyclical meditations on destruction and regeneration" (La Rocco 2005). Audiences were treated to a host of images:

> In *Before the Dawn*, Yoshioka's body became a menagerie of strange creatures . . . she appeared in voluminous red robes, her face masked. When her hands emerged from the fabric, they skittered over her body like spiders or pecked at her flesh like birds.
>
> (La Rocco 2005)

Kasai referenced Genet with his piece *Flowers—Lovely Jean Paul*, in which he performed as a drag character. "A meditation on innocence and violence, this solo opened with Mr. Kasai in a sparkling pink ball gown, feathered headdress and fake eyelashes, moving about the stage to driving techno music like a crazed vogue dancer" (La Rocco 2005). La Rocco was particularly taken in *Eros and Thanatos* by

> the masterly Daisuke Yoshimoto, covered in white paint and naked except for a thong, his taut body bent double, he walked in painstaking, tremblingly slow fashion. . . . It was easy to forget that this spooky, otherworldly creature was human.
>
> (La Rocco 2005)

LaRocco's review echoed earlier critical assessments of butoh: *The New York* Times arts writer Margarett Loke noted in 1987, "If butoh's message is sometimes bewildering, the visual impact is raw and direct" (Loke 1987). Loke profiles the showing of the first butoh documentary by Ethan Hoffman, *Butoh: Dance of the Dark Soul*, which features the wide-ranging work of butoh's first and second generations as seen through a Westerner's lens. There are now iconic clips of Kazuo Ohno, Sankai Juku, Min Tanaka, Yoko Ashikawa,

Dairakudakan, and Byakko Sha. When taken in total, the film reveals the aesthetic variety of the artists who claim the butoh mantel.

The New York Butoh Festival also fostered this diversity of expression. Not only did they position themselves as major producers through these premieres, but they also stayed close to their community-building ethic; the festival also showcased local artists, including former Poppo and the GoGo Boys dancer Celeste Hastings, in outdoor events at the 2nd and B Community Gardens in the Lower East Side.

Fortuitously, Japan Society concurrently hosted Ko Murobushi's all-male company Sebi in *Bibo no aozora* (*Handsome Blue Sky*). The piece bore the same name as one of Hijikata's books and was intended as an exploration of Hijikata's ideas. The performers—Daiji Meguro, Yukio Suzuki, and Sadayuki Hayashi— were all painted in silver and interacted musically and quite dramatically with three large sheets of copper. The rawness of the men's bodies hitting the metal sheets evoked Hijikata's similar actions in *Nikutai no hanran* (*Revolt of the Flesh*). As part of the 2005 New York Butoh Festival, CAVE co-presented workshops with Murobushi, thus beginning one of the most significant artistic relationships for Garnica with this master artist.[23]

Bolstering the audience education component of the 2005 festival, Anthology Film Archives co-presented two days of butoh-themed films, including famed film director Daniel Schmid's (*La Paloma*, *Tosca's Kiss*) 1995 mini-documentary on Kazuo Ohno, Masaki Iwana's feature-length film *Vermillion Souls*, a surrealist story of living in post–World War II Japan, video artist Eric Koziol's *The Duchess*, featuring Shinichi Koga's inkBoat in German castles and ruins, and Berlin-based filmmaker Peter Sempel's feature-length documentary on Kazuo Ohno, *Just Visiting This Planet*, shot in numerous locations while he followed the artist around the world.

Several important relationships were formed during the 2005 festival: Kaseki was introduced to Japan Society producer Yoko Shioya, who later booked her and Shinichi Koga's *Ame to Ame* and built a lasting relationship with these two artists. Additionally, Murobushi would return to teach several extended workshops through CAVE over the next decade as it developed into its Butoh-Kan training model, and he became a mentor of sorts for Garnica. He also collaborated with Garnica on her company's 2009 piece *Furnace*. Murobushi's dancer Meguro would also return to appear in Garnica's 2007 piece, *A Timeless Kaidan*.

Garnica spent the whole of 2006 in Japan, studying with Akira Kasai. A group of about 20 students committed to a year of training at his studio. She says that this time made her realize the limitations of the two-week intensive workshop structure that was the longest model that CAVE had presented to date, because students started over with each new workshop. She craved building a true ensemble and working intensively over time. Garnica also says that she held a romantic idea of theatrical ensembles that emerged in the 1970s, such as Grotowski's Theater Laboratorium (Poland), Ariane Mnouchkine's Théâtre du Soleil (France), Teatro de la Candelaria (Colombia), Tadashi Suzuki Company of Toga (SCOT, Japan), and the Japanese butoh ensembles: Dairakudakan and Sankai Juku. She wanted to develop a similar, deeply connected ensemble that had its own style. During this formative time, the seeds of her company and a new training format coalesced. In addition to the creative inspiration Garnica gleaned from Kasai's "voice power" techniques, she also recognized the importance of what she calls "a group grammar."

In an effort to build her own ensemble upon returning to New York, Garnica recruited a large cast for her next work, *A Timeless Kaidan*. She invited three prominent Japanese dancers: Yuko Kaseki (Berlin), Daiiji Meguro (Tokyo), and Takuya Ishide (Tokyo). There were also 16 local dancers included in the piece. Though the effect of such a large group onstage was impressive, Garnica and Moriya quickly realized that it was too large of a group to sustain as an ensemble. Says Garnica, "You notice that after [Dairakudakan and Sankai Juku], it's mostly solo butoh artists. I don't think that was a choice but rather a circumstantial need for survival and how hard it is to sustain an ensemble." She notes that Tadashi Suzuki is a successful contemporary example of a Japanese ensemble; however, "his option was to live in the middle of nowhere, and he had to create everything himself." What Garnica did have to help structure and organize her work, however, was the New York butoh community that she had a large part in continuing to develop. She drew from students in workshops and supporters of the festival, and began to carve out her own vision of a company. The first stage of that was presented at the 2007 festival.

That next cycle, the New York Butoh Festival program featured a robust offering of events including performances, workshops, film screenings, and symposiums. Eight different venues across the city were involved. Perhaps most importantly, the 2007 festival coincided with Japan Society's Centennial celebration, playfully titled "New York is Turning Japanese." Japan Society's stage hosted Dairakurakan and two of their offshoot companies, the all-male one directed by Kumutaro Mukai (later to become a collaborator with Espartaco Martínez in Mexico City) and Yuko Kobayashi. They also presented Eiko and Koma, Basil Twist's puppet spectacular *Dogogeshi*, and several important contemporary Japanese dance artists including Mika Kurosawa, considered by many to be the "godmother of contemporary dance in Japan" (Kourlas 2016) performing at The Kitchen, and Hiroshi Koike's company Papa Tarahumara in *Ship in a View*, a large-scale spectacle at Brooklyn Academy of Music. The 12-member company balanced impressively on a thick wooden post resembling a ship's mast amid fog and tiny boats seemingly floating across the stage. In addition to Basil Twist, there were other Americans that were apparently "turning Japanese," including Paul Lazar and Annie B. Parson's Big Dance Theater, and Brooke O'Hara's Theatre of the Two-Headed Calf, both known for their intercultural works. There was also a restaging of composer Harry Partch's *Delusion of Fury*, directed by John Jesurun and choreographed by New York-based Japanese choreographer Yasuko Yokoshi, who was also a curator at The Kitchen, where Big Dance Theater and Two-Headed Calf had frequently performed. Kurosawa, who had been involved in the experimental New York dance scene since the 1980s, greatly influenced by Judson Dance Theater and working with artists such as Bebe Miller, invited American dancer Jennifer Monson and New York-based Barcelona dancer Margarita Guergue to join her onstage. Japan Society's season was a heady mix of superstar performers and cross-disciplinary works that highlighted just how interconnected the New York and Japanese performing arts have been since the 1960s.

CAVE's contribution to the Japan Society season drew those linkages forward to a new generation of American-based dancers. They curated a program at Japan Society entitled "Butoh Marathon," a role which sealed their prominence in the field as butoh presenters and also bolstered the careers of several key American-based butoh artists, namely, Degenerate Art Ensemble, Shinichi Koga, and Ximena Garnica, all of whom performed solos. The marathon culminated in a headline performance of *Kuu* (*Emptiness*) by Yoshito Ohno, and then a Birthday Party featuring Yuko Kaseki and experimental percussionist Tatsuya Nakatani in an improvisational performance at Japan Society.

As with the collaboration in 2005, CAVE again co-produced the 2007 workshops affiliated with Japan Society's programming. Additionally, CAVE presented their own slate of workshops and performances at Theater for the New City, Noguchi Museum, Dance Theater Workshop, and Movement Research. Artists featured included Ko Murobushi, Toronto-based Denise Fujiwara, Seattle-based Degenerate Art Ensemble, San Francisco-based Shinichi Koga/inkBoat, and the last generation of Japanese dancers to train at Asbestos-kan—Taketuru Kudo and Takuya Ishide. These two dancers brought important lineage and history to the festival; Kudo toured with Sankai Juku for five years, and Ishide performed with Tanaka in Hijikata's last piece in 1985 and danced with "post-butoh" choreographer Saburo Teshigawara. The 2007 festival was also the debut of Garnica and Moriya's company, LEIMAY, in *A Timeless Kaidan*. The set consisted of transparent fabrics that formed a maze and were also used as projection screens. The Japanese word *kaiden* is a reference to staircases and, as Garnica says, "the illusion that you have to get somewhere" (Ximena Garnica, pers. comm., July 17, 2019). The theme was perhaps ironic in the midst of the scale and success of the festival and Garnica and Moriya's growing company.

The 2007 Butoh Festival continued the relationship with Anthology Film Archives, which screened Misao Arai's 1973 documentary *A Summer Storm*, featuring Hijikata's last public stage performance at Kyoto University, the 2001 NHK documentary on Kazuo Ohno titled *Beauty and Strength*, and the 1929 silent surrealist short film, *Un Chien Andalou* by Spanish director Luis Buñuel and artist Salvador Dalí, which drew connections to Hijikata's early influences in the creation of butoh.

Further cultivating an educated audience and emphasizing the academic study of butoh, the 2007 New York Butoh Festival collaborated with the Graduate Center of the City University of New York (CUNY) and its director Frank Henschger to present a day of lectures. Featured speakers were Sondra Fraleigh, one of the first scholars after Susan Blakely Klein to write about butoh in English, dancer Yukio Waguri, who was until his death in 2017 one of the primary living archives of Hijikata's butoh-fu dance notation, and noted Japanese dance critic Tatsuro Ishii, a Professor Emeritus at Keio University who has written and lectured extensively on butoh. This panel lent heft to the image of the New York Butoh Festival as the US nexus of butoh (a name they would later adopt for a resource-sharing website). It also distinguishes this festival from the San Francisco and the Mexico festival that followed, in that the Keio University Hijikata Tatsumi Memorial Archive did not do a presentation or exhibition as a part of the festival. The organizers were never interested in lineages and butoh as historicized form, though they were most certainly interested in studying its historical influences, such as *Chien Andalou.*

Garnica and Moriya's program note makes their interests quite clear: "Almost half a century since Hijikata's Ankoku Butoh Project, butoh dancers have been appearing like mushrooms across the world taking myriad forms and paths; some retain the butoh label as a marketing strategy," a decision Garnica has said that she understands because "they need to eat" but that she herself eschews. The program note continues: "Others continue the teachings of their masters, make crucial discoveries, and perhaps later become susceptible to stagnation in these once-vital realizations." Garnica is critical of ossified notions of butoh; as an example she talks of dancers in Colombia throwing themselves on the ground in imitation of Murobushi, yet having little understanding as to Murobushi's motivation for performing this action so that their own performance is self-absorbed and created for shock value (Pers. Comm. July 17, 2019). The program note now turns to where Garnica positions her company's work:

> Still others have gained great inspiration from their studies, evolved their training and art process to create their own butoh. This Festival celebrates the life-work of dancers whose bodies demonstrate the pursuit of honesty, moving beyond found styles or forms.
> (NYBF 2007; Ximena Garnica, pers. comm., July 17, 2019)

Through their company LEIMAY, Garnica and Moriya focused purposefully on the development of their "group grammar" in pursuit of their own signature style.

As part of its Centennial in 2007, Japan Society also presented Akira Kasai's *Butoh America*, a piece he choreographed on five American women. The cast included Sara Baird and Erin Dudley (formerly Anemone Dance), Alissa Cardone (a student of both Kasai and Tanaka), Celeste Hastings (Poppo and the GoGo Boys, Butoh Rockettes), and Stephanie Lanckton, who would go on to dance for LEIMAY. The piece was not well received. *The New York Times* dance writer Gia Kourlas criticized it for "fail[ing] to build a tangible portrait of 'Butoh America,' whatever that is" (Kourlas 2007). Audience members, the author included, were equally confused and the applause was tepid. The images presented were of the five American dancers in somewhat interesting but static, "self-conscious" (Kourlas 2007) poses with limbs akimbo for prolonged periods of time, accented by dramatic but seemingly disconnected lighting changes. Excitement peaked when Kasai himself was revealed from behind a stage backdrop, "quivering" in a white porcelain bathtub. Says Kourlas, Kasai "commanded the stage . . . until the dancers switched from worship to revenge, pretending to devour his body like ravenous wolves" (Kourlas 2007). Kourlas concludes that Kasai was "swallowed up whole, along with his dream for a butoh America" (Kourlas 2007).

A closer look at the *Butoh America* program notes, as well as consideration of the New York Butoh Festival program noted earlier, might reveal Kasai's intention. As Kourlas comments in her review, Kasai writes, "Butoh in America is the most beautiful and fragile, the most complete form that contains both fulfillment and destruction, the life and death of the dance" (Kourlas 2007). Perhaps Kasai did not dream of a Butoh America at all but rather was marking the dance's ultimate death is its seeming success, as it grew to prominence in the quintessential consumeristic culture: America.

Indeed, in a 2006 article entitled "Is Butoh's Big Season Good for Butoh," La Rocco posed a similar question. She wrote,

> In the dance world, practitioners and critics often fret that codified techniques, like Martha Graham's, will diminish over time as individual steps are lost or misinterpreted. With a non-technique-based art like Butoh, the danger is that its spirit will curdle into a set of stylistic clichés—all aesthetics, no guts.
>
> (La Rocco 2006)

She had asked Kasai through Japan Society producer Yoko Shioya his opinion on the matter, and he had replied that hip-hop was "America's most authentic butoh," as the closest to the original concepts of rebellion and movement invention as butoh had been at its inception. According to La Rocco, Shioya laughed that definition off as too broad. But there is also some truth to it. Butoh was born of the same impulse that made punk, before clothing companies started selling t-shirts held together with safety pins. As soon as something becomes a marketable trend, a part of its vitality dies. La Rocco also interviewed Japanese dance critic Takao Norikoshi for her article; he responded to her that Butoh "was born in 1960's, dead in 70's, reborn in 80's, and it has diffused to the undercurrent of Japanese dance" (La Rocco 2006). Considered in this light, butoh is seen as a cultural moment that influenced what came after but is no longer a contemporary expression. Whether Kasai's *Butoh America* was a response to La Rocco's commentary or not, I would argue that his piece could be seen as an indication that he did not see the impulse of butoh surviving well in this country.

In an effort to push their own artistic exploration forward, in 2008 CAVE formed a new framework for training through which they hosted fewer visiting artists for longer periods of time. The project was called the New York Butoh-Kan Initiative, and it was funded by the National Endowment for the Arts.

Through this structure, students were able to spend two to four weeks studying daily with artists such as Ko Murobushi and Mari Osani, teacher of Noguchi gymnastics. The Phase 1 brochure advertised:

> The integrative training is based on Butoh Dance philosophy and practice, Noguchi Gymnastics—a Japanese gymnastic method on relaxation of the body, and Voice and Actor training especially those akin to the traditions of Grotowski.
>
> (NYBK 2008)

There were workshop showings at CAVE which gave participants performance experience. Garnica undertook a larger project with Murobushi through this program, which became their collaboration directing LEIMAY piece, *Furnace*, which premiered in the 2009 Butoh Festival.

As Phase 2 developed, the producers became increasingly interested in Mari Osani's work with Noguchi Gymnastics and no longer mentioned Grotowski's work, nor did any physical theater experts with Grotowski training teach in either one of these workshop cycles. The mention of Grotowski's work is still significant though, as it foregrounds Garnica's developing practice of training for the physical actor, including integrated voice and movement practice.

Indeed, Garnica embraced her background in Theater with a capital "T" with the creation of her powerful solo work *Antigones*, presented at Joyce SoHo in September 2008. The piece drew on the metaphor of Antigone's resistance: "her transgression gathers force in silence," write Garnica and Merchan in the program note for the work (Garnica LEIMAY 2008). She ties Antigone's refusal to accept Creon's oppression with "women in conflict sites, who live in the consequences of absence and kidnappings, and to those bodies in the shadow of oblivion" (Garnica LEIMAY 2008). In particular, she drew the connection to Colombian French contemporary activist Ingrid Betancourt, who had been kidnapped for six years and chained to a tree for three of those years before she was rescued in June 2008. The stage was littered with white shoes, in a scene reminiscent of memorials to Los Desaparecidos and victims of cultural genocide (US Holocaust Museum), made heavier by the sheer multiplicity of what it represents.

The 2009 NY Butoh Festival organizers framed the festival that year as the "Butoh-Kan Phase" to point to the shifting emphasis away from producing and toward training. They nonetheless delivered high-caliber performances by Ko Murobushi, Daisuke Yoshimoto, and Mari Osani. Murobushi performed the iconic *Quicksilver*, which had also been presented in the 2007 Butoh Festival and has become one of the artist's signature works, Yoshimoto performed *Ruined Body*, and Osani presented *Seesaw*, all at Dance New Amsterdam. But the real emphasis was on training and exploration and the extended workshops that were a part of this festival. In addition to introductory and intensive workshops with the aforementioned artists, CAVE also co-presented a three-day introductory and nine-day intensive workshop with Yuko Kaseki.

The collaboration between Murobushi and Garnica, *Furnace*, premiered at Dixon Place, which also hosted New York-based artists Mana Yoshimoto, Leigh Evans, and Zack Fuller. Garnica drew students from the year-long Butoh-Kan trainings to cast in *Furnace*, including Stephanie Lanckton, Denisa Musilova, Irem Calikusu, and Teerawat Mulvilai (Kage), a dancer who frequently works in Thailand for Theater B. Further demonstrating the fruition of the year of dedicated training, there were two programs of New York-based artists presented at CAVE.

Even as it became clear that CAVE was the go-to local outlet for the butoh community, the producers signaled an end to their large-scale presentations for other artists. In the festival program note, they wrote:

> By no means does this festival attempt to give an overview of the state of butoh in the 21st century New York . . . we have always avoided the classification of fellow artists or the constriction of the spirit of butoh . . . If water and air do not circulate, they spoil.
>
> (NYBF 2009)

As the producing team did after every festival, Garnica and her collaborators met to evaluate their work and chart a path going forward. It became apparent that they were interested in expanding the training focus beyond butoh. Says Garnica, "Butoh-Kan" was an appropriate name for what we had just done, because the training centered around *butoh*. However, over time, they realized they had to change the name to reflect the research they were now doing. Hence, a new vision for training emerged: Ludus.

The formation and naming of LUDUS was an attempt to distance the work from the word "butoh" as well, and to start to look through a personal lens (Garnica et. al. 2016, 13). Says Garnica:

> All these programs were an attempt to keep the creative energy flowing, shake the boat a little, find how you create your own questions, especially with teachers that become exoticized, [and idolized with] guru culture, and we were always trying to invoke the road that the question wasn't in those teachers, that these people that we presented were resisting things from their culture, times. Identity, etc., and *why* they were doing was sometimes was more important.
>
> (Ximena Garnica, pers. comm., July 17, 2019)

In 2010, CAVE launched the Ludus Training Season, "the educational program of CAVE and its resident company LEIMAY" (CAVE 2010). They built on the recognition of New York Butoh-Kan (NYBK) as the core program but expanded to include other art forms beyond butoh. In particular, the interest in Noguchi taiso deepened significantly, through collaboration with Noguchi Taiso teachers Imre Thormann and Mari Osani. Osani lives in Aomori in

Northern Japan, and mostly learned by practicing for thousands of hours on the tatami by herself. She sought permission to teach from Noguchi's student— Hatori (who took the somatic application of Noguchi work, while the other main student took the practice into dance)—and now does so internationally. While teaching in New York, Osani met Yuko Kaseki and now the two are teaching together in Europe. Thormann also works with Noguchi Taiso from the somatic perspective, combined with his training in Alexander Technique. He lived in Japan for eight years and studied with Noguchi directly.

The training format under Ludus matched the NYBK: three-day introductory sessions and 10-day intensive sessions. The first season featured Osani and Thormann teaching Noguchi gymnastics and Waguri and Yukio Suzuki teaching butoh. The second season in 2011 featured several butoh luminaries including the formidable Hisako Horikawa, who had been a key partner to Tanaka's development of Body Weather, as well as Kasai, Iwana, Wakamatsu, Waguri, and Meguro, who was in a year-long residency at CAVE. With the exception of Kasai's performance, co-produced with and presented at Dance New Amsterdam, the performances by these visiting solo artists were on CAVE's studio stage, small scale, without all the fanfare of local presenting partners. LEIMAY and Moriya had begun to shift their producing heft toward their own work, creating *Trace of Purple Sadness* and *Floating Point Waves*, solos for Garnica, the latter of which was created as artists in residence at HERE Arts Center. They were also building up toward the company's run at BAM Fisher Space, a third stage for the Brooklyn Academy of Music that hosted competitive residencies for local artists to develop and self-produce their works.

For the next couple of years, the programming continued with butoh and Noguchi gymnastics as the main forms of study, with a wider variety of visiting artists in extended training sessions. Wakamatsu, who had been a collaborator back when they founded the New York Butoh Festival and had then relocated to Paris to become a principal collaborator with Iwana, returned to New York several times during this period to teach in the Ludus workshops. Garnica and Moriya also built a relationship with Sherwood Chen, a former member of Tanaka's Mai Juku and Body Weather teacher who had also collaborated with inkBoat on projects with Halprin and Murobushi.

Throughout this period, Garnica honed her company style. She built on vocal work she had begun in acting training and deepened her exploration of Kasai's Voice Power work, which he himself had derived from Rudolph Steiner's Eurythmy. It should come as no surprise then, that in 2014 Garnica circled back to her interest in Grotowski and invited Mario Biagini to teach three weeks of extended workshops as a LEIMAY Ludus Lab. Garnica was inspired by Biagnini's work with "entering realms and connecting to vibratory powers" (Ximena Garnica, pers. comm., July 17, 2019). While she hasn't adopted Grotowski exercises into her own company training routine, she "does jive with the physicality of the body, and the power of the environment and the space" (Ximena Garnica, pers. comm., July 17, 2019).

LEIMAY

Originally, what attracted Garnica to butoh was not the lifestyle and the radical edginess, because, she says, "CAVE already had that energy . . . Kenta Nagai was doing crazy things with the guitar and breaking the strings, Carlo Altomare, a musician with The Living Theater, was playing a prepared piano" and she notes that there were numerous experimental Japanese artists involved in the space. Instead, what drew Garnica to continue her research in butoh was

> not the theatricality or the costumes and the red lips and all that, but the ambiguity . . . For me this is interesting because I was struggling with being a Colombian but I didn't fit because I don't look like a Colombian.
> (Ximena Garnica, pers. comm., July 17, 2019)

She had come to the United States in part to expand past typical roles for women, and instead found herself marked by ethnicity. When she watched performers such as Akira Kasai and Ko Murobushi, she noticed the slippage of identity: "I felt like, are you a thing? An animal? What?" She also notes that these moments were fleeting: "when it happens, they are very quick, they don't stay for a long time" (Ximena Garnica, pers. comm., July 17, 2019). And yet it was enough to make her look further, in search of that in-between-ness.

Garnica's interaction with these artists shaped her own artistic vision. She was not searching for a style; she was searching for an experience. Some of the tools she found through her engagement with butoh artists like Murobushi and Kasai, as well as Osani and Biagini, are what helped her find her own unique expression. "When I thought about creating the training for Ludus, I was concerned with how I get those moments of ambiguity; what procedures that were transmitted to me will lead to those moments?" (Ximena Garnica, pers. comm., July 17, 2019). Drawing from her extensive study with all of these artists, she at last felt as if she had conceived of a group grammar.

In the creation of each new work for LEIMAY, she likens the search for these ambiguous moments to the Japanese idea of *ma*. Says Garnica, "That doesn't belong to butoh, it belongs to a larger conversation of Japanese spatio-temporal aesthetics" (Ximena Garnica, pers. comm., November. 8, 2018). Through their work, they attempt to "disclos[e] the invisible, whether through an architecture of strings that reveals the dynamics of the sky, or a latex skin imprinted with a fleeting moment of the body" (Garnica et. al. 2016, 21). Both Garnica and Moriya sensed this search in each other's work from the beginning, and approach the work from their different disciplines. The result is a true blend of bodies and objects into inhabited environments in performance. Each project has more than one modality of delivery: installation, theatrical performance, and even publications.

Seminal works by the company appear in series, with iterations spread over multiple years of research and public events. The *Qualia* series features an installation in which a single rock is suspended by thin threads above a rock-covered floor, hanging precariously above the spot where one rock is missing in the floor pattern. The performance piece *Qualia Holometaboly* cleverly attached dancers to similar strings, which quivered and bounced as they jumped from crouch to full height, positioned carefully on the support beams of the glass ceiling in the Brooklyn Museum.

The *Floating Point* series includes an installation version with projections of refracted light on fabric suspended from the ceiling of CAVE gallery and in trees at Watermill Center. *Floating Point Waves* showcased Garnica as a performer in a shallow pool of water, interacting with a number of different set elements including the same video projections from the gallery installation.

Becoming Corpus (2013), *Borders* (2016), and *Frantic Beauty* (2017) all belong to a trilogy of work that "deals with matter's constant state of becoming through growth and decay, beginnings and endings" (LEIMAY 2021). Presented in BAM Fisher's flexible Fishman Space, each piece made thus far showcased LEIMAY's prowess in blending evocative physical action with stunning visuals and haunting vocalizations. The dancers appear fearless, launching themselves through the air, riding the waves of sound and light. Loud, industrial music keeps the audience on the edge of the experience along with the dancers, in that delicate place between beginnings and endings.

In 2017, the company began work on *Correspondences* (see Figure 4.9), an installation that intensified the element of risk. Performers encased in plexiglass and clad in only rubber shorts and a gas mask are periodically pelted with sand from a blower in the floor. They crumple and sink as the blast begins, and their fetal bodies are semi-buried. They rise slowly and laboriously as the dust settles, only to repeat the cycle again. In addition to LEIMAY's search for spaces "in between" that make one ponder the nature of existence, *Correspondences* touches on environmental ethics and our precarious contemporary moment. The piece premiered in the plaza at Astor Place in New York City in October 2020, in the middle of the COVID-19 pandemic. The eerie scene of the encased dancers matched the uncanny moment; people were distant, masked, unable to touch, and under constant threat of a new surge. *Correspondences* played again in Socrates Sculpture Park in August 2021, in the middle of Hurricane Henri. Again the work felt prophetic, touching on the nerve right below the surface of this unique cultural moment.

Additional Gen X Artists

As I have mentioned previously, there is a multitude of artists who became active butoh artists in the Americas in this same time period, more than I could possibly do justice to in one volume. Among them are Atsushi Takenouchi, who trained under Hijikata and claims influence from the Ohnos. He worked in Upstate New York for many years and trained a variety of dancers from the United States and Mexico, and he is now more centered in Europe where he teaches at the Pontedera Center, the Workcenter of Jerzy Grotowski, and Thomas Richards (Jinen-Butoh, n.d.). Oguri trained under Min Tanaka and

Figure 4.9 Correspondences by Ximena Garnica and Shige Moriya featuring the LEIMAY
Ensemble (From left to right: Derek DiMartini, Andrea Jones, Krystel Copper).
The Watermill Center (2019).

Source: Photo by Shige Moriya, reprinted with permission of LEIMAY

emigrated to the United States in 1991, where he and Roxanne Steinberg
teach Body Weather Laboratory (Bodyweather, n.d.). Jennifer Hicks (student
of Katsura Kan) founded CHIMERAlab Dance Theater and developed a
butoh community in Boston, Massachusetts. Julie Becton Gillum studied with
Diego Piñón, Yoshito Ohno, and Natsu Nakajima and founded her own company Legacy Butoh in Asheville, North Carolina. Nicole LeGette has a similar
pedigree through Piñón, Ohno, and Nakajima, and founded Blushing Poppy
in Chicago. Mizu Desierto studied with Piñón, Nakajima, and the Tamanos,
and is instrumental in the butoh community in Portland, Oregon. Interestingly, *mizu* means water in Japanese, and *desierto* means desert in Spanish; her

chosen identity bridges the three cultures which she inhabits. José Bravo studied with Piñón, Nakajima, and Anzu Furukawa, and founded a movement arts center that combines butoh with somatic studies and tai chi, called Butoyolotl (*yolotl* translates to "heart" in Nahuatl) (Butoyolotl, n.d.). Carlos Ivan Cruz Islas was a student of Eugenia Vargas at La Universidad Autónomo del Estado de Hidalgo and has continued to be a close collaborator, studying with nearly every butoh artist LEDTR has produced in Mexico; he founded his own collective, Grupo Cultural Internacional Teatro Cuerpo Social, through which he creates community-based performance. In Guanajuato, Mexico, Pájaro de Nube is directed by husband and wife team choreographer Beatriz Garcia and composer Marcos Garcia; their blend of disciplines and fairytale subject matter makes them a distant cousin to Degenerate Art Ensemble, though they share no similar teachers. There are many more artists one could name. I invite others to continue recording their contributions to the butoh diaspora.

Notes

1 www.fundacionunam.org.mx/donde-paso/conoce-el-espacio-escultorico-de-la-unam/.
2 www.derevo.org/common/int/actions/projects/wheelofpower/info.html.
3 It would be 2005 before Mexico would launch its first Bachelor's degree program in dance. The degree is called Licenciatura and is equivalent to the 4-year bachelor's degree in the United States.
4 Ellen Stewart herself joined the group in Mexico to ensure the success of the production. The performance was produced by Bellas Artes at Ex Teresa Arte Actual in Mexico City. In the cast was then-17-year-old María José Loyola, a now-famous pop star and TV personality who is a coach on *La Voz* [*The Voice*, Mexico] (Suga, Pers. Comm., December 5, 2020).
5 http://tlatelolco.unam.mx/.
6 See www.uabjo.mx/celebra-shinzaburo-takeda-sus-82-anos-con-opera-prima-documental.
7 Shinichi took the last name Iova-Koga in 2006 when he married Dana Iovacchini, who also took the last name Iova-Koga. I will refer to him primarily as Iova-Koga throughout the text; however, when discussing he and Dana together, I will refer to them by their first names in order to distinguish them.
8 Ralph Lemon was a mentor for Koga through Margaret Jenkins CHIME program. He felt a kinship to the vision of Lemon's work as what Koga calls "anti-dance": an exploration of movement that is beyond stylized movement vocabulary. For example, he says, "skilled dancers flailing their bodies around for 20 minutes. It's not choreography per se but they go through a process by going through the situation. Or Lemon taking a sock on and off his foot repeatedly" (Pers. Comm. 5 25 18). Koga relates Lemon's aesthetic to *Kinjiki* in the way that "dance" is turned on its end, and the performance of everyday actions is presented as dance.
9 US Koga trained the US Olympic team and lead them to a gold medal in October 1979.
10 There were other dancers in the company, including Ken Rice, who performed locally however they didn't tour.
11 Barrons was also Flournoy's Production Assistant on numerous SF Butoh Festivals.
12 Jean Viala and Nourit Masson-Sekine, Shufunotomo Co/Tuttle Publishing, 1998.
13 Principal dancers were Shinichi, Mullin, Yoshioka, and Dana Granitz.
14 Principal dancers in the first iteration of Test Labor were Shinichi, Mullin, Yoshioka, and Dana Granitz, and then in subsequent performances, Mullin left the company and Yoshioka took herself out to direct the work. Shinichi and Granitz remained for a number of years touring and performing the work.

15 This is where my story with butoh begins. I knew nothing about butoh before I met Koga. His exact words to me: "I'm doing a show called *Cockroach* and you have an expressive face, I think you'd make a good bug. We are going to Germany. Do you want to join?" I only heard "Germany" and I wanted to travel so I said yes.

16 Koziol collaborated with inkBoat over a period of 20 years, on projects including *Glass Head* (2005), *95 Rituals* (2015), and *Storm in My House* (2019), and made a film about the Dance on Land workshops in 2009. Sadly, he passed away from COVID complications on September 24, 2021. His films are online at https://eyelasher.media.

17 See Wangh, Steven. 2000. *An Acrobat of the Heart: A Physical Approach to Acting Inspired by the Work of Jerzy Grotowski*. New York: Vintage Books/Random House.

18 Presented online through Luzerner Theater May 2021. Created by choreographer Ann Carlson in collaboration with inkBoat. Performed by Shinichi Iova-Koga and Dana Iova-Koga "We Meet Again" Created and Performed by Shinichi Iova-Koga + Dana Iova-Koga, Music by: Sleepytime Gorilla Museum, Joan Jeanrenaud, Kevin MacLeod, an inkBoat production "These Are the Ones We Fell Among" (excerpt of a work in progress to premiere in November 2021 at ODC Theater in San Francisco); Directed by Ann Carlson; Performed by Dana Iova-Koga + Shinichi Iova-Koga; Work in Progress; Music by Shahzad Ismaily; Produced by inkBoat and ODC Theater, San Francisco.

19 I am honoring the artists' wishes to publish this cheeky response to my query, when were you born? (Shige Moriya and Ximena Garnica, pers. comm., October 3, 2021). It suits them.

20 Commenting on the Comprehensive Annenberg Report on Diversity (2016), Felix Sanchez, co-founder of the National Hispanic Foundation for the Arts notes that he has been tracking these stereotypes for the past 20 years, and there has been little change. He comments that "according to the report, [Latina actresses] are the most sexualized identifiable minority group" (www.nbcnews.com/news/latino/latinos-hollywood-few-roles-frequent-stereotypes-new-study-finds-n523511).

21 See Barba, Eugenio, Nicola Savarese, and International School of Theatre Anthropology. 1991. *A Dictionary of Theatre Anthropology: The Secret Art of the Performer*. English-language ed. Published for the Centre for Performance Research by Routledge.

22 Dancers in *Illo Tempore* were Garnica, Merchan, Moeno Wakamutsu, John Schneider, Taylor Kuffner, and myself.

23 The relationship between CAVE and Japan Society developed as mutually beneficial, as CAVE brought a large following of students and Japan Society lent credibility to CAVE's endeavors.

Works Cited

Arn, Jackson. 2018. "The Japanese 'Demon of Painting' who invented Manga in 1874." *Artsy*, Nov. 22, 2018. www.artsy.net/article/artsy-editorial-japanese-demon-painting-invented-manga-1874. Accessed Mar. 15, 2021.

Bodyweather. n.d. www.bodyweather.org/oguri Accessed Sept. 28, 2021.

Butoh Archive. n.d. "Butoh Artists." https://butoharchive.herokuapp.com/. Accessed Sept. 28, 2021.

Butoyolotl. n.d. https://butoyolotl.wordpress.com/quienes-somos/. Accessed Sept 28, 2021.

Brito, Jaime Luis. 2011. "The March Advances to Mexico City Amidst Silence and Cheerfulness: Raúl Vera, Rius, Eduardo Gallo, Julián Lebarón, and Francisco Rebolledo Attend." *La Jornada*, May 6, 2011.

CAVE. 2010. "Ludus Training Season: Teaching Residency & Training Initiative." Brochure, August—December 2010.

Felciano, Rita. 2007. "25 to Watch." *Dance Magazine*, Dec. 27, 2007. www.dancemagazine.com/25-to-watch-2306862399.html. Accessed May 1, 2021.

Garcia-Gomez, Patricia. 2019. "Door to Heaven: Mexico Off the Beaten Path." *East Hampton Star*, July 4, 2019. www.easthamptonstar.com/201974/door-heaven-mexico-beaten-path-0. Accessed Jun. 15, 2021.

Garnica, Ximena, Lucy Kerr, and Hiram Pines. 2016. *Borders*. Brooklyn: LEIMAY. Exhibition book.

Garnica LEIMAY. 2008. "Antigones." Performance Program, September 18–20, 2008.

Holburn, Mark. Ethan Hoffman photographer. 1987. *Dance of the Dark Soul*. New York: Aperture. 1987.

Iova-Koga, Shinichi. 2020. "Burn Butoh: Start Again." In *The Routledge Companion to Butoh Performance*, edited by Bruce Baird and Rosemary Candelario, 533–539. New York: Routledge.

Jinen-Butoh. n.d. www.jinen-butoh.com/profile_e.html. Accessed Sept. 20, 2021.

Keene, D. 1966/67. "The Portrait of Ikkyū." Archives of Asian Art 20: 54–65.

Kourlas, Gia. 2016. "Mika Kurosawa, Leading Figure in Japanese Contemporary Dance." *New York Times*, Dec. 11, 2016.

Kourlas, Gia. 2007. "A Quest to Put Butoh on the US Map." *New York Times*, Oct. 27, 2007. www.nytimes.com/2007/10/27/arts/dance/27akir.html. Accessed Sept. 29, 2021.

La Rocco, Claudia. 2006. "Is Butoh's Big Season Good for Butoh." *New York Times*, Oct. 22, 2006. www.nytimes.com/2006/10/22/arts/dance/is-butohs-big-season-good-for-butoh.html. Accessed Sept. 29, 2021.

La Rocco, Claudia. 2005. "Plumbing the Depths in Vast Inner Landscapes." *New York Times*, Oct. 26, 2005. www.nytimes.com/2005/10/26/arts/dance/plumbing-the-depths-in-vast-inner-landscapes.html. Accessed Sept. 29, 2021.

LEIMAY. 2021. https://leimay.org, Accessed Mar 17, 2021.

Loke, Margarett. 1987. "Butoh." *New York Times*, Nov. 1, 1987.

Martínez, Espartaco. 2013. *Bitácora de Oriente: Compendio sobre la visión y procesos creativos en la danza butoh*. CDMX: Centro Nacional de las Artes.

Museo Universitario del Chopo. n.d. "*The News: Danza Butoh*," www.chopo.unam.mx/anteriores/danzabutoh.html

Museo Universitario del Chopo. n.d. "Residencia Artistica de Tadashi Endo." www.chopo.unam.mx/danza/TadashiEndo.html

Nuevo Siglo. 2018. "Ganadores del Premio Iberescena en Mapa Teatro: 'Temblor o la consagración de la nada' con la danza Butoh y teatro." *Nuevo Siglo*, July 2, 2018. https://elnuevosiglo.com.co/articulos/07-2018-temblor-o-la-consagracion-de-la-nada-con-la-danza-butoh-y-teatro. Accessed Jun. 22, 2021.

NYBK. 2009. "CAVE New York Butoh Festival: The butoh-kan phase." *Brochure*, October 23–November 25, 2009.

NYBK. 2008. "NY Butoh-Kan Training Initiative Program." *Brochure*, October 3, 2008–January 5, 2009.

NYBF. 2007. "3rd Biennial New York Butoh Festival." *Performance Program*, October 21–November 21, 2007.

NYBF. 2005. "2nd Biennial New York Butoh Festival." *Performance Program*, October 4–26, 2005.

NYBF. 2003. "New York Butoh Festival: First." Performance Program, October 11–19, 2003.

LEDTR. 2019. "Umbría." Press Release, 2019.

Luzerne Theater. 2021. "Friendly Takeover." www.luzernertheater.ch/friendlytakeover.

Registro de Danza. 2013. "Espartaco Martínez Cárdenas." Registro Nacional de Danza, Sociedad Nacional de las Artes y Ciencias Cinematográficas, June 2013. www.registro dedanza.com/perfil/2013/722-4.html. Accessed Jan. 1, 2019.

Sanford, James H. 1980. "Mandalas of the Heart. Two Prose Works by Ikkyu." *Monumenta Nipponica* 35:3, 273–298.

Teatrounam. 2020. "Acción + Aislamiento: 15 ejercisios de liberación virtual—#12—Espartaco Martínez." YouTube video, 9:59. www.youtube.com/watch?v=mSrqyHuRxHA. Accessed Mar. 19, 2021.

Upchurch, Michael. 2009. "It's a Show, It's a Spectacle, It's Degenerate Art Ensemble's 'Sonic Tales.'" *Seattle Times*, Oct. 25, 2009. www.seattletimes.com/entertainment/its-a-show-its-a-spectacle-its-degenerate-art-ensembles-sonic-tales/. Accessed Mar. 15, 2021.

5 The Future of Butoh Is . . .

The preceding two chapters addressed two generations of American artists who have adopted the mantel of butoh. In many cases, the butoh moniker has fallen away, while the methods have continued to inform their practice. Several of the artists also infuse their process with additional methodologies, including physical theater and healing arts, and still others have developed their own pedagogies through an amalgam of forms and experimentation.

In this final chapter, I want to highlight two artists who intentionally engage the term butoh, building on the form's history and identity while at the same time grafting a modifier to the term. Their work is markedly different from one another, and yet both aim to support a sense of community. French-born New York-dwelling artist Vangeline has assumed a producing role under the name the New York Butoh Institute; the tagline on the website is of key interest: "Carrying Butoh into the 21st Century" (Vangeline, n.d.). Her curatorial vision carries a decidedly feminist voice, and she works to address the overwhelmingly male dominance of this art form. Mexico-City-born Puebla-dwelling Tania Galindo directs Butoh Chilango, a term used to refer to residents of Mexico City, where she has lived most of her life. Now as the Director of Tourism and Culture at the Gobierno Municipal de Tecali de Herrera, she continues years of community work and connects contemporary artistic practice with Mexico's indigenous past. Both artists signal a new iteration of what Rosemary Candelario has termed new local butohs. Candelario defines this as "a framework to think about choreographers who . . . have adapted the [Japanese butoh] training to their own cultural contexts in order to develop their own particular performance modes that work through local or personal problematics" (Candelario 2019, 250). She argues that this "contributes to the vitality of the form" (Candelario 2019, 250). Because both Vangeline and Galindo have amplified their creative voices through highly visible producing, I would add curating to Candelario's formulation. Much in the way that Brechin Flournoy sought to situate Japanese New Wave as an iteration of butoh that was engaged with the digital age just as the cultural tide was turning in San Francisco toward the dotcom boom, Vangeline has engaged with butoh curation in ways that speak to social movements ranging from #MeToo and gender inclusivity. Galindo

DOI: 10.4324/9780429028472-5

amplifies pre-colonial Mexican culture that is itself a form of resistance against an increasingly Western neoliberal capitalistic trend in her country.

Vangeline/New York Butoh Institute (b. 1970, France)

In an interview in October 2018, Vangeline expressed her concept of "contemporary butoh" as distinct from its historical antecedents. She commented: "Contemporary butoh is growing and changing so fast it's hard to keep up. We are playing catch up" (Vangeline, pers. comm. October 23, 2018). In addition to the tagline "We carry butoh in the 21st Century," the company website proclaims to "Engage, Educate, and Empower through Butoh" with a goal of "gender equality and social justice" (Vangeline, n.d.). The decision to form the festival under the New York Butoh Institute name was informed by her desire to create a component of her company that is focused on research and education, as opposed to her own creative work. Vangeline's artistic background is informative in understanding her curatorial directions, however, and is valuable in appreciating her artistic goals.

Vangeline studied a wide range of arts in Japan and London and in 1993, devoted more seriously to dance. She moved to New York and was quickly engaged in work in the Downtown scene, in cabaret, burlesque, and musical theater during the burlesque revival in New York City. She was also a model and was involved in the fashion industry in France and New York. One of her first jobs in New York was working for Isaac Mizrahi as his key makeup artist. She points to that experience as pivotal in her professionalization as an artist. She says:

> These were people who would debate the color of a lipstick for hours . . . always the aesthetic choices were very important. There's a team of eight art directors sitting behind a monitor who might ask me to change the makeup five times before a shoot.
>
> (Vangeline pers. comm. October 23, 2018)

This was a significant moment in developing her own aesthetics and sense of costume and makeup which is so important in her work (see Figure 5.1).

She was cast in a performance at La MaMa in a show called *Sin*, directed by Ami Goodheart, who Vangeline credits with formally introducing her to butoh. Goodheart, now an award-winning film and music video costume designer based in LA, had been raised in New York City in the 1980s and had her own vintage store by the age of 18 (Goodheart, n.d.). An innovative artist, she cites avant-garde artists such as Jean-Michel Basquiat and Keith Haring as influential to her development (Goodheart, n.d.). In making *Sin* at La MaMa, Goodheart wanted the sin called Sloth to be inspired by butoh, and the dancers went to see Sankai Juku's *Hiyomeki* at BAM Opera House in 1999 as a company. Says Vangeline, "I had a complete epiphany and a visceral reaction to the performance" (Vangeline, pers. comm. October 23, 2018).

Figure 5.1 Butoh Beethoven at Lincoln Center Rose Theater (2017). Dancer: Vangeline.

Source: Photo by Darial Sneed courtesy of Vangeline Theatre, reprinted with permission from Vangeline Theatre

It would be a few more years before Vangeline would commit to butoh as her art form. She continued working in the burlesque scene for some time, and then after 9/11 happened in New York City, she took a touring job as a brand ambassador for a makeup company and traveled across the United States. When she returned, she sought out her first butoh teacher, Diego Piñón, with whom she studied and also presented in New York for many years. After Piñón, she found her main teacher in Tetsuro Fukuhara, with whom she lived and worked in Japan and continues to produce in New York.

Her burlesque performances fell away as she discovered a more expansive range. She says,

> doing burlesque and musical theater was very empowering but I also felt it was very limiting for me as a woman . . . working in the nightclub scene and the downtown scene, it's fun when you're in your 20s but as you get older you want to explore what's possible for you as a human being . . . being pretty and sexy is nice but that's not all there is to life.
>
> (Vangeline pers. comm., October 23, 2018)

Her work has taken on a decidedly feminist voice. With her all-female company, her vision concerns "women and women's beauty, and contrasting that with what's inside us as human beings. We also have violence, we also have darkness, and we also have contradiction" (Vangeline pers. comm., October 23, 2018). She continues that work in her curation as well.

The 2021 New York Butoh Institute Festival showcased luminary female dancers, including Natsu Nakajima, Saga Kobayashi, Hiroko Tamano, Minako Seki, Yumiko Yoshioka, Yuko Kaseki, Joan Laage, and Eugenia Vargas. The festival further elevated the role these women have played in the development of butoh but honoring Nakajima, Kobayashi, and Tamano with Lifetime Achievement Awards. Each recipient offered an acceptance speech via Zoom that shared more about their lives, work, and artistic visions that they developed independently of their male colleagues. Offering this platform to female pioneers was more than a gesture; it was a chance for their voice to literally and figuratively be entered into the archive of butoh history.

In fact, the four New York Butoh Institute Festivals to date—2018, 2019, 2020, and 2021—have all featured women or queer artists, particularly highlighting the feminine in butoh because "women have been systematically invisibilized," says Vangeline (Vangeline, pers. comm., October 23, 2018). This echoes Flournoy's 1996 curatorial choices for the San Francisco Butoh Festival, highlighting Akiko Motofuji (Hijikata's widow), Setsuko Yamada, Saga Kobayashi, and Hiroko Tamano. However, for Vangeline, this focus has been her priority. She also wanted to make sure it was international in focus, beyond artists from the Japan and the United States, as she herself is an immigrant. She has reached out to artists through Latin America in particular, including Natalia Cuéllar (Chile) and Eugenia Vargas (Mexico).

For Vangeline, the desire to use the word butoh to describe her work was a conscious choice. It came out of a conversation with Katsura Kan after he spent an evening watching more than five hours of footage of her performances. Afterward, he asked her why she referred to her work as only "butoh-influenced" and not just as "butoh." He told her: " 'To study butoh and not call your work butoh is sort of a cop-out' . . . and it really resonated with me when we are studying butoh we are already stepping into the lineage" (Vangeline, pers. comm. October 23, 2018). After this conversation, she began to think about her "responsibility in my community, to the students I was teaching, and what part I was playing in all of that" (Vangeline, pers. comm. October 23, 2018). The decision to form the festival under the New York Butoh Institute was informed by the desire to create a component of her company that is focused on research and education, as opposed to her own creative work.

In terms of her curatorial decisions as to who to present in workshops and performances, Vangeline was curious in sampling the great diversity she saw in the second and third generations of Japanese butoh dancers. She asks herself: "Can we produce work at the same high caliber of the originators of butoh?" She is clear that her vision to move butoh into the 21st century involves producing work at a high caliber:

> I don't want to see another work-in-progress in a garage in Bushwick. If that's the case. then we should just say "butoh was really great" and then

move on. Either we are doing experimental work and we are inspired by butoh and it's another story altogether, or we are really going there and making something worth seeing, and taking performance to the next level.
(Vangeline, pers. comm., Oct. 23, 2018)

Her vision of butoh in the 21st century is one in which a community, brought together by the nexus of a festival, can mutually push one another to define and craft their own work.

Tania Galindo/Butoh Chilango (b. 1977, Mexico City)

Tania Galindo is a powerhouse of an artist, activist, and producer. She received her Bachelor's degree in Latin American Studies from la Universidad Nacional Autónoma de México (UNAM), where she focused in particular on urban and rural community development. In addition to her performance work, she makes herbal products and is cultivating a plot of land according to Mayan principles known as *milpa*, a method which involves pesticide-free crop rotation of complimentary plants like corn, beans, and squash (Mann 2005, 197–8). More than just an alternative lifestyle, the farming, botanicals, and artwork are woven into her spiritual practice and manifest her cosmological view that is deeply connected to the Earth, and by extension, rituals originating in indigenous culture.

Galindo started in ballet and contemporary dance but it became clear that this was not her path. She encountered the teaching of dancer Lola Lince and studied with her for four years. Through Lince, Galindo met Nora Manek, a German dancer who was trained with Susana Linke and in Pina Bausch's school and subsequently studied with Diego Piñón.

Galindo herself began dancing with Piñón in 1998. Manec and Galindo had a group called Viandante at the time, and Manec had introduced Galindo to his work. Says Galindo, "Working with Diego in eight hour workshops, she was in another state. She was completely transformed" (Pers. Comm. March 14, 2018). Manec and Galindo began to organize workshops for him in Mexico City. They studied with Piñón for two years and then in 2000 when he constructed his space in Tlalpujahua, they joined the cast of his project *Espíritus en Tránsito*, which was funded by FONCA and culminated in a performance in 2003. Galindo was a student of Piñón's for many years, during which time she came to know some of the Americans who were also studying with him, including Nicole LeGette from Chicago. Students of Piñón's are a major part of the cross-pollination among US and Mexican butoh communities; Galindo continues to collaborate with several different US-based artists in her current work.

After that process was completed, Piñón began working on solo work again and all of the other dancers went their separate ways. Galindo worked a while with Jaime Razzo, José Bravo, Lola Lince, and other Mexican butoh dancers. During this training process, she had undertaken her Bachelor's degree in Latin American Studies at the la UNAM, for which she focused on the iteration of butoh in Mexico. Lince provided a critical impulse for Galindo especially when she was working on her thesis, making her participation in many workshops with visiting Japanese artists possible. Galindo was able to stay in Lince's house or do work exchange for a workshop that Lince's company produced, including with Natsu Nakajima, Akira Kasai, Susana Reyes, and many others. That community helped her develop in new directions. Says Galindo, Guadalajara has a very experimental performing arts scene (Tania Galindo, pers. comm. March 14, 2018). In addition to Lince, other experimental dancemakers include Gabriella Gallego, Paloma Díaz, and Sandra Soto (a Mexican dancer who worked for five years in Japan with Kazuo Ohno). Beatriz Cruz, who danced with Lince, formed her own group Pájaro Nube.

Galindo developed her own teaching practice and has taught consistently through El Piramide Center in Mexico City, a center which she says is an important part of her support system as an artist. El Piramide is an alternative activist space, with artists of many different disciplines working together. In 2017, right-wing politicians tried to take the space away from them due to the political nature of their work, but the artist collective joined forces with the Cultural Secretary of Mexico and formed a semi-governmental arts organization that ensured the success of the project.

Galindo founded her company Butoh Chilango in 2005 with students who studied with her at El Piramide. The dancers in her company are Maria Zato, Sofía Deveaux, Priscila Miranda, Jesica Quintana, Klarissa Pineda, Leticia Becerril, and Antonieta Fernández, and they are a photographer, writer, a news anchor, two muralists, and visual artists. Most are involved in different projects on their own. The name Butoh Chilango occurred to her after a workshop and encounter with Akira Kasai. They were discussing his experience at the Museo de Antropología; he did not see the past but rather the future. He saw the mutation of butoh, the same way that she did, says Galindo, and he told her that Mexican dancers should put their last name on it. Her response was to the addition of Chilango, referring to citizens of Mexico City. To her, Chilango refers to the scrappiness of living in a city of 10 million people that is as much marked by poverty and decay as it is by globalization. One civilization has literally built on top of another, and from the sedimented layers of indigenous, colonial, and contemporary, Galindo pulls inspiration. It is in fact the multiplicity that drives her, in an effort to find balance with what is, rather than yearning for something that once was.

Galindo previously worked with Teatro Sensorial, founded by Héctor Fernández Piña and Demian Lerma. The company creates tactile and olfactory experiences for audience who are frequently blindfolded. The idea is that the audience member themselves—their inner experience—is the mise-en-scene of the performance. One project was titled *Labyrinth*, a reference to the double entendre of the event, as the company members guided blindfolded audience members on a walking sensorial journey through the space, and simultaneously the audience member experienced their own internal labyrinth of sensations during the event. Says Galindo, a wide variety of people are attracted to the performances, which provide a space to get back in touch with our sensuous lives in ways that fast-paced capitalistic, city life does not promote. The founders of the group are musicians and visual artists who explore sensation and perception. Says Galindo, "It is also related to spiritual path, not related to any particular religion" (Tania Galindo pers. comm. March 14, 2018). Her own work is connected with an animist perspective of the natural world, particularly the sun, the earth, and the water. For her they are not as gods in the true animist sense but she engages with their energetic forces.

After she studied with Piñón, she met a Japanese dancer named Chika Omoishi, who had worked with Kazuo Ohno and later emigrated to Mexico. She worked with him intensively for a period, and then Omoishi invited her to travel to Colombia and Ecuador with him in 2005. It was the first time she toured as a butoh artist. Galindo stayed in Colombia for half a year, during which time she developed *La Serpiente*, a solo work based on the Aztec god Quetzalcóatl. With this solo she returned to South America from 2008 to 2010 performing in different cities, giving workshops, and building connections. The students she encountered had not studied butoh previously and were fascinated. One workshop led to another, and she found herself on a nearly two-year tour beginning in Bogota, Colombia, and ending in Mendoza, Argentina. She also made this into an experiential work for the audience, so they each went through the journey of transformation of the snake.

Galindo has traveled and performed extensively throughout Latin America, and the community she has made in the region is quite closely knit. In particular, she has worked with Susana Reyes (Ecuador), Carla Lobos (Chile), and Juan José Olavarrieta. Reyes hosted the Primero Encuentro Latinoamericano de Butoh and was involved in the second one that Galindo organized in Mexico in 2012.

When developing the Segundo Encuentro Latinoamericano de Butoh, Galindo and her fellow organizers were invested in the question of how butoh has "mutated" as it has become a global diaspora. They were of course most interested in the Latin American iterations of the form (Tania Galindo, pers. comm. March 14, 2018). To address this vision, they curated artists from throughout Latin America, including Carla Lobos and her company Aucabutoh (Chile), Fuchen (Concepcion, Chile), Joao Butoh (Brazil), Susana Reyes (Ecuador), Lola Lince (Mexico), Eugenia Vargas (Mexico), Cocobioreal, Tania Galindo, and Butoh Chilango (Mexico). It was a group effort, with everyone paying for their own plane tickets, and most of the events were free. Isabel Beteta offered the artist room in her Los Talleres center to help with lodging. They held events in El Chopo and Foro Coyucanense, and in the Teatro del Pueblo. Workshop spaces were provided by El Piramide. They produced this large-scale international festival on a shoestring budget of 800,000 pesos ($35,000 USD), with Galindo selling her car to put in 70,000 ($3,000 USD) of her own money. Though rewarding in terms of fellowship and dialogue among like-minded artists, it was an exhausting effort that she has not since repeated on this scale on her own.

Galindo notes that funding for dance has tended to circulate among the same companies over and over (as it has in other countries as well), making the dance field rather homogenous. She believes that butoh has had a breakthrough influence on dance in Mexico, opening up expressive possibilities. Butoh has been met with great audience interest, and through the acceptance of these other expressions, butoh has also helped to open up the field of artists who receive funding. Previously, the accepted techniques in contemporary dance were quite rigid. The arrival and popularity of butoh, particularly in the past 20 years, has revolutionized everything, says Galindo.

> It's been a very powerful encounter, bringing us back to indigenous culture. The Mexican body has suffered through colonization, all of this domination, and the stratification of classes which is still very strong here, more so than in other Latin American countries where there is more immigration and diversity. Butoh has opened a channel of liberation, especially to this part that has been denied, violated, enslaved. Butoh has helped us reconnect to our territory.
>
> (Tania Galindo, pers. comm., March 14, 2018)

One dance in particular that Galindo incorporates into her own company's work is the Mexica Danza de la Luna, and also Concheros, a dance of the Chichimecas, a group who were based in the North of Mexico. The Chichimecas were one of the last tribes to succumb to Spanish colonizers, partially due to their isolated location from the capital city and also due to their own fortitude. When they finally did agree to lay down their weapons and submit to Spanish rule, the bargain they struck was that they be allowed to keep their dances and songs. As a result, says Galindo, this cultural knowledge was never lost and still is a part of Mexican traditions today. They may have been mixed with Catholic traditions and now carry the words referring to La Virgen (The Virgin Mother), but the steps and the rhythms are the same as always.

Says Galindo, these traditions have influenced her in her own dance practice. For example, when she paints her body she frequently uses earth, mud, and clay rather than the butoh white (see Figure 5.2). For her, this practice has more to do with the land she occupies than the white paint that for her relates to the atomic bomb but also Japanese traditional dance. Her focus is more on territories and land than on political boundaries and nationalities. She says, "Of course, my work is political, but not in the same way as to be defined by national boundaries" (Tania Galindo, pers. comm. March 14, 2018). Her company has performed in protests, particularly on social issues like access to water and violence against women. In Mexico, the stakes are much higher than they are in the United States for political protests, even in our current social unrest. One of her students was arrested for being in a protest and held for two months in jail.

Galindo is an environmental activist. She is involved in conservation and re-forestation efforts. She has a plot of land outside the city on which she is

Figure 5.2 La tierra es crudo y sin embargo se mueve (2018). Dancer: Tania Galindo.

Source: Reprinted with permission of Tania Galindo

growing food and building a small structure with other artists. She also is a skilled herbalist and has her own business making products. She credits her study in butoh, particularly Diego Piñón's center in Tlalpujaha, for her current path. She says, before studying butoh she was rebellious and angry with society, involved in many social protests. Her work in nature with Piñón enabled her to find a channel for her rebelliousness, toward creating an alternative life.

During the COVID-19 pandemic, she focused intensively on her farming plot and spent more time outside of Mexico City. Her land is on the outskirts of Tecali, where one of the oldest theaters in Mexico stands. The building housing the theater was under reconstruction, and Galindo reached out to the President of the organization because she wanted to encourage them to use methods that would preserve the building's original materials rather than cover it with concrete. The President surprised her by listening to her ideas and also asking her to accept the position of Director of Tourism and Culture at the Gobierno Municipal de Tecali de Herrera. She accepted the role as a part-time position so that she could continue her own work in performance and cultivating land. Says Galindo, the blend of civil society, government organizations, and artists is precisely the connection she enjoys making with her work (Tania Galindo, pers. comm. September 30, 2021). In her position, she organizes presentations of music, traditional dance, and artisanal crafts.

Fueled by multiple crises—the COVID-19 pandemic, recent earthquakes in Mexico, and ongoing violence in her country—Galindo created a new work entitled *Cielo Cae*. The title translates literally to "The Sky is Falling" but also references the Aztec Goddess of the Moon, Coyolxauhqui, as she journeys to the underworld. Galindo revived a large-scale puppet made by Edwin Salas for their collaboration in the Segundo Encuentro Latinoamericano de Butoh. Dancers operate the limbs, head, and torso independently. Initially, the puppet referenced the alarming rate of femicides and lack of rights for women in Mexico. In the latest iteration of the work, the dance with the puppet also signifies the ways in which people come together to heal from tragedy and trauma, paired with Los Angelos-based multimedia artist Jim Ovelmen's piece *Silencio Extraño*, about the 1985 and 2017 earthquakes in Mexico City which were 32 years apart to the day. Writes Ovelmen, "The profound collective-rescue efforts by civilians, as well as the dysfunction and corruption of larger infrastructures, are subjective aspects of the work" (Kyotoagreement). The project was presented in September 2021 by Quipo, a team of international curators, artists, and cultural producers, who focus on "promoting dialogue and social engagement" (Quipoinfo). Indeed, this is the tenor of Galindo's oeuvre to date, and her use of butoh is in service of the fostering profound dialogue with the living things that sustain us.

Butoh as Commons: Concluding Thoughts

Returning to the idea of butoh as a commons, I want to underscore the notion that there is great diversity in the aesthetics, methods, and aims of artists connected to the global butoh diaspora. At the same time, there is a touchstone at the core and a shared act of resistance. Whether it be the abstract notion of *ma*, or in-between-ness, that has captured the attention of artists like Garnica and Moriya of LEIMAY, or the literal between-ness of existing at a crossroads of cultures and identities, as artists such as Galindo, Martínez, and Iova-Kogas are in their life and work, there is a shared activity of stepping outside, defying categorization, and eschewing identities.

Kinji Hayashi offers yet another example to consider of how butoh artists refuse to behave as expected. In the 2003 duet *West* choreographed by paige starling sorvillo, Hayashi performs a butoh cowboy, a *vaquero* (see Figure 5.3). It is an iconic American masculine role, the kind that says "live free or die." His legs are spread wide to assert dominance; however, his lack of pants in this posture just makes him more vulnerable. At the same time, the sneer on his face and finger jabbed forward tells us he knows that and he wants a fight anyway. It is this punk attitude that sustains those who live outside the mainstream.

That is not to say that alternative lives are necessarily aggressive or angry. What they are is persistent. Dana Iova-Koga has developed a fascination for eggshells, and their dichotomy of strength and fragility. Similar to her deep dive into farming and taking care of land, she engages in a labor-intensive process with eggs, in which she boils the half eggshells from family meals and

Figure 5.3 West (2003). Duet choreography by paige starling sorvillo. Pictured: Kinji Hayashi.

Source: Photo by Ian Winters, reprinted with permission of Ian Winters

then makes them into performance elements. Dismayed at throwing away an elaborate paper and wood set that had been soaked in fire retardant (and thus not recyclable) for inkBoat's *Line Between*, she decided she wanted to work with more simple elements that could be composted. In the course of performance, she crushes them into a fine powder which sparkles in the stage light. "By the time I get on stage with the shells I have already put tons of hours into handling them" she says, and in a way "they represent the human act of labor" (Dana Iova-Koga, pers. comm. June 7, 2021). Moreover, she reinvents the eggshells, fashioning them from the mundane into something unexpected.

Akira Kasai contends that butoh is dead because it is no longer the *hanzai* [crime] dance it once was, thumbing its proverbial nose at the establishment and promoting uselessness in a production-oriented economy (Akira Kasai, pers. comm. October 29, 2010). The "bad check called democracy" that Hijikata railed against so vehemently has not changed much since the 1960s (Hijikata 2006, 43); it has only become a more well-oiled machine. Artists in such a society have had to become increasingly clever in order to navigate the economics of production if they are to survive with any longevity and still maintain the integrity of their protest and resist societal pressures to "domesticate."

One way in which contemporary butoh artists walk the fine line between institutionalization and the avant-garde is to participate in the *experience economy*. The product they offer is singular and difficult to replicate; thus, at the very least it is a product of immediacy and an experience that can only happen once.

Butoh as *training experiences* that have emerged in the Americas in the last 20 years emphasizes artistic process and personal journey. Some, such as ink-Boat's Art on the Land and training camps in sacred Incan Lake Titicaca, are modeled after Min Tanaka's farm training (with a less punishing regimen). Others, such as CAVE/LEIMAY's LUDUS, offer eclectic arts workshops including vocal and gymnastic training akin to Grotowski's Plastiques and other early theater experiments. Still others, such as San Francisco-producer BareBones-Butoh and Mexico City's alternative community at La Pyramide, offer the open, non-curated performance spaces as a platform for artistic exploration.

The *audience experience* is something that Hijikata's butoh has stressed since inception, as in The 650 Dance Experience, with 650 indicating the number of seats in the performance hall. Indeed, the transformative experience of watching butoh is something that Western presenters continue to employ as a marketing tool. In contemporary practice, Teatro Ritual Sensorial in Mexico City, in which Mexican butoh artist Tania Galindo performed for many years, offers their audiences a truly unique and evocative journey. Their work is riding the twin waves of immersive theater and cognition studies within theater. The audience is blindfolded and led through a series of olfactory experiences, and invited to develop the narrative of the "play" in their own dreamlike state.

In sum, I wanted to capture the trajectories of the artists profiled in this book because of their sheer ingenuity and tenacity. Their stories are inspirational for future generations. More specifically, Burt draws our attention to the commons at play in "the study of dance and labor, economy, relationality, and institutional critique" (Frankfurter, 2019, 100). While I do not disagree with Kasai that butoh as *hanzai* dance no longer exists, I also do not think butoh in the Americas has sold out. As the pathways and creative expressions of these artists attest, resistance to categories and commodification is still at the heart of butoh practice in the Americas.

Works Cited

Burt, Ramsay. 2017. *Ungoverning Dance: Contemporary European Theatre Dance and the Commons*. New York: Oxford University Press.

Candelario, Rosemary. 2019. "Now We Have a Passport: Global an Local Butoh." In *The Routledge Companion to Butoh Performance*, edited by Bruce Baird and Rosemary Candelario, 245–253. New York: Routledge.

Frankfurter, Sariel Golomb. 2019, December. "Ungoverning Dance: Contemporary European Theatre Dance and the Commons (Review)." *Dance Research Journal* 51, no. 3, 98–100.

Goodheart, Ami. n.d. www.amigoodheart.com/bio. Accessed September 1, 2021.

Hijikata, Tatsumi. 2006. *From Being Jealous of a Dog's Vein*. Translated by Elena Polzer. Berlin: Mori-Ôgai-Gedenkstätte der Humbolt Universitat zu Berlin. Originally published as *Inu no jomyaku ni shitto suru koto kara* (*Bijutsu Technō*, 1969 May).

Kyotoagreement. 2021. "Silencio Extraño (pt.1) Jim Ovelmen." Youtube, www.youtube.com/watch?v=O6IrsEqXd6Q. June 9, 2021.

Mann, Charles C. 2005. *1491: New Revelations of the Americas before Columbus*. First ed. New York: Knopf.

Quipoinfo. n.d. https://qipoinfo.wordpress.com/about-2/. Accessed September 30, 2021.

Vangeline. n.d. www.vangeline.com/what-we-do. Accessed June 3, 2021.

Index